FIGHT TO LIVE,
LIVE TO FIGHT

SUNY series in New Political Science

Bradley J. Macdonald, editor

FIGHT TO LIVE, **LIVE TO FIGHT**

Veteran Activism after War

Benjamin Schrader

SUNY
PRESS

On the cover: Detail from "War Is Trauma for Humans and Otherwise," by Roger Peet (Portland, OR), courtesy of IVAW (www.ivaw.org)

Published by State University of New York Press, Albany

© 2019 State University of New York

For information, contact State University of New York Press, Albany, NY
www.sunypress.edu

Library of Congress Cataloging-in-Publication Data

Names: Schrader, Benjamin, 1980– author.
Title: Fight to live, live to fight : veteran activism after war / Benjamin Schrader.
Description: Albany, NY : State University of New York Press, [2019] |
    Series: SUNY series in new political science | Includes bibliographical
    references and index.
Identifiers: LCCN 2018036280 | ISBN 9781438475196 (hardcover : alk. paper) |
    ISBN 9781438475202 (ebook)
Subjects: LCSH: Veterans—Political activity—United States. | Iraq War, 2003–2011—
    Veterans—Political activity—United States. | Afghan War, 2001– —
    Veterans—Political activity—United States. | Veterans—United States—
    Biography. | Political activists—United States—History—21st century. | Social
    movements—United States—History—21st century. | Protest movements—United
    States—History—21st century. | United States—Politics and government—21st
    century. | Militarism—United States. | Critical theory—United States.
Classification: LCC UB357 .S347 2019 | DDC 322.4086/970973—dc23
LC record available at https://lccn.loc.gov/2018036280

10 9 8 7 6 5 4 3 2 1

Veterans are the light at the tip of the candle, illuminating the way for the whole nation. If veterans can achieve awareness, transformation, understanding, and peace, they can share with the rest of society the realities of war. And they can teach us how to make peace with ourselves and each other, so we never have to use violence to resolve conflicts again.

—Thich Nhat Hanh

Contents

Abbreviations and Acronyms

1SGT	First Sergeant
AO	Area of Operation
AWOL	Absent Without Leave
BDU	Battle Dress Uniform
CIA	Central Intelligence Agency
CMS	Critical Military Studies
DCU	Desert Camouflage Uniform
DUI	Driving Under the Influence
EMDR	Eye Movement Desensitization and Reprocessing
FOB	Forward Operating Base
GED	General Equivalency Diploma
GMACC	Gangsters Making Astronomical Change in the Community
GWOT	Global War on Terror
IED	Improvised Explosive Device
IMF	International Monetary Fund
IRAP	Iraq Refugee Assistance Program
IVAW	Iraq Veterans Against the War
JROTC	Junior Reserve Officers' Training Corps
Lt.	Lieutenant

Lt. Col.	Lieutenant Colonel
MILES	Multiple Integrated Laser Engagement System
MEPS	Military Entrance Processing Station
MK19	Mark 19 Automatic Grenade Launcher
MRAP	Mine-Resistant Ambush Protected vehicle
MST	Military Sexual Trauma
NAFTA	North American Free Trade Agreement
NOLB	No One Left Behind
OG	Original Gangster
OPFOR	Oppositional Forces
OpFree	Operation FREE
OWS	Occupy Wall Street
PL	Platoon Leader
POG	Person Other than Grunt
POGO	Project of Government Oversight
PTS	Post-Traumatic Stress
PTSD	Post-Traumatic Stress Disorder
QRF	Quick Reaction Force
REMF	Rear Echelon Mother Fucker
ROE	Rules of Engagement
ROTC	Reserve Officer Training Corps
Sgt.	Sergeant
Sgt. Maj.	Sergeant Major
SFC	Sergeant First Class
SSG	Staff Sergeant
TBI	Traumatic Brain Injury
TC	Truck Commander

UCMJ	Uniform Code of Military Justice
VA	Veterans Administration
VFP	Veterans for Peace
VFW	Veterans of Foreign Wars
VGJ	Veterans Green Jobs
VVA	Vietnam Veterans of America
VVAW	Vietnam Veterans Against the War

Acknowledgments

First and foremost, I would like to thank all the veterans who participated in this research. I can only hope that the narratives here inspire others as much as you have all inspired me. As a large part of this book contains accounts from my own life, this appreciation and love extends to my parents, Mark Schrader and Marykay Deveraux—I am who I am because of you both, thank you—and to my sisters Eryn Brady and Kelsie Foxx, as well as my brother, Brett Brady, rest in peace, and to my stepmothers and all who had a hand in raising me: Randi Schrader, Joan Schrader, and Shauna Atkins. They also extend to all my brothers and sisters with whom I served in the army. Within this group of people I would especially like to thank my closest friends: Garett Reppenhagen, Jeff Englehart, Thomas Cassidy, and Mark Lachance. Also to the rest of the 2/63 Scout Platoon shitbags: Matt Frank, Ron Holmes, Nestor Martinez, John Flynn, Kentner Scarborough, Matt Stroup, Jesse Smith, Abraham Stanfill (honorary scout), Brian Porter, Robert Brown, Michael Zugg, Zacarey Davis, Daniel Carter, Alfred Luna, Timothy Williams, Jody Casey, James Dolph (Doc), Thomas Ervin (wishes he was a scout), Josef Merritt, Gregory Bedingfield, John Casey, John Preston, Lt. Joshua Kaiser, Lt. Matthew Caldwell, Lt. Jon Genge, and all the others I missed, sorry. . . . But definitely a very special thanks to SFC David Jenkins, you changed my life in more ways than I can express here.

A very special thanks to my friend and mentor, Eric Ishiwata. None of this would have been possible without you encouraging and pushing me to be better and do more! Once I left Colorado State University, I found a new family at the University of Hawai'i. Thanks so much to my dissertation chairs Kathy Ferguson and Michael Shapiro, as well as to the rest of my committee, Jairus Grove, Manfred Steger, and David Stannard. And to all my fellow comrades from UH: Francois-Xavier Plasse-Couture, Rex

Trombley, Anjali Nath, Katie Brennan, Sharain Nayler, Tani Sebro, Rohan Kalyan, Noah Viernes, Iokepa Cusumbal-Salazar, Melisa Cusumbal-Salazar, Guanpei Ming, Lorenzo Rinelli, Sam Opondo, Irmak Yazici, Adam Foster, Jimmy Weir, Sankaran Krishna, Sami Raza, Nicole Sunday Grove, Tuti Mary Baker, Nevzat Soguk, Alvin Lim, Akta Kaushal, Aubrey Morgan Yee, Bettina Brown, Brian Caldwell Gordon, Debora Halbert, Duyen Bui, Eri Kiyoko, Kim Compoc, Kyle Kajihiro, Ryan Knight, Heather Frey, Gitte Du Plessis, Julia Guimaraes, and Sophie Yeonhee Kim. A very special thanks goes to Brianne Gallagher, who always inspired me, made me a better person, and was able to make me understand complex things like no one else could. And thank you so much for pushing me to not put off turning this into a book; I am forever grateful and indebted to you.

And to my friends who are fighting the good fights: Kristen Grigsby, Alan Pitts, Mitch Trebesh, Ian Overton, Carlie Trott, Laura Bruner, Therese Inman, Phil Linkchorst, Jodi Edmonds, Cheryl Distaso, Marketa Rumlena, Irene Vernon, Micah Lease, Adam Bracky, Ambeur Johnson, Jennifer Dobb, Sara Gill, Jeff Key, Eli Wright, Kelly Dougherty, Lovella Calica, Barb Kistler, Sean Jaster, Jeni Cross, Rachael Martel, Melanie Amoroso-Pohl, Maggie Martin, Matt Howard, Rachel Darden, Megan White, Katie Gleeson, Mark Settle, Dan Palmer, Jason Green, Sadie Conrad, Trevor and Katie Trout, Megan Skeehan, Rachel Johnson, James Sander, Mike Marion, Emily Yates, Shawna Foster, Mike Flaherty, Vrnda Noel, Dom Mullins, Kim Grubbs, Jess Dyrdahl, Peter Dearth, Casey Boczon, Colleen Bannon, Matt Stys, Robin Guthrie, Wendy Barranco, David Mann, Nick Velvet, Jose Vasquez, Charon Hribar, Phil Guzy, Kevin Levad, Kevin Kirchner, Ramon Mejia, Lance Wright, Roe Bubar, Karina Cespedes, Doreen Martinez, Cori Wong, Rachel Kennedy, Denise Ondaro, Monica Rivera, Carmen Rivera, Laura Osteen, Emily Ambrose, Caridad Souza, Ray Black, Bobby Kunstman, Norberto Valdez, Carl Olsen, Maricela DeMirjyn, Nancy York, Claire Ryder, Erica LaFehr, Avondine Hill, Kevin Cross, Krista Martinez, Shelby Williams, Michele Frick, Pam Norris, Jen Johnson, Chris Leck, Sam Bowersox-Daly, Taylor Smoot, Ben Prytherch, and so many more! (I'm missing so many here . . . just know you are loved.) And to the Bouncing Souls, whose music saved me from many dark places, as their friendship has always been amazing, and their lyrics inspired the title of this book.

Much thanks to Central European University for the opportunity to work on this in my postdoc. To Yoav Galai, I don't care what anyone says, you're a good officemate. I will always remember the Budapest spas with Kata Hudry and Mate Tokic. As well as all the late nights with the Edison and Retox crews: Balazs, Jonny, Bori, Smike, Dana and Shane, Peter, Bryan, Josefine, Hannah, Luke, Aditya, and Tito! Also, to my ISA/EISA/Critical Military Studies peeps, you're my favorite! Hopefully there will be many more fun conferences with the likes of Kateřina Krulišová, Kevin McSorley, Synne Dyvik, Linda Åhäll, Shannon Brincat, Bree Rhodes, Stephanie Fishel, Paul Kirby, Ben Tallis, Ben Meiches, Henri Myrttinen, Catherine Baker, Annick Wibben, Chris Rossdale, Joanna Tidy, Jesse Crane-Seeber, Marsha Henry, Meera Sabaratnam, Sarah Bulmer, Victoria Basham, Mark Salter, Julia Welland, Can Mutlu, Christopher Leite, Lauren Wilcox, Mauro Caraccioli, and so many more! And to all my students who helped me think through many of these ideas.

Finally, I would like to thank everyone who made this book possible. Brad Macdonald, thanks for believing in this project, being a good friend and mentor, and making it a part of your book series. Again, to Synne Dyvik for your detailed review of the book, as well as to the other blind reviewer. And to SUNY Press for publishing it.

To all those I forgot, to all those we've lost, and to all those fighting for a better tomorrow, thank you all very much, this book is dedicated to you!

An earlier version of chapter 1 appeared in the *Journal of Narrative Politics*, volume 1, issue 1.

Introduction

As the Iraqi man lay in front of me cold and lifeless, the veil of ignorance was removed from my eyes. The actions of my deeds swarmed through my head like a beehive disturbed on a hot summer day. Was this man a father? Was he fighting to free his country? Was he fighting so that he could put food on the table for his family? I would never know. It was there on that hot, hectic, and deadly day that I had resolved the conflict that kept me up at night: that we should not be in Iraq. As I lay in my bunk after the heated battle, I discovered my passion to seek social justice for all, to fight for those too weak to fight for themselves, to give voice to those without a voice, and to show those with power and privilege how their actions affect those they don't see.

Every day in Iraq I felt like a hypocrite, and it tore me apart inside to fight in a war I didn't believe in. I wanted to throw down my weapon and refuse to promote the injustices I executed. My integrity to fulfill my oath and the compassion for my comrades kept me at my post. The battle within raged, but the light at the end of the tunnel was near. I swore to myself that I would one day make a difference in this world. On May 31, 2005, I was honorably discharged from the United States Army, though in my heart and mind I felt I had been part of a dishonorable action. I would spend the next nine years going to school, learning to understand my experience, and the reasons I feel the way I do. I would also spend that time as an activist, fighting to make the world a better place, as well as seeking penance for the things I felt I had done wrong. I knew I was not alone in this quest, as the other veterans I worked with to create change had stories similar to mine. Therefore, I am writing and sharing some of those stories, to show the battles we face, how they relate to the wars we fought, and how our current fight seeks to heal the nation, our communities, and ourselves.

This personal experience—of being soldier, having fought in war, and then becoming an activist directly combating the very war I fought in—gives me special insights not only into the struggles faced by returning veterans but also allows me a certain level of understanding and intimacy with the veterans I interview. I have been interviewed by journalists and academics many times, and there was always a tension between the interviewer and me as I would have to constantly stop and explain little things, or I would hold back this detail or that sentiment, because I knew they just would not understand. Many of the people that I interviewed relayed similar stories and told me how much easier it was to talk with me, because I had been there. Therefore, there is a different layer of thinking I bring beyond what many other amazing academics can—with my own story, my more contemporary view, and the subsequent way I am able to analyze these issues.

Since I began working on this project, there have been a great number of events that have directly impacted veterans, making it hard to focus on it. Events such as the release of the documentary *The Invisible War*, which subsequently brought to light the high levels of sexual assault in the military, prompting government officials to take action; the reporting of the high rates of suicide and homelessness among veterans; whistleblowers Chelsea Manning and Edward Snowden releasing classified military documents; the release of POW Bowe Bergdahl; the Veterans Administration (VA) health care scandal; the shift to drone warfare; and last but not least, the recent return to Iraq as the US continues this seemingly endless "war on terror," and even the election of Donald Trump as president. Many of these issues have been highly publicized since I began writing this book, only to be forgotten months after their occurrence. I do bring some of these topics into the fold as they relate to veteran activism; however, I am not able to cover all areas of veterans' issues and activism, as it is a dynamic and ever-changing field of study that is rarely examined.

While there has been some work on contemporary veterans' issues, most scholars have focused on issues around post-traumatic stress (PTS), like Erin Finley's *Fields of Combat: Understanding PTSD Among Veterans of Iraq and Afghanistan*.[1] Many of the veterans I interviewed were dealing with PTS, but they often sought alternative forms of dealing with it, as opposed to seeking help from the Veterans Administration. Many of the current engagements with veterans and PTS have been framed either medically/psychologically or administratively (i.e., whether or not the VA is sufficiently meeting needs).[2] However, these works have failed to recognize that veterans are engaged in other agency-driven modes of being, which are political. Many examinations of veterans fail to fully recognize the ways in which veterans are *subjects* (political agents fighting to reshape the lives of themselves and others) rather than *objects* (waiting for medical/administrative attention). While this sort of veteran advocacy is done with the best of intentions, it unwittingly renders veterans as objects/dependents (helpless and in need), robbing them of agency. It is ironic because the veterans themselves are contesting their militarism through an active de-objectification, through re-humanization, connection/relationship-building, and agency. Therefore, this project discursively examines a series of interviews that I conducted with veterans who identify as activists and seek to create this agency.

There have been two books that specifically examine veteran activism, Dahr Jamail's *The Will to Resist: Soldiers Who Refuse to Fight in Iraq and Afghanistan*, and Lisa Leitz's *Fighting for Peace: Veterans and Military Families in the Anti-Iraq War Movement*.[3] Both books primarily focus upon the organization Iraq Veterans Against the War (IVAW), which I was and still am a member of. While I utilize both their works, and am inspired by their writings, neither author seems to reach a critical/theoretical analysis that is needed to understand contemporary veterans' issues. Jamail's book is more of a brilliant piece of journalism chronicling the events of IVAW, while Leitz's book is an in-depth ethnography aimed at understanding the dynamics of social movements, specifically the peace movement. What I seek to do is different.

I take a critical, analytical lens in order to examine post-9/11 US veterans who are now social justice activists. As soldiers, these veterans were trained and formed in specific ways, for specific purposes, primarily to perpetuate violence. While this training affects every individual differently, there are similar themes and ideals that come to light, which tell us much about the military, the US government, Western liberal democracy, the affects and effects of war, and subjectivity. Furthermore, veterans are able to articulate these concepts and ideals differently than civilians because their lived experiences exemplify the ramifications of war and American policy. Often, veterans feel the effects of US policy before society does, thus acting as the miner's canary, and yet they are rarely the locus of enunciation. As Victoria Basham points out, soldiers act as "geocorporeal actors that are necessary for waging wars that harm some populations while preserving the life of others."[4] The veterans that I interviewed have been these "geocorporeal actors" in times of war and continue to be so, though in different ways, as they interact and often resist the very institutions that, as soldiers, they were a part of.

The contextual shift from "soldier" to "activist veteran" highlights the aims of my project. With veterans being separated from the military, this time often gives them the space for critical reflection that is often difficult to achieve when in the thick of military service. These veterans are able to find ways to heal through different forms of resistance within these veteran activist communities, as their reflection and their activism work hand in hand to help them understand their experiences.[5] This not only works to heal the traumas of war within the veteran, but also pushes the veteran to try and alter the war dispositif, thus attempting to heal the impacts of war on society.

The aim of this book is both to try and disentangle the messiness of war and politics at times, and also to make it more complicated and messy at others, as I seek to break with the normative analytic constructions by examining veterans' narratives. I also want to understand how these veterans came to become activists. Embedded within this *how* is a narrative that falls outside the empirical normative expectations for war veterans, in which we can see a resignification of patriotism take place. This resignification of patriotism is the pushback against militarism, which many within the general public might normally see as problematic; however, since it is war veterans who are doing the pushing it blurs the boundaries of *who* and *what* signifies as patriotic. My ultimate goal is to locate when resistance takes place and to understand what it looks like.

Critical Military Studies

My work falls within the field of critical military studies (CMS). This fairly new field is an interdisciplinary approach to interrogate "conceptions of military power, militarism, and militarization," both inside the military and outside of it.[6] Therefore, CMS is often drawing from a wide range of theoretical backgrounds from modern schools of thought such as postcolonial feminism to classic fields of study such as Marxism. This work has consistently tried to extend beyond the fields of military and security studies that is often "atheoretical, apolitical, and largely quantitative," in order to problematize systems of militarism and show how they pertain to everyday social and political realities.[7] Furthermore, this approach of study "warrants complex and messy interpersonal qualitative encounters with those who articulate and are themselves articulations of military power, including the researchers themselves."[8] I feel this statement perfectly conveys the approach to this book, especially within a CMS framework. There are multiple layers of militarism that are examined, from the personal to societal, as I look not only at other veterans' stories but also at my own embodiment in the military, as well as my interactions with the veterans I interviewed.

As many within CMS have explained, embodied experiences should be central to our understanding of war and militarism as it shows the ways in which the security dispositif has "generative effects."[9] As Synne Dyvik points out, the embodied experiences of soldiers and veterans "offer narratives of war and combat that should be listened to—not necessarily because they provide 'the truth' about war, but because of how they frame 'their truth' through the body and numerous potent, prevailing and powerful discursive frames."[10] Thus, when we hear the stories and narratives of soldiers and veterans, we connect the unknowns of war and combat with the feelings we know and have experienced, and we can begin to empathize. While most veteran and soldier narratives that are portrayed are primarily gendered and militarized stories of combat meant to highlight heroism, the narratives here often push against these stories that become normalized by the security dispositif.[11] These veterans are attempting to have a reciprocal relationship with the security dispositif; because it has shaped them into the bodies and soldiers they are, and it also put them in situations that had them face-to-face with the traumas of war, they now hope that their narratives can be used as tools to transform the security dispositif through activism.

In using the term "security dispositif," I draw from a Foucauldian concept in which a dispositif is a "thoroughly heterogeneous set consisting of discourses, institutions, architectural forms, regulatory decisions, laws, administrative measures, scientific statements, philosophical, moral and philanthropic propositions—in short, the said as much as the unsaid."[12] Foucault goes on to explain that it is the strategic interaction between these mechanisms of power and different types of knowledge that he was interested in.[13] Therefore, the security dispositif consists not only of structures like the military and governmental policies tied to military actions but also to more abstract ideas such as military masculinities, which are examined in chapter 5, or war imaginaries, examined in chapter 6. Thus, this book is a collection of the ways in which the security dispositif has affected and still is affecting the embodied experience of the veterans I interviewed. It navigates how they understand the dispositif, how they relate to it, and how they are trying to change it based on their embodied experiences.

The concept of militarism, which is examined throughout, can also be seen as a part of the security dispositif mentioned above, as it is the "normalization and legitimation" of the security dispositif.[14] Militarism can also be seen as what Chris Cuomo calls a *presence*.[15] This presence is a force that can be felt and seen at all times because it is inherent within the military structure. Cuomo's aim is not an examination of war in and of itself, but rather a critique of militarism in general and the military institutions whose goal is ultimately to make war. In this critique, she shows how the military propagates violence not only in times of war but also in times of peace, specifically along gender and environmental lines. This is better explained by Laura Sjoberg and Sandra Via, who sum up Cuomo's argument by stating, ". . . war is best seen as a process or continuum rather than a discrete event. Where an event has a starting point and an ending point, militarism pervades societies (sometimes with more intensity and sometimes with less) before, during, and after the discrete event that the word 'war' is usually used to describe."[16]

Cuomo's use of the military as a presence not only shows the violence perpetrated on women's bodies by men, but also shows that there is a similar effect as the violence and harm of militarism is perpetrated upon the environment—which is examined in chapter 4. Cuomo explains that the military is one of the most harmful institutions against the environment.[17] She illustrates that the military is inflicting violence on both human and nonhuman entities, not only in times of war but also in times of peace—or in other words, the everyday.[18]

Similarly, in Michael Shapiro examines "the presence of war" through an intervention of theory and aesthetic montages. Shapiro shows that there is a "spatio-temporality of war" that cyclically connects war and the home-front.[19] In this analysis he states:

> Both texts disclose not only the way the homefront delivers bodies
> to the war front but also the degree to which war takes place on
> the home front. They evince an equivalence that frames "war"
> within a critical politics of aesthetics inasmuch as they reparti-
> tion the sense of war as they challenge the boundary between
> war and domesticity.[20]

In other words, there is not only an intimate link between the battlefield and those at home, but there is an effectual relationship between the two. Those at home are driven to war for a variety of reasons; similarly, those at war come home to fight for a number of different causes, and often there are links to their time in the military. My project examines these frames of war as these veterans are coming home and fighting these new wars through their activism. Their activism "challenge the boundaries between war and domesticity."[21]

Besides the physical and mental traumas that can come with military service, a veteran's whole being has become militarized, from the ways they navigate space to their social interactions.[22] As Zoë Wool explains, the affect of the "soldiers' experience of movement as suffused with the experiences of war zones, the way their experience of being and moving in one place has changed their experience of being and moving anyplace, including when they are not soldiers anymore."[23] Therefore, the affect of war and militarization is continually carried in the body and mind long after they have left the war zone.

Cynthia Enloe's construction of militarization is useful here. While Enloe is examining militarism as more of a cultural phenomenon, in which the militarization of the soldier seems to be a given, it helps lay out the effect of militarization on soldiers. Enloe describes militarization as a:

> step-by-step process by which a person or a thing gradually comes to be controlled by the military or comes to depend for its well-being on militaristic ideas. The more militarization transforms an individual or a society, the more that individual or society comes to imagine military needs and militaristic presumptions to be not only valuable but also normal. Militarization, that is, involves cultural as well as institutional, ideological, and economic transformations.[24]

Enloe goes on to state that the road to demilitarization is partially tied up with an unraveling of masculinity. A number of issues come about in the militarization processes, from dealing with PTS to issues of masculinity.[25] The military does a poor job dealing with these issues once a soldier comes home from combat, as there is little time to heal and no real attempt to deprogram a soldier from the training meant to dehumanize and kill the perceived enemies of the state. However, throughout this book we will see veterans begin to demilitarize as they critique the security dispositif and become less dependent upon militaristic ideals and beliefs.

One important critique of this project, coming from the critical military studies literature, is of the privileging of soldiers' and veterans' voices in activist movements, since the privileging of masculine militarized identities can be problematic.[26] Joanna Tidy shows that this becomes especially problematic in activism such as antiwar movements, where militarized masculinities such as combat soldier stories become seen as authentic in comparison to other stories that are often pushed aside but are just as important to understanding the implications of war and militarism. This focus on militarized masculinities in turn can have the ability to militarize the very groups that are attempting to dismantle militarism. I do not refute this criticism, as I think that there is the intent of many of these veterans to fight militarism, especially militarized masculinities, yet the intent can often have the opposite impact. This speaks directly to the messiness of war and politics. One of my close friends, Jeff, would often leave IVAW meetings angry, telling me, "Sometimes I hate IVAW. Many of those guys in the meeting are the same hypermasculine assholes that I hated in the army pushing the same army bullshit." I have no doubt that this occurs in many of the movements that veterans are a part of, and due to the hierarchy of military masculinities (discussed in chapter 5) it is easy to imagine that while these veterans may believe that they have become demilitarized, they still have much work to do.

While these veterans still have personal work to do (as we all do), one thing that they are cognizant of is how they are treated throughout the US. Since 9/11, there has been a "heroization" of soldier and veteran identities, from the media attention to cultural events such as sporting events.[27] Within this heroization is a discourse of patriotism in which those who have served are understood to be patriots who love their country and uphold "American values."[28] Oftentimes this idea of patriotism is framed within politically conservative and nationalistic ideals, whereas liberal ideologies—including social justice issues—are not often seen as patriotic.[29] Therefore, the soldiers and veterans who fight for social justice causes are often seen as having oppositional identities. Being cognizant of this they often work to leverage their identities in order to try to reframe the work they are doing, which would often be viewed as not patriotic, into something that is patriotic.[30] As can be seen throughout the book, this leveraging of their identities and reinscription of patriotism extend beyond issues directly pertaining to war, as many veterans can see the presence of militarism throughout society and they are able to make the connections of their service to these issues and attempt to create positive social and political change.

The activism that these veterans are engaged in is wide ranging, from environmental activism to participating in the Occupy Wall Street movement; it sometimes involves participating in protests, as well as taking paid community organizing positions with nonprofit organizations. While all these veterans began and ended up in different places, the one common point I am starting from is their military service; so, while I hope that my work can be helpful to social movements literature, the work itself is not necessarily about social movements. While the work of authors like Sydney Tarrow, Charles Tilly, Kevin McDonald, Donatella della Porta, and many others is very important not only to social movements but also to understanding the collective identity formation process, they are not particularly interested in the singularity of particular experiences because they are trying to build "theories" of social movements. Furthermore, I am not so much interested in the process or how contentious politics becomes formalized into movements; rather, I am turning it inside out as I seek to understand the affective relationship between these veterans' activism in relation to war and trauma. So, while normative social movements literature is conceptually helpful to define what has been done, it is not useful for understanding the micro politics of veterans, who already share a collective identity that bonds them. Hopefully my work can be seen as an alternative way to examine social movements, as a micro-political analysis is very useful to examining the meso and macro levels of social movements. Furthermore, these veterans often see their activism not necessarily as a product of the social movements, but rather a function of their subject position within the Social Contract, which I am labeling as the "Soldiers' Contract." Throughout this book, the terms "Social Contract" and "Soldiers' Contract" are capitalized, as they are transcendent concepts related to Enlightenment thinkers and the construction of the Social Contract.

This concept of the Soldiers' Contract can help to expand the current critical military studies literature, as it shows the ways that these veterans and their activism enact a similar approach in their critique of the state, militarism, and systems of power. Their embodied experiences before, during, and after war, as well as their relationship to the security dispositif, are what constitute the Soldiers' Contract as well as the Social Contract, which, as I will explain, have a reciprocal relationship.

The Soldiers' Contract

One of the foundations of modern society rests on the idea of the Social Contract, as there are important developmental relationships between the concepts of the nation and subjectivity within the Social Contract. This theoretical construction highlights the legitimacy of authority the state has over individuals. While many have written and theorized about the proper relationship between the state and individuals within this contract, and there is a range of viewpoints on where the limits of freedom, care, and security begin and end, the one clear point that comes through is that in exchange for legitimacy and sovereignty it is the duty of the state to protect and care for its citizens. One of the first theorists to develop the idea of the Social Contract, Thomas Hobbes, states, ". . . covenants, without the sword, are but words and of no strength to secure man at all."[31] It is within this line that we find the basis of the Soldiers' Contract, because it is the sword that defends, upholds, and enforces the relationship between the state and individuals in the Social Contract. But a sovereign is not a lone actor wielding the sword; it is through police and military force that the sovereign exercises the ability to maintain sovereignty. Thus, this concept navigates the relationship between the liberal state and people who are a part of military institutions.[32]

Two classical thinkers dominate current political thought when it comes to war and society, Niccolò Machiavelli and Thomas Hobbes. While Machiavelli predates the Social Contract, his ideas around the use of force are dominant in political thought. Machiavelli preferred a Roman-style standing military comprised of citizens, whereas Hobbes preferred mercenary soldiers.[33] The difference between these two is important, as one relies on the patriotism of the people to defend the state (Machiavelli), whereas the other works to protect citizens from the violence of war (Hobbes).[34] While Hobbes would help form the Social Contract, it would seem that most Enlightenment thinkers would follow Machiavelli's ideas on who should be defenders of that contract, as Rousseau, Kant, Hamilton, and many others would all advocate for citizen militias as forms of national defense; even Napoleon would use citizen patriotism as a way to create an "imperial military juggernaut."[35] However, while the use of citizen soldiers has been important to defending and forming the Social Contract, there has always been an element of a professional army within the formation of the nation.

Carl von Clausewitz believed there was no escaping the value of a professional army. This becomes especially clear with modernized weapons, as the technological complexity of weapons requires a professionalized component.[36] Because of this, there is a balance that has formed between a citizen/militia-style military and a professional/mercenary-style military in most nations. In the US there was a draft through the Vietnam War, but due to the unpopularity of the war and the draft, there was a shift to an "all-volunteer army," thus shifting the "political economy from post-war welfare statism to neoliberalism."[37] So in many ways the US is a mix of the two forms of thought. In some countries such as Israel, Iran, and many others, there is a forced conscription. So, what does the composition of one's military say about a country's system? The composition question must go beyond volunteer versus non-volunteer, as political aims of a nation easily become entangled within the formation of the soldier identity, thus shifting the Soldiers' Contract.

As Charles Mills points out, the Social Contract is not only political and moral but also racial.[38] Looking at the US military historically, we see that it has not only been used to "protect" the nation from foreign invaders, but that it has primarily been used to maintain the Social Contract internally—from employing the military to put down slave revolts to the use of the National Guard to stop black children from entering white schools in the 1950s. Carl Bogus goes as far as showing how the Second Amendment of the US Constitution was meant to protect and arm militias that were used as slave patrols, thus showing how the founding rights were meant to uphold white supremacy.[39] Or we could easily see the ways in which the US military was used to exterminate and/or control Native American and Hawaiian cultures, or as Mills puts it, anyone seen as "Savage."[40] This brings into question another aspect that Mills examines, that of beneficiaries versus signatories of the contract, because while not all white folks are signatories of the racial contract, all are beneficiaries of it. So, what does this say about those who enforce the racial contract, soldiers? While they are usually beneficiaries of the contract as well, are they all signatories since they are enforcing it? Again, we see this shifting throughout time dependent upon space, place, and current political climate. For example, the Soldiers' Contract in relation to the Social Contract looks extremely messy and different depending upon which side of the Civil War one was on; or the differences between a segregated US military force during World War II versus military forces today; beyond race, the contemporary debates over women serving in combat roles, as well as folks who identify as transgender serving at all. The aspect of women being excluded from military service for so long shows how the Soldiers' Contract upholds Pateman's Sexual Contract in the maintenance of a patriarchal society. So, the composition of the military is an important reflection of the relationship between the Soldiers' Contract and the Social Contract.

Introducing Racial and Sexual Contracts into the Soldiers' Contract—as Pateman and Mills do for the Social Contract—suggests that it will vary dependent upon space and time. So, at the height of the Enlightenment, the Soldiers' Contract can arguably be seen as crucial to the formation of the United States. The contract between the varied states and soldiers at this time was primarily what Pateman refers to as the "settlers contract," wherein the goal of soldiers was to occupy and establish authority beholden to the soldiers' state authority.[41] In return, soldiers received land rights—often called military bounty lands—which, in the case of the United States government, partially established a basis of being a citizen protected by the Constitution.[42] This practice continued through the middle of the nineteenth century.

Ideologically speaking, the American Civil War marked a dividing point for the Soldiers' Contract, as the Union worked to maintain the nation, which was heading toward the abolition of slavery, and the Confederacy fought to uphold states' rights in order to maintain the institution of slavery. The Emancipation Proclamation would be the tipping point, as it not only pushed slavery to an end, but it also opened the door for black Americans to fight for Union forces.[43] The vast majority of those who fought in the war were the poor, who were drafted to fight for either the North or the South, depending upon where they lived or arrived in the country. The Union had an easier time drafting folks as they had a wider pool of people to draft from, especially considering that New York City was a major port city where large numbers of European immigrants arrived. Citizenship was often offered in exchange for service in the military.[44] With the Union victory, slavery ended, and while black Americans would partially be brought into the fold of the Social Contract, equality remained elusive, as there was still mass discrimination and Jim Crow laws that kept half of the country segregated, including a segregated military force.

While the Soldiers' Contract may have shifted to be a bit more inclusive, it still worked to maintain colonial white supremacy within the US, as it used the ideology of Manifest Destiny to expand westward and decimate many different indigenous cultures.[45] Once "sea to shining sea" was accomplished, the US began empire building and its gaze shifted outward. It is in empire building that the Soldiers' Contract really begins to shift and become not only more complex but also more noticeable. When war is on your doorstep it is much easier to justify, from tactics such as fear and control of an "other," to the opportunity of land and riches to be gained through bounty land warrants, you are constantly face-to-face with why you should fight.[46] But the farther away from war one gets, the reasons become more rhetorical, and the wealth and resources fall into fewer hands. Nothing drives this point home more than Maj. Gen. Smedley Butler's short 1935 book, *War Is a Racket*.[47] Butler is one of the most decorated US Marines of all time, a two-time Medal of Honor recipient who served tours of duty all over the world. In this antiwar political manifesto, he highlights the ways that the military is used in order for US businesses to profit, at the expense of soldiers' lives. This critique would be echoed years later by President Eisenhower, once a military general himself, in his famous warning about the military-industrial complex. So, what kept soldiers fighting and risking their lives so far from home for the profits of a few? While some were conscripted, many joined due to the economic hardships of the times; military service did not pay much, but it was guaranteed food and shelter for many. Furthermore, as will be highlighted in chapter 6, the US military has a long history of enlisting foreign-born citizens with the promise of citizenship. While natural-born citizens are born into the Social Contract within the US, foreign-born citizens are not, and thus they are agreeing to two contracts when they sign up. First is the US Social Contract, second is the Soldiers' Contract, which is meant to defend the first. Thus, empire building also relies on foreign-born labor, with the promise of inclusion in the US Social Contract.

Empire building requires many allies, so when war broke out in Europe during World War I, the US eventually answered the call, although in both World War I and World War II it did so reluctantly, as faraway war for other people's land is hard to justify, especially with the onset of the Great Depression. Bonuses were promised to soldiers, but when the US government and the US upper class pushed to not uphold the promised bonuses, the veterans organized into the Bonus Army, which turned into a series of protests in Washington, DC, that had the participation of more than 40,000 veterans.[48] While the Bonus Army would be violently removed, the seeds of dissent were sown, and the rights of the soldier began to shift. It is my contention that *it is in the protest of soldiers and veterans that we can best see the state of the Social Contract that the people have with the state.* Since soldiers are the sword and the strength of the Social Contract, their dissent acts as the miner's canary and shows that there is something amiss in the Social Contract. Soldiers and veterans have led the way for progress not only in the military but across the nation, as the reciprocal relationship between the state and soldiers has been important for either to succeed.

One example to see the relationship between the Soldiers' Contract and the Social Contract is to examine the imbrications of the military and the civil rights movement. The Bonus Army was not racially segregated, as the military at the time still was. Veterans both black and white stood side by side and came together to advocate for what the state owed them. The push by the Bonus Army would eventually lead to better care and benefits, such as the GI Bill, for veterans.[49] This unity could also be a sign of a shift within the military as the civil rights movement taking place in the 1940s sought to desegregate the US military. The fight to desegregate the military was long and arduous, and lasted from World War II to well into the Korean War. The "Double V for Victory, at home and abroad" sent the message that black soldiers were just as courageous and patriotic as their white counterparts—though in the "Banana Wars," World War I, and World War II, most black soldiers were relegated to noncombat service and hard labor positions, despite the fact that there were some very prominent black fighting units, such as the Buffalo Soldiers and the Tuskegee Airmen.[50] In 1948, President Harry Truman would issue Executive Order No. 9981, which ordered the desegregation of the military. However, due to the cost and difficulty of maintaining a segregated military, it would not be until the Korean War that it would become fully integrated.[51] That this took place during the Korean War means that these gains happened a decade before the civil rights movement would be at its peak; however, it was soldier and veteran activism that pushed Truman to pass the executive order.[52]

One cannot talk about the civil rights movement without understanding the connections to the 1960s antiwar movement; and one cannot understand the antiwar movement without knowing about the veterans' peace movement that led the way within the antiwar movement. But veterans were not only a part of the antiwar movement; with the creation of organizations such as Vietnam Veterans Against the War, veterans came home and were also prominent members of civil rights groups such as the Black Panthers and Brown Berets.[53] The draft, and the soldiers who came home opposed to the war, brought about a critical engagement concerning the war, civil rights, class warfare, racism, and imperialism. It would be this critical engagement that would end the draft, as the US would shift to an "all-volunteer force." Thus, these soldiers saw a flaw in both the Social Contract and the Soldiers' Contract, and their protest worked to renegotiate the terms of the contract as it ended the draft and forced the government to shift not only its strategy for enlisting soldiers but also the rhetoric used to uphold both contracts. As others have shown, however, the shift in the security dispositif to more privatized and neoliberal systems of securitization does not come without its own sets of problems, some of which the activist veterans discussed in this book are now addressing.[54]

While the shift away from the draft would make internal dissent more difficult, as would a rhetorical shift by people who worked to shame dissent such as President Reagan when he stated that "the country has turned its back on veterans, and we'll never do that again," the legacy of dissent by soldiers and veterans has lived on.[55] In the wake of the Iraq War, veterans would start the organization Iraq Veterans Against the War, who again worked to bring a critical engagement to America's military engagements. But many of the veterans who are critically engaging in protest are not only covering issues about war. The activism they are engaged with is a critique of the state, and it is heavily involved with identity politics as they are rooted in issues of race, class, gender, and sexuality.[56] So reframing this within a contractual framework, veterans' and soldiers' protests seen throughout this book are not only a critique of the state, but also a critique of both the Soldiers' Contract and the Social Contract.

Mills highlights that there are de jure and de facto elements within the Social Contract. Similarly, there are de jure and de facto elements within the Soldiers' Contract. First and foremost, soldiers sign a legally binding contract and swear an oath when joining the military. Once they have signed their contract, they are under constant threat from their superiors about maintaining their contract. This threat comes from the recruiters, drill sergeants, and their chain of command. Threats range from imprisonment to death—though the latter is usually a more idle threat, usually in war zones to comply with orders. The threat of breaking the de jure contract plays into the formation of the de facto contract as it is a set of informal practices, ideals, and beliefs that create the subject of the soldier. The contract is used as a consequence during the indoctrination process, as soldiers in boot camp are constantly reminded of what will happen if they do not meet their "obligation," that is, their "duty" to fulfill the oath they swore and the contract they signed. Therefore, the process of militarization becomes a part of the contract, and while this point probably seems obvious, the implications are not as obvious. The terms of the de facto contract then are to be militarized and to follow the directives of the chain of command. This is done and maintained not only through the threat of the contract but also through indoctrination. As I describe in chapter 1, the indoctrination process happens in boot camp and is a mental, emotional, and somatic process meant to break down the individual so that he or she becomes part of a militarized group. The aims of the de facto contract are clear: the weaponization of the body and the ability to create weapons of and for the state. The de facto contract can be seen throughout military culture, from the cadences that are sung to the hypermasculinity and racism that is often promoted. The de facto contract contributes to the Soldiers' Contract; however, it does not constitute it, as the Soldiers' Contract also has a relationship with society and the Social Contract.

To be clear, the Soldiers' Contract stands between the state and the Social Contract. Thus, when soldiers protest, it shows that they feel there is something wrong with the Social Contract. Soldiers are the defenders of the Social Contract as well as participants in it. When the state violates the Social Contract, soldiers and veterans are in a prime position to critique the state, as well as to work to repair the contract, as they could still be seen as upholding the Social Contract by being a part of the Soldiers' Contract. As the US enlistment oath holds, soldiers are sworn to defend the country from enemies both foreign and domestic. The domestic can include the state if the politics of the time is incongruent with the will of the people. One recent example of this is the organization Vets Vs. Hate, which has worked to counter the divisive rhetoric of President Donald Trump, both before and after his election. This indictment of the state by these veterans shows the violation of the Social Contract that President Trump enables through his rhetoric and policies. While there are soldiers and veterans who work to uphold the ideals and policies of Donald Trump, they too are enabling their understanding of Soldiers' Contract in favor of their political view of the Social Contract. Therefore, individuals' political outlooks can shift their views of both contracts, and thus it is not as much about their actual politics but rather their collective positionality as veterans and soldiers as opposed to subjects of the Social Contract, because no matter their politics they are drawing from similar discourses.[57]

Methods

It is not necessarily the norm for veterans to become activists, especially social justice advocates.[58] However, it is important to hear these voices because they represent a different view from the average veteran precisely because their activism is an articulation of an as-of-yet unmarked phenomenon: the embodiment of political agency to contest the objectification by the military (during service) and the VA (through treatment).

To conduct this research, I started compiling a list of veterans who I considered activists. These were mostly veterans who were part of Iraq Veterans Against the War (IVAW). I then used a snowball method, having them reach out to contact their networks or other veterans that they knew who considered themselves activists on any issue. This led to a large list of veterans who were interested in participating in in-depth interviews, with open-ended questions, that discussed their personal history, their time in the military, and their current activism. The interviews typically lasted two hours, and at times I spent the day with the participants observing them in action, which allowed for extensive field notes. I would ask each participant if there was someone else they knew that could be interviewed, which led to more interviews. From August to December 2013, I drove from coast to coast across North America (the United States, Mexico, and Canada) to conduct interviews with twenty-two self-identified veteran activists. I then transcribed all of the interviews and conducted thematic discursive analysis, which I coded and compiled, primarily into six different categories of activism that I had found among the participants: antiwar, class, environmental, gender, citizenship, and veteran healing.[59]

As I recruited and interviewed participants, my personal identity as a combat veteran helped on numerous levels. First and foremost, many of these veterans were excited to be helping a fellow veteran with a project that was strengthening the community for veterans. Second, the veterans expressed that they were more at ease in relating their experiences with me compared to other interviewers (academic or media), because they knew I had experienced similar things and that I therefore not only understood them better but also would not judge them for their past actions. This is partly due to my opening the interviews by relating my own experiences and explaining how I came to formulate my project. There was also a lot of interaction within the interviews, as we would often echo similar experiences and stories to one another about our time in service. Third, there was no real language barrier, as many of the acronyms, duties, and structures did not have to be explained to me.[60] Throughout the book, all names are the participants' actual names, as veterans wanted their work and activism to be exposed so that others may know of it and hopefully be inspired to do the same. However, pseudonyms are used for any third-party nonpublic figures discussed.

I began the interviews by telling my story and explaining my initial theoretical framework of the overall project. This led to a number of open-ended questions about their time prior to joining the military, in the military, and after the military. This allowed me to ask a range of questions about their subject formation from civilian to soldier to activist. While most of the interviews began the same, they all took on a life of their own, exploring many different paths. Some interviews were held in coffee shops, some at the veterans' places of business, and others just after an activist action or event. Whenever possible, I would observe their activism in action, taking field notes of the event, watching the reactions of others, and analyzing the literature used to promote or explain the event.

My collection of narratives from veteran activists works to make discursive arguments meant to shift the ways in which we understand and view issues around the security dispositif. The initial narratives led into questions that would highlight their current activism, how it tied to their experiences as a soldier, how the issue that they are fighting is tied to the military, and the ways in which their activism has affected them since their exit from the military. I utilized grounded theory; as I traveled and interviewed, I would find common themes to build upon, as well as new questions to ask based upon past interviews. I came into the project solely wanting to interview activist veterans, with no other parameters, but as I traveled themes around identity began to form. While I started with antiwar activists, I found that many of these veterans' activism bled into other forms of activism. One example is the veterans I interviewed who were a part of the Truman Foundation. This group consists of a wide array of veterans, from those who were in no way antiwar but were very environmentally conscious, to those whose activism took them back to Afghanistan to meet with local peace groups there. While I often drew from my own war experiences to relate to those I interviewed, I also used stories I heard from other vets to relate to those I was currently interviewing. This allowed for a further development of the themes that became the chapters of this book.

While there are thousands more veterans who are activists with different stories and experiences that could have contributed to this project, it was obviously not feasible to interview them all. And while I could have done a survey to get a wider representation, the in-depth interviews provide a more intimate account of the everyday violences that these veterans face. Furthermore, a part of what many of these veterans are trying to do is to speak their truths to power, and the details of those truths can easily get lost in surveys and quantitative studies. My project displays these intimate stories and then cuts them open, showing how they relate to theoretical concepts and, most importantly, what we can learn from these veterans. Most of the interviews were very helpful for me personally in understanding how their activism is directly connected to their time in the military.

All of my interviews and field notes were transcribed, tying together those common themes with the different interviews and to various literatures and concepts. My project shows how the veterans' embodiments are not only self-reflexive but also transformative. Many of the veteran activists I interviewed understand the subject-formation processes and the ways that they interact with ideals of masculinity, racialization, and liberal democratic governance, but what they seek is to change those interactions, as they find them deeply problematic and the source of much trauma. The veterans I interviewed seek to resist regular embodiments of militarization, even if they were once a part of and reinforced those same identities.

Furthermore, I am staging encounters with theory and these narratives—which are genealogies—as I seek to create histories of the present. As Foucault explains about genealogies:

> We have both a meticulous rediscovery of struggles and the raw memory of fights. These genealogies are a combination of erudite knowledge and what people know . . . we can give the name "genealogy" to this coupling together of scholarly erudition and local memories, which allows us to constitute a historical knowledge of struggles and to make use of that knowledge in contemporary tactics.[61]

Similarly, my use of the narratives of these veterans and their activism highlights "the discursive construction of social subjects and knowledge and the functioning of discourse in social change."[62] These veterans hope to construct new ways of knowing with their activism and narratives, which is counter to the hierarchical knowledges or systems of thought. These systems often use empirical data, which more often than not works to dehumanize the issues that these veterans are passionate about. These are not just flat stories; they are dynamic narratives inviting us to think about the concepts discussed throughout in different ways. Furthermore, similar to how Michael Shapiro describes the creation of an encounter between data or events and theory, I seek to show how these narratives interact with theory, and vice versa, throughout the book.

Finally, an important aspect to these narratives is the way I engage them with my own experiences. I feel that this can provide a new way of not only understanding the stories and theories I weave in and out of, but also could be seen as a more intimate way to conduct research. In many ways it is a blend of ethnographic and autoethnographic approaches that is engaging with theory. Just as the field of critical military studies works to understand the relationships between the researchers and forms of militarism, this book constantly interacts on multiple levels as we look at my embodied experience, the people I interviewed and their embodiment, as well as the theories and events that are taking place locally, nationally, and internationally.

Road Map

In the first chapter I locate myself within my work through an autoarcheo-logical account of my time in the military. This chapter explores my own subject formation in boot camp, then goes on to show the effects of war. By relating my own experiences, I am able to problematize the ways in which masculinity and racism are used within military training, and how individuality is stripped in order to form the soldier subject. Upon leaving boot camp, an examination of my time in Kosovo and Iraq shows that the soldier subject is not completely stable, as it becomes fractured in war, which then leads to the subsequent struggles to heal and to understand my experience through academia and activism.

Chapter 2 examines the organization that got me interested in activism, Iraq Veterans Against the War (IVAW), as well as my own experience with the group. It not only explores the history of IVAW and their tactics but also focuses upon how their primary tactic, parrhesia—speaking truth to power—represents a perceived threat to Western liberal governance. This form of nonviolent action works to expose the lies as well as the truths that have been hidden from civil society, while also healing by releasing the burden of their truths. Finally, the chapter illustrates the similarities between the dangers these veterans represent with their words to the threat that Chelsea Manning posed by releasing top-secret documents.

Chapter 3 shifts more to others' narratives, as it engages with IVAW members Scott Olsen and Shamar Thomas, and their work with and beyond the Occupy Wall Street movement. This chapter considers the effects of neoliberalism, particularly its effect on communities of color, and the ways in which neoliberalism is maintained by the police state. Occupy Wall Street reflects these problems as it seeks to confront these systems of power through nonviolence, even in the face of heightened state violence. These veterans' activism was produced by neoliberal policies as social programs are stripped and communities become impoverished. In response, they seek to better their situation through resistance, and they are able to relate these functions of neoliberalism to their experiences in the military.

Chapter 4 moves to the *presence* of neoliberalism and war in environmental activism. Many veterans have left the military disgusted with the resource wars that have violently claimed the lives of their brothers and sisters in arms. This in turn has pushed them into becoming advocates for alternative energies and a nonviolent geopolitical stance. This advocacy for the environment has had multiple effects, from shifting the debate from global warming to a position of national security, to veterans finding new forms of healing in and through the power of the nature they aim to preserve. It follows the narratives of veterans Garett Reppenhagen, who has worked as a "veteran coordinator" for a number of nonprofit organizations, and Jon Gensler, a veteran who works to bridge the private sector and the military in order to protect the environment and end America's dependence on foreign oil.

Chapter 5 examines veterans Jessica Kenyon and Brian Lewis in their fight around the sexual assault epidemic that is taking place within the military, which, as mentioned earlier, is one of the violent effects of the presence of war. These veterans seek to change the policies within the military through the US Congress. While it is often thought that this is a problem that primarily impacts female veterans, this chapter also examines the high rate of sexual assault experienced by men. Such sexual assaults act as a marker of the inherent violence of the hypermasculine subject formation that takes place within the military, which also occurs throughout our militarized society.

Chapter 6 continues with the theme of a presence of war and neoliberalism as it juxtaposes three veterans' stories about service to their country, citizenship, and the idea of the "American Dream." The first narrative is that of a Mexican immigrant who honorably served in the US Army and who has now been deported, like many other veterans in his position. Today, he seeks reentry to the US, pleading his case to anyone who will listen as he marches up and down the rows of cars entering the country through the border town of Tijuana. The second story is that of the son of migrants whose family members have all served in the military. After his deployment to Afghanistan, he refused to be redeployed and fled to Canada to become a war resister. He now seeks asylum but has been labeled a criminal and faces deportation and imprisonment for being absent without leave (AWOL). The chapter then relates the story of a veteran who has fought to have his courageous Afghan interpreter given asylum in the United States. These three stories demonstrate how the racial imaginary within civil society is formed, and who is deemed worthy of being part of that imaginary.

Finally, chapter 7 engages with veterans who are trying to "remake sense" of their experiences in the military through art and poetry. This chapter offers new, alternative ways to combat the PTS and other traumas they experienced while in the military. These practices are used to deprogram the violent identity formation produced by the military and the traumas of war. While the inscription of war is a permanent scar that the veteran cannot erase, these activists seek to transform the experiences of war into something that the veteran can understand and live with.

1

Autoarcheology of War

In Michel Foucault's series of lectures entitled *The Hermeneutics of the Subject*, he outlines a number of methods related to an introspective line of understanding that looks to locate the intricacies that are tied between the concepts of the subject and truth. Within this journey, he examines the concept of knowledge and "true discourse" when he states, "making the truth your own, becoming the subject of enunciation of true discourse: this, I think, is the very core of this philosophical ascesis."[1] It is in this spirit, of making my experience the subject of enunciation, that I hope to draw out why my work is important. By turning the gaze inward, hopefully a new discourse can be found and a personal account of political affect, as described by John Protevi, may be seen. Furthermore, by examining this particular narrative through different lenses, the political can shift as a different understanding of the Iraq War can be told and used as a lesson of war and violence. The narrative thus becomes its own body politic as similar stories can be heard from veterans across the nation, highlighting how war and veterans' subsequent return has affected society. This account can be seen as a model for examining narrative accounts, which highlight the politics of narrative international relations. However, it should be noted that Foucault's appeal to "true discourse" and "the subject" contains multiple layers. For Foucault, truth is a contentious claim, not solely focused upon accuracy, because my truth may look very different from the truth of those who I interview throughout this book, or even different than those I fought beside. Our subjectivities and truths become sites of struggle that work to contest and complicate the everyday narratives. Our stories and our activism are a struggle toward a truth that can serve us, and a subjectivity we can inhabit, as it becomes a poignant field of struggle. Ultimately, this narrative is an insight into my own construction of how I came to understand

23

my relationship to the Soldiers' Contract, as well as my relationship to the military dispositif.

Joining the Army

One day while driving down Patterson Road in Grand Junction, Colorado, my best friend, Garett, told me he had a dream in which he saw himself in the military. "I'm thinking of joining," he said, "which is crazy because I told myself that I would never join after the torture that my dad put me, my brothers, and mom through." His father had been a drill sergeant in the army and had received a Purple Heart, among other medals for his time in Vietnam. He died from complications with shrapnel that eventually formed cancer after being in his body for more than twenty years. I told Garett that I had tried to join many years before, but as I was overweight at that time I was not able to join. I knew the recruiters, and told him, "Well, if you want to go, I would be down, let's go talk to them." I had spent the prior year in college but knew that I could not afford to continue to take out loans, as well as I knew I was not ready for college since I had spent the last few years partying and not taking my studies seriously.

Initially we tried contacting the Colorado National Guard but only got the answering machine and didn't hear back from them, so we went to the regular US Army recruiters. I had been to the recruiting station before and recruiters SSG Fortenberry and SSG Petty greeted us; the latter would die at the same time that we were in Iraq. The job of the recruiter is to be your best friend; he is there to reassure you, make you excited to join, and make sure that you qualify. The first time I had attempted to join a couple years before, I was barely overweight and told to come back the next month, which discouraged me. This was the first time I had seen the recruiters since my initial rejection, though they had called me regularly. The two men seemed genuinely happy to see me, perhaps because they knew that besides my past weight problems I was a quality candidate, as I had a high school diploma and no criminal past.

SSG Petty was a Cavalry Scout, and one of the videos that he showed us was actually a Special Forces video, but he said that this would basically be our job if we chose to be Cavalry Scouts. The video was very exciting as soldiers zipped around on dirt bikes and dune buggies and were shooting weapons neither of us had seen before. We decided that this would be a fun option if they offered it for the Army Reserves. Within a couple of days, we were on a plane to Denver to go through MEPS (Military Entrance Processing Station). They flew us over the night before and put us up in a hotel. Early the next morning we would be rushed through breakfast and then put through a number of lines, tests, background checks, and paperwork. I had gone through the process before and knew that much patience was needed to get through the long day. Once we had both passed all the tests and were done being poked and prodded we were taken to the contracts office. Garett went ahead of me, and when he came out he told me, "So I decided to sign up for active duty for three years, but got guaranteed to be stationed in Germany. Do you want to do the same, because if you do we can go on the buddy program?" It didn't take me long to decide that it would be fun going to Germany, so I agreed, and within an hour the contracts would be drawn up and we would sign our lives away for at least the next three years.

What we were told, but not very clearly—and which would later become a very stressful aspect of our service—was that our contract was actually for eight years, three years of active duty service, then five years of Individual Ready Reserve. Furthermore, what they quickly say while reviewing the contract with us was that during those eight years, at any time, we were at the will of "the needs of the Army." Meaning, if they needed us to stay longer, they would extend our service beyond the three years of active duty service, which did end up happening. However, at the time all of this seemed a distant possibility since there was no reason why they would need to extend our service; we weren't at war, as it was July of 2001. We also decided to go on the delayed entry program, not leaving until October of that year.

About a week after we had signed up, our buddy Jeff had decided that he wanted to join us in Germany, so he went through the same process and we were all then on the buddy program together. Once we had signed up, the recruiters kept in contact to ensure that we were preparing for basic training. We did so primarily by working out and watching Stanley Kubrick's famous film *Full Metal Jacket*. By repeatedly watching the film, we built up an idea of what boot camp would be like, which on one level terrified us, but we felt that it prepared us for the worst. The recruiters assured us that boot camp would be much easier than it appeared in the movie, but that it definitely did resemble it in many ways. And like generations of soldiers before us, we turned to popular culture to build conceptions of war. Previous generations had looked up to John Wayne and Audie Murphy; we had directors like Kubrick and Oliver Stone.[2] While the tenor of the films changed, the glory and excitement had not. Movies prior to Vietnam seemed to glorify the soldier as a hero, and while many post-Vietnam movies showed layered complexities of war, the masculinity of being a soldier still shone through.

Less than two months after signing my contract to join the military, I was awakened one morning by my roommate telling me that there had been an attack on the World Trade Center in New York. I told him to fuck off, and he said, "Seriously, come check it out." I got up and went into his room as the first tower fell. My mind began to swim and my stomach knotted up, as I knew that this would change everything with my upcoming entrance into the military. At the time, I was working at a river rafting company and was scheduled to lead a trip that afternoon. The trip was different than any other trip I had guided, as the shadow of the moment ominously loomed over the day. To add to the awkwardness, the family who was on the float trip was from New York. The silence was piercing, and I remember asking, "Have you been in touch with your friends and family?" The father replied, "Yeah, we're actually from Upstate New York, but we have talked to most of our friends and family back home."

That night I went to hang out with Garett and Jeff to discuss the situation. While we were all scared about the future, we were still adamant about joining the military—I more so than Garett and Jeff because of my conservative political leanings, but Garett was still determined, and Jeff decided he was still along for the ride. There had been some talk of what could happen if we didn't go, and we thought that we probably didn't want to find out. Our recruiters had called the next day to see how we were doing, but they also called to tell us that we had signed contracts and that we could go to jail if we didn't go, which confirmed our thoughts. We would later find out that our recruiters were lying to us, since our contract was not solidified until we were sworn in before we left for basic training, but either way we planned on going. I was proud to be going, as I thought at the time that we were doing the right thing. On October 15, 2001, we would leave Grand Junction, fly to Denver, be sworn in, and fly out to Fort Knox, Kentucky.

Boot Camp

. . . there are psychiatrists who recommend fear, violence, and threats in every case. Some see the fundamental imbalance of power as sufficiently assured but the asylum system itself, its system of surveillance, internal hierarchy, and the arrangement of the buildings, the asylum walls themselves, carrying and defining the network and gradient of power.

—Michel Foucault, *Psychiatric Power*

Much as Foucault points out in the preceding quote, basic training was an imbalance of power. After a week of waiting for space to open up in a new training company, we were given our initial physical test; those who passed would go on to the training company, and those who failed would have to wait longer and try again. We were told that the next chance we would have to do this would be a month away, so it motivated us that much more to pass the first time. The sergeant who was in charge of us until we went to our training platoon was now unleashed and was finally allowed to "smoke us" now that we had passed our physicals. He had us going back and forth between the "front-leaning rest position" (better known as the push-up position) and standing at attention for hours. He would call out "Bawk-Bawk," to which we were to reply "Chicken-Chicken"; he would then call it out again and we were to reply, "Chicken Head."[3] The cadence was from a popular rap song that came out that year, meant to degrade women, which seemed like a taunt he enjoyed directing at us.[4] Later that morning we would get on a bus and go get all of the issued equipment that we would need, and then on to our training company, Echo Company.

As the bus pulled up, the drill sergeants were waiting outside for us; they then boarded the buses and began screaming at us to get off the buses. It was a torrent of yelling, as curse words and degradations were being thrown at us as we tried to exit the buses and get in line as quickly as possible. Once outside we were told to empty our duffle bags on the ground for their inspection, though they barely looked at the contents strewn across the lawn, yelling at us to "get our shit back in our bags." One smaller drill sergeant walked around with a clipboard and got the recruits' names, and told them which platoon they would be in. Once we were told our platoon, and all of our stuff was back in the duffle bags, we were told to get our stuff up to our barracks as quickly as possible and to get back downstairs for formation. I was put into 3rd platoon, while my friends Garett and Jeff were put into 2nd platoon, which was distressing, but it seemed that I had much bigger problems to worry about at the time.

The first few weeks of basic training were known as "black phase"—so named because it reflects the status of being completely out of supplies, or more particularly ammunition, regarding which we are seen at this point as starting from zero—and it is the most difficult portion of basic training. It is in these first few weeks that the initial imbalance of power is formed, primarily through a somatic process that includes discipline centered on the body and psychological degradation meant to break down the soldier. Punishments were usually focused on individuals, but if an offense was big enough one's whole platoon would be punished. Often there was no real cause for a punishment; rather, it was a statement being made that we were not individuals. We were now property of the US Army. Drill sergeants would scream in our faces, call us names, and make us do hours of bear crawls, push-ups, sit-ups, running, etc. We would be kept up late and awoken early to ensure that our mental and physical capacities were worn down to a bare level of survival.

Throughout these first few weeks we were constantly exhausted, and it seemed that everything we did was incorrect. A button would be undone on our pockets, and we would be punished; someone next to you would fall asleep during a class, and you and he would have to do push-ups. It got to the point where I questioned which way was up and which was down. I questioned why I joined, why I was there. It is in the first few weeks that the highest attrition rate takes place, but with the attacks of September 11 having just occurred, our drill sergeants aimed to make it very difficult for anyone to get out of their contract, which made us hate them that much more.

One night in the first few weeks, my "battle buddy" Jared told me that he "couldn't take it anymore" and that he was going to tell the drill sergeants that he was gay.[5] I asked him if he was telling the truth, and he said he had a whole black book of contacts to confirm his story. The confrontation must not have gone well because the next time I saw him he was in tears and wearing a bright orange vest that read "SUICIDE WATCH," and we had to take shifts to watch him. He later told me that he had threatened to commit suicide if they didn't let him out, which later created a spectacle as the drill sergeants would berate him as "weak," "a pussy," and "a faggot." The obviously gendered insults were intended just as much for us as they were for him, as they insinuated that a man is not like him, and that he was acting like a woman.

The military relies on creating and maintaining these gender roles during training, as it is an easy way to control and build the militarized masculine subject.[6] This berating was prior to the repeal of the military's policy of "Don't Ask, Don't Tell," which had made coming out as gay a crime within the military; but while gays can now openly serve, the maintenance of masculinity is still a very important aspect of training. This punishment was also a purposeful humiliation as Jared was used as an example of the hell that they could put us through, because if we thought we had it bad, they showed us that they could still make it a lot worse. He was eventually sent to an out-processing unit and kicked out of the army, but the message was clear: it may just be easier to finish training than to get kicked out like Jared was. A part of me looks back and sympathizes with him, but another part of me feels like he is the one who got off easy.

In Foucault's *Psychiatric Power* lectures, the construction of the soldier as a subject can be related to his description of subject formation in the asylum, which occurs in progressive steps. The first step that Foucault identifies is the creation of an imbalance of power between the doctor and patient, whereas the doctor demonstrates force in order to make the patient conform to his will and the patient learns to "accept the doctor's prescriptions."[7] Similarly, black phase is meant to perpetuate this imbalance of power, from the constant punishment, which broke down not only our bodies but also our will, to making an example of my battle buddy. The laws had been set as to who was the doctor, and to survive, the drill sergeant's prescriptions must be taken. It was a constant mix of emotions that drove me the first few weeks: fear of being punished or, even worse, being recycled and having to start all over; a deep anger and hatred at the drill sergeants and what seemed like cruel punishment; the feeling of pride, whenever a task was completed, or when we overcame an obstacle; and the constant, extreme exhaustion. While the latter wouldn't seem like an emotion, it definitely was one; perhaps it was an anti-emotion because when you become too exhausted you become completely devoid of all emotions, and you start to move on automatic pilot, which is what they wanted. Furthermore, this emptiness of emotions helps build the path toward hypermasculinity; the hypermasculine subject is supposed to be devoid of emotions as they were seen as a weakness.

A Reuse of Language

. . . it is equally a matter of re-teaching the subject to use the forms of language of learning and discipline, the forms he learned at school, that kind of artificial language which is not really the one he uses, but the one by which the school's discipline and system of order are imposed . . . making the patient accessible to all the imperative uses of language: the use of proper names with which one greets, shows one's respect and pays attention to others; school recital and of languages learned; language of command.

—Michel Foucault, *Psychiatric Power*

In our right cargo pocket, we were to have with us at all times our *Soldier's Blue Book*. We were to memorize our chain of command, ranks, the seven core US Army values, how to address our superiors, etc. We were expected to be reading and reciting it whenever we had free time. At any time, day or night, we were subject to examination, and an incorrect answer would result in corporal punishment. The *Soldier's Blue Book* contained everything from the definition of a soldier to the national anthem. It was the go-to guide for any questions we had for the first half of our training.

When we would run or march anywhere, we would chant military cadence as a group to ensure that we were all in step with one another. Protevi describes this as an "entrained acculturation through rhythmic chanting to weaken personal identity in order to produce a group subject."[8] This was especially effective because it made one feel more powerful as a group and not alone as an individual when chanting the different cadences, which as William McNeil calls it, "muscular bonding."[9] The loneliness that came with basic training, the feeling of alienation, seemed to disappear as the group became more proficient at running and marching while singing cadence. Furthermore, as previously mentioned, it helped us to stay in step with one another when marching in formation. As the cadence caller would sound off, the first word is supposed to be simultaneous with when your left foot hits the ground. The most basic cadence, that most soldiers first hear, and is often used as filler between cadences, is the simple "left, left, left right." It is through this basic coordination that a somatic reflex begins to be formed so that the individual ceases to be and thus becomes a part of a group as they march as a single organism. To this day when I go for a run, cadences go through my mind; even at times when I walk I hear the "left" as my foot hits the ground. There was a sense of unity in this constant drilling, especially when we practiced for parade drills. This unity was both positive and negative because when someone would mess up and we would have to start over, we would all be angry, but when we perfected our parade steps, a unified smile could be seen. While it seemed that I was losing myself, I was gaining brothers in arms, who knew the feelings I was feeling because they seemed to be experiencing the same.

A few weeks later, while training, Drill Sgt. Mendez was yelling at us and said something that I will never forget: "Listen here privates, you need to take this shit seriously. Many of you will be going to Iraq and some of you won't come back. You need to know how to kill those Haji's so that you can come back." The main reason this has always stuck in my head was because at the time there was no talk of going to Iraq, as Afghanistan was the primary focus. I have always wondered, was this a premonition or did he know something that many did not? Perhaps it was neither and in his own ignorance he was lumping the whole of the Middle East into one enemy; there is no way to be sure. However, in this quote can be found a number of things regarding the concept of the reuse of language that is seen within basic training: first and foremost is a dehumanization of the enemy. As Protevi points out, this is done primarily through creating sterilized euphemisms that can make it seem as if one is not killing a fellow human but rather a wild beast that would kill you otherwise.[10] Protevi uses names of past "enemies" of the US such as "Kraut, Jap, Reb, Yank, Dink . . ."[11] But none of these were used when I was in training; instead it was "Sand Nigger, Haji, Camel Jockey, Dune Coon, etc." This updated version of racial epithets is fairly spatially and ideologically specific, making the enemy of the state not only those who live within the Middle East but also those who are of the Muslim faith and dark-skinned, since, for Americans, "nigger" and "coon" are unmistakable. At the time, I had no problems with these sorts of terms because I had grown up in a very conservative town, where many of these terms and worse were commonly used. However, racial epithets were not always tolerated. As a soldier in 2nd platoon, whose name was Polaski, would say, he wouldn't "take orders from that fucking nigger," talking about Drill Sgt. Rivers. The word got back to Sgt. Rivers about what Polaski had said, and within an hour he was sent up to 3rd platoon, where Drill Sgt. Mendez made him hate life, after which he was eventually kicked out. The contrast of using racism to create a foreign "other" versus not tolerating internal racism creates an interesting hierarchy. As Basham points out:

> These accounts suggest that military training could mitigate the association of racial difference with inferiority that so often characterises racial stereotyping and racism within the institution and more widely. However, it is important to remember that as long as the military as an institution continues to facilitate stereotyping based on seemingly fixed notions of culture in its recruiting and institutional practices, then traces of the myths that sustained the military's imperial past will continue to mark its present. Such myths not only facilitate divides between sub-groups of the military population but echo a wider biopolitics that prioritises some ways of life over others on the grounds of perceived and often immutable cultural differences. These supposedly unassailable differences sometimes materialize war.[12]

Therefore, according to how the military frames it, it is okay to be racist toward the enemy but not toward the hierarchy or the structure of power, as the hierarchy is what maintains both the Social and Soldiers' Contracts. However, because the military perpetuates racism within its training, it creates spaces for racism to persist and thrive, so long as one does not get caught being racist toward another within the military; so instances of racism are thus often tolerated and go unaddressed.

Polaski's leaving meant that 2nd platoon needed another soldier, and as it was known that my friends were in 2nd platoon, I was sent down, which seemed to be both a blessing and a curse. I was near my friends but with Drill Sgt. Rivers, who not only scared the crap out of me but also had a reputation for being the most difficult drill instructor. This fear was most likely tied to my own racism and fear of black men, who were a stereotype in my mind, a stereotype that was perpetuated throughout my childhood by the town I grew up in and by American society and culture in general.

Returning to Drill Sgt. Mendez's "premonition," the idea of needing to know our jobs because otherwise "Hajis" would kill us, is how a dichotomy of life and death is formed. You must kill, or else be killed. It will be a "Haji" trying to kill you. It is on this point that I feel I must push against Protevi in that, as a 19D Cavalry Scout, which is a combat arms specialty, there were no sterilized euphemisms for killing. We were expected to be killers, trained to be killers, told consistently that we were killers. On the whole, other military occupation specialties were trained differently, specifically the support specialties that were not combat arms—because they were not expected to be killers—but our training glorified combat and killing. One example of this killing instinct, which is specifically drilled into soldiers using raw emotions, occurs during the bayonet training course. While Protevi points out that rage is ineffective for the contemporary soldier, that emotion is still tapped during training, though only briefly, and only at specific times. Like a powerful drug, the authorities dole it out when necessary.

The first half of the bayonet training consisted of pugil stick training. The pugil stick is meant to act as a replacement for a rifle. There was about an hour of training in different moves that were to be performed if we were attacked in hand-to-hand combat, such as a butt stroke and a thrust; and while the initial training seemed important I eagerly anticipated what was to come. I could see it in others' eyes as well, and I could hear the hypermasculine calls for the pugil sticks. Everybody was given a football helmet and put into a circle. In the circle two soldiers would come together and were told to rage upon one another. It was a primal feeling that you could feel in your gut with emotions going wild and everyone around the circle was chanting and yelling, hoping for blood. Like the movie *Fight Club*, everyone must fight, but it doesn't end until the drill instructor says it's over. Because I was one of the larger soldiers, I was matched up with another large guy, Anderson. The lessons that we just learned had been quickly been forgotten, and I swung the pugil stick with a wild rage as if trying to hit a home run and pretending Anderson's head was the ball. I was reminded of my time playing football, with everybody screaming and yelling, and the blood pulsing through my head drowning out the sound. He hit me hard in the jaw, which knocked me backward. He lunged forward, but as he lunged he tripped, and like a tiger pouncing on its prey, I attacked, hitting him on the back of the head. As I went to swing again the drill sergeant called the match, but I couldn't hear him as my adrenaline pumped. I swung again at the man on the ground only to be tackled by the drill sergeant. While in another arena this behavior may have been discouraged and looked down upon, here it was encouraged as the drill sergeant slapped my ass afterward and told me, "Good job."

The second half of the training was just as intense. Soldiers are given a fake rifle but with a real bayonet. We were again instructed on how to stab someone with it, while it was affixed to the rifle. The drill instructor would yell out, "What is the spirit of the bayonet?" We promptly replied, as loudly as possible, "TO KILL-KILL-KILL WITH COLD BLUE STEEL, DRILL SERGEANT!" The drill instructor then asked, "What makes the green grass grow?" To which we respond, "BLOOD-BLOOD-BLOOD MAKES THE GREEN GRASS GROW, DRILL SERGEANT!" This was done many times over the course of the day, and we were taught that with every thrust of the bayonet we were to scream with our "battle cry," like in the movie *Full Metal Jacket*. Like the marching and cadence, this repetition works to erase the individual and replace it with a group identity, one that removes the moral ambiguity of killing, and instead normalizes it. We were then sent to a mile-long obstacle course in the forest, where we were to jump logs, crawl under concertina wire, run up to a large, human-shaped wooden targets, scream, stab, twist, and pull. There were at least five different dummies along the course and if it was completed in a certain amount of time, we were awarded expert in the Bayonet Achievement Medal.

In hindsight, this day seems to have been an important turning point; not only was it a confidence booster after so many days of being mentally, emotionally, and physically beaten down, but we were also given constant positive reinforcement throughout the day. The act of killing was being transformed from what I had always been taught it was, as bad, to something that was righteous, powerful, and good. It was the first time in weeks that we had all been in high spirits, and we all joked and laughed before going to bed that night.

Management or Organization of Needs

> The third maneuver in the apparatus of asylum therapy is what could be called the management or organization of needs. Psychiatric power ensures the advance of reality, the hold of reality on madness, through the management of needs, and even through the emergence of new needs, through the creation, maintenance and renewal of needs. . . . Basically it involves establishing the patient in a carefully maintained state of deprivation: the patient's existence must be kept just below a certain average level.
>
> —Michel Foucault, *Psychiatric Power*

One of the most basic and consistently drilled management of needs comes in the form of shining boots. The appearance of a soldier's boots is to be scuff-free and shiny at all times in garrison and as much as possible in the field.[13] If the boots are not adequately shined, as per usual, the soldier will more than likely be punished; I am not sure how many push-ups I was subjected to throughout my time in the military due to "not shiny enough boots," but it was definitely a lot. Throughout basic training and the rest of my time in the military, countless hours were spent shining boots. While the boots are the focal point for this entrained action, the whole uniform is to be honored, which is thus creating a need, as Foucault highlights in the passage above, within the reorganization of needs that is a part of this process of subject formation. There should be no wrinkles, all pockets should be buttoned, the beret should be properly formed, etc. As stated in the *Soldier's Blue Book*:

> Personal appearance is important—it demonstrates the pride and self-discipline you feel as a Soldier in the U.S. Army. Being neat and well groomed contributes to the esprit in your unit. Your uniform should fit well and be clean, serviceable, and pressed as necessary.[14]

This passage highlights that the US Army sees a fluid exchange between the individual and the group, wherein they are affective upon each other. Personal appearance becomes a statement of one's feelings and emotions toward the military and the country. The soldier who is "ate up" or, in other words, looks like a slob, shows a lack of respect for him- or herself, the uniform, and for the military. It is thought that the morale of the unit is affected, which then becomes a reflection upon the leadership.

Probably one of the most somatic aspects of the management of needs comes by way of nutrition and is also alluded to as a tactic by Foucault as meals are targets of making the subject become more docile.[15] This is done in a number of ways and begins in basic training. All meals are set at specific times, with a specific amount of time allotted to consume each meal. Soldiers who are larger are regulated as to what they can eat, while soldiers who are underweight are forced to eat more than they normally would. This is to put soldiers at an "ideal" weight, but in reality it is a transformation of the body into a productive subject aimed at being able to complete the tasks the military requires.[16] Soldiers who are overweight are highly scrutinized and face punishment as extreme as expulsion from the military, but that is only for those who cannot achieve an ideal weight through rigorous, often forced, exercise. I was one of these soldiers, as I have always been heftier than most people. I had entered the army weighing 250 pounds, and by the time I left basic training I weighed 180 pounds, the result of many extra miles of running, additional push-ups, sit-ups, food being taken off my plate at dinner, and other forms of punishment. At times it felt like punishment; at other times it fueled me to lose more weight and become stronger. My body had changed, and, to use a football analogy, I no longer looked like an offensive lineman but more like a running back or a linebacker, or more to the point, like an "ideal" soldier. When I went home on hometown recruiting in the following month, my transformation inspired two of my female friends to also join the army. At the time this seemed cool, but I later regretted it, since they would have very difficult experiences in the military; though I know they do not regret their choice to join. Either way, I was transformed into a new man. I was a soldier, and I was a 19D Cavalry Scout.

Transitions

After graduation I went home, as mentioned, to do two weeks of hometown recruiting. After hometown recruiting, and a bureaucratic battle with the army, I finally arrived at my unit in Vilseck, Germany, where Garett and Jeff were waiting. Having just finished basic training "a new man," my previous conservative ideals were further solidified. Garett and Jeff, on the other hand, were both fairly liberal going into the process, and while they too had been physically transformed, they maintained their liberal ideals. Yet even though we had different political ideologies, we were much closer after our experience in basic training because we were able to constantly give one another mental and emotional support.

Within the coming months we would spend much time traveling around Europe, experiencing the world and soaking in new cultures. Many of our friends in the platoon would stay close to base, as it provided everything an American craves: bars, bowling alleys, movie theaters, and restaurants. We were constantly told about the dangers of going off-base and told to stay within a fifty-mile radius. This meant that soldiers could go as far as Nuremberg, but no farther without written consent. However, having each other as pillars of support emboldened us to go where we pleased. Many of our fellow soldiers expressed their fear of going too far, especially without permission, but we felt that one of the main reasons we had joined was to see Europe, and we did. We often tried to stay away from places that soldiers went, because all too often that would be the center of trouble as fights often broke out due to drunken soldiers.

Our refuge came from a small Irish Pub in Nuremberg called P. J. O'Shea's. We became family with the staff, sometimes spending the night at different staff members' homes. We seemed to be experiencing Germany and Europe very differently than our compatriots, as we became embedded within the German economy, and made many friends from all across the world. It was this time that probably softened my ideals of American exceptionalism, which would be shattered upon our first deployment to Kosovo. We trained to be the battalion's Quick Reaction Force, and in September of 2002 we were sent to a small town near the Macedonian border called Vitina, Kosovo.

The training leading up to our deployment consisted of preparing for mortar and sniper attacks. We were to be prepared for everything, and were told the worst; so on our first day in sector, when going on a "ride along" with the unit we were relieving, I was shocked when a little girl came up to the Humvee and threw flowers at the window. Immediately the sergeant on my truck yelled at me, saying, "That's why we keep our windows up! For all we know that could've been a grenade and we would all be dead." I wasn't sure how to react; a part of me was fearful that this place was as violent as the sergeant made it seem; another part of me was angry because what was said made no sense since it was a little girl. She couldn't be the enemy, but it is this type of rhetoric that had become so common in the military.

Over the next six months I would be assigned to drive the platoon sergeant around, Sergeant First Class David Jenkins, or Sgt. J. Our time driving around Kosovo together changed me in ways I hadn't thought possible. Sgt. J was a black man from "Hot-lanta, Georgia!" And this was my most intimate experience with a black man as we spent thousands of hours together. I grew to not only respect him, but I also looked up to him as a sort of father figure. All my preconceived notions of race were thrown out the window as the stereotypes I had once grown up with, believing as facts, were dispelled as things that would infuriate me when I heard them. To this day I still try to track down Sgt. J, and hope to someday reconnect with him and tell him how much he meant to me personally, as well as thank him for his contribution to my transformation into the person I am today. I would later work to understand racial politics, social justice, and white privilege, which might never have happened had I not spent so much time with Sgt. J. While the army isn't trying to make people more liberal, it does need for soldiers to work together across racial boundaries with minimal friction. So, the military's production of subjectivity can take unpredictable turns, as some young white men recalibrate racism in system-challenging ways as evidenced here.

Another incident that made me question the identities and stereotypes I had grown up with came that winter, as it was especially cold and there were multiple blizzards that brought a lot of snow. While on patrol one day I noticed that none of the houses in the area had windows. This thought blew my mind, as I could not imagine living in this climate, in a house with no windows. Having grown up in Colorado, I knew about the cold, but everybody I knew lived in a house with windows. To stay warm people had trash barrels in these windowless concrete homes. To add injury to insult, one of our tasks was to stop smugglers—not smugglers of drugs or weapons mind you—but smugglers of wood. This left an awful taste in my mouth and made me question my privileges as an American.

As we sat in Kosovo, George W. Bush and company ramped up for a war in Iraq. With the walls of my ideologies falling, I didn't know what to believe anymore. I stayed up at night watching the news, listening to Colin Powell's speeches to NATO, and I even went as far as printing out the transcripts of different speeches justifying the reasons we were being given for going to war with Iraq. If these reasons held up, then it seemed justified, but as time went on the justifications for why we were going to Iraq fell, as did my conservative leanings as I followed my friends and became more and more liberal. This caused a lot of personal tension as I slowly lost faith in our cause, which eventually made me not only angry for being sent to Iraq, but I also felt betrayed by my government for sending me to a war that seemed to be justified by lies. In many ways, I felt that I was being told by the state that in order for the state to be safe, in order for the Social Contract to be fulfilled, my duty in the Soldiers' Contract was to go to Iraq and fight. But as I began to see that the reasons they were sending us to Iraq were not factual, I felt there was a violation of the Soldiers' Contract by the state, which meant there was also a violation of the Social Contract.

Upon our return from Kosovo we were told we would be deploying to Iraq within six months, and we promptly returned to training. This time we had much more intense weapons and reaction training. As Cavalry Scouts, we were constantly at different firing ranges learning different weapon systems throughout our time in the military. My own personal weapon throughout my time was an M4A1 semiautomatic carbine rifle. While I was a driver, my rifle had an M203 grenade launcher attached to it, but once I became a gunner this was removed. When I was a gunner I served on two primary weapon systems, the .50 caliber machine gun, and the MK19 automatic grenade launcher. Both weapons were mounted to the tops of our Humvees, and I was considered an expert marksman with both weapon systems. When training with our personal weapons, the silhouettes we fired at were pop-ups at various ranges, which resembled human targets. We would fire from a standing position and lying in the prone position. When firing a crew-served weapon such as the .50 cal. or the MK19, we would fire at vehicle silhouettes. I fired at numerous different firing ranges, and it was always exhilarating to shoot those weapons. The adrenaline rush I experienced when shooting automatic weapons was amazing; I would fire and see things destroyed before my eyes. As Protevi highlights, shooting targets that resemble actual bodies and vehicles raises the probability that soldiers will fire upon real targets when faced with a threat, because the protoempathic identification processes have been bypassed such that killing an enemy becomes no different than killing a target.[17] Furthermore, Michael Shapiro explains that these depersonalized targets create an ambiguity around the target, so that when and if a noncombatant is killed there are less legal and ethical impacts for those who not only pulled the trigger but also for those who ordered the killing.[18] Therefore, if an innocent civilian is shot, the casualty can be brushed off as collateral damage or forgotten as a silhouette.

Protevi also points out that the purpose of using automatic weapons is to kill at a distance through the use of technology, because it is more effective. Soldiers will be more likely to pull the trigger since the distance keeps them from being able to identify with the subject.[19] The military does not label or think of it in this way but rather conceives of the technologies as "combat multipliers," whereas the better our technology and the farther away we can kill from, the fewer soldiers it will take to neutralize a greater number of enemy soldiers. It is in this sense that a sterilization of the terms has shifted the most when examining the act of killing, which has a double effect: one on the soldiers, and the other on society in general as the act of killing then sounds less morally reprehensible.

Another form of target practice we frequently prepared for was known as "room-clearing tactics." While in Germany, preparing to go to Iraq, our platoon did a full day training of with a Navy Seals unit on room clearing, which we would repetitively practice for the next few months. We started practicing room-clearing tactics with no ammo, then with blank bullets, and finally with live ammo. This repetition helped to create a muscle memory, or as Protevi puts it, "direct access of the military machine to reflexes embedded in the spinal cord of the soldier—as clear an instance of political physiology as one can imagine."[20] This training would prove useful in Iraq as our platoon was tasked with a number of house raids, and we were able to safely clear rooms with no casualties on any side. While there were no deaths, however, there were definitely physical, mental, and emotional casualties. We were good at what we did, which was quick, efficient, and terrifying. I have no idea how many people we frightened, made cry, slammed on the ground, or butt-stroked with our rifles. We tore apart families as we often took the males away for questioning, not knowing when they would return. It was all a very traumatic experience for those who were our "targets," often based on poor intelligence.

The last form of reflex training we conducted before leaving for Iraq was a month-long training exercise in Hohenfels, Germany. Hohenfels, a former German Army training site, is an expansive area where brigades can hold training exercises that have a "home" brigade that plays as oppositional forces (OPFOR). Throughout the month numerous live-action scenarios were played out, all while wearing MILES gear (Multiple Integrated Laser Engagement System). The MILES gear consisted of a laser system attached to our weapons that would fire if we fired (when we fired we were using blanks, so it still sounded like we were firing an actual bullet) and receiving sensors that we put on our vehicles and our bodies so if someone fired at us we would know we were hit by "enemy" fire. With each platoon, there was a referee who would tell us the extent of the wounds if someone shot at us and it hit the receiving sensors, and we then had to react accordingly. This simulation is meant to try and match the intensity of real combat situations, as local actors are brought in to act as civilians, small cities are erected and given names of towns we will be deployed to, and past events are re-created.[21]

At the time, though, it felt like an extreme waste of time to me, partially because it was snowing most the time so most of us were more concerned with staying warm; and secondly, knowing that none of it was real when we would soon be facing the real thing made it seem less glamorous. However, the simulation would often spark the adrenaline that I would face in the combat zone—even if it was only a fraction of the intensity; even an unconvincing practice produced a version of the desired militarized affect. The month before we left was nerve wracking as we packed up all of our equipment and had a constant ear on the happenings in what would become our AO (area of operation). At the time I had thought there was a chance that I would be getting out of the military in October, since my three years would be up in the middle of our deployment, but all hopes were lost when we were told we were being put on a stop-loss that would last until three months after our deployment. When I heard the news, it was like somebody had kicked me in the stomach. Not only was I being sent to a war that I no longer believed in, but I would be stuck there after I was supposed to get out. It looked like the needs of the army had won out and I was on the receiving end of what we called the "big green weenie."

Iraq

Our mission in Iraq was to be somewhat similar to the operations we had conducted in Kosovo for nine months, just six months prior to this deployment. We were told that while we would primarily serve as the battalion's Quick Reaction Force (QRF), we would also be tasked with the brigade's QRF duties. This task would be split up into three sections, two sections from our Scout platoon and one from the battalion's Mortar platoon. Each day, one of the sections would be on call for twenty-four hours, and it would then rotate to the next section. When on call, we had to be prepared to leave the base within five minutes and get to any situation to respond to IEDs (improvised explosive devices), ambushed convoys, mortar attacks, etc. On days off, we were tasked with regular patrol missions, convoy escort missions, house raids, and a number of other operations. When we were not out on mission we would have to do maintenance on our vehicles. So needless to say, there was little to no personal downtime for my platoon, making our year there a constant adrenaline high that was very physically, mentally, and emotionally strenuous, which contributed to my own PTS. In relation to PTS, Protevi states, "Many of the problems have to do with the sustained high cortisol levels and the high endorphin-release thresholds of the traumatized body. In other words, PTS is at least as much physiological as it is psychological disturbance, though neither nor the other exclusively."[22] This has played out in a number of ways throughout the years; I will now try to discuss some of the events and situations that led to the different elements of my PTS and my symptoms in general, which in turn show the affective somatic relationship between the individual body and war.

Many of our missions were conducted at night: home raids, counter-mortar operations, patrols, overwatch operations, etc. At least half of our encounters when we were fired upon occurred at night. This has had a lasting effect on me, which is one of the symptoms of my PTS. To this day, my anxiety level is usually higher at night, especially while driving. Whether walking or driving, I usually feel like someone is following me. The darker and quieter it is, the more I am at unrest. Years after exiting the military, I was riding my motorcycle the day before the Fourth of July when a loud "BOOM" went off, followed by a number of small "pops." It sounded as if an IED went off followed by small arms fire. I nearly drove my motorcycle off the road. I pulled over and cried for nearly two hours. Protevi links this crying to a "reprograming . . . joy/endorphin triggers, which are set at a very high-level due to the intensity of battle."[23] It may have worked in some sense, because ever since this situation my sensitivity to fireworks has lessened over the years to a level where it does not really bother or surprise me anymore. However, my anxiety levels and vigilance at night are still a problem, as I am often hyperaware of my surroundings.

Another anxiety trigger is driving slowly. When driving, I usually try to drive as quickly as possible, without getting a ticket. I attribute this to two things that stem from my time in Iraq. The first is the fact that we had to drive as fast as possible to avoid IEDs, which hit us frequently in Iraq; however, because we drove so fast, we usually came out of the situation unscathed. The second is when we were assigned movement to contact missions or, as we liked to call it, "Trolling for Fire" missions. Whenever a particular road or stretch of highway became an area of high contact, we were sent out to drive slowly up and down that area to try to draw fire. After the first few times of this, it became ineffective as the Iraqis realized what we were doing, which then proved dangerous for us, as we became regular targets of IEDs. The command made us do this every few months; they thought it might be effective since we did kill some Iraqis the first couple of times, but it never was.

With only a few months left in our deployment, my section was on QRF duty. One day at around 9 a.m. we were spun up and told to be on standby as the city of Ba'quba was being overrun by insurgents. While this may sound fairly exciting or dangerous, it was just another day to us, as it seemed that we had been constantly on mission and in danger since we had arrived. We got into our trucks and moved to the front gate. It seemed very chaotic as we waited to get our orders. Our platoon leader (PL) came out and told us the situation. We were to get into the city square and secure the location until the areas that were overrun could be retaken. In some ways I was excited because it seemed like this was a legitimate mission to get rid of some actual bad guys, but it also carried a bit of fear since we could hear the chaos from the radio and the booms of explosions outside the wire. As we approached the edge of the city a tank battalion was parked in the middle of the road blocking our entry. We contacted their PL who told us that there was an IED ahead and that we shouldn't proceed until it was cleared. While waiting for them to clear the IED, we started to take automatic fire from a nearby building. The gunner in front of me opened fire with his .50 cal. on a nearby building that subsequently was the local hospital. This angered me at the time because nobody was clear as to where the fire was coming from at that point, but we opened up fire anyway. The fire continued for what felt like an eternity, as time seemed to slow down. We took more small arms fire that I could hear pass over my head and then an RPG was fired and exploded near the tank, which caused all of us to open fire to the southwest as the sun was high overhead. A few minutes later the fire stopped. We waited for about ten minutes; at that point, the tankers disarmed the IED by shooting at it and blowing it up. We regularly used this tactic to disarm IEDs, and every time it seemed gratifying to me.

We slowly crept toward the city center, leaving behind the tankers that were cordoning off the city. The city, heavily populated and normally very active, was like a ghost town. We would go one block and stop and wait for a minute or two. My truck was in the rear of the convoy so my sector of fire was anything behind us, and about halfway to the city center we took fire from the west. We stopped as the drivers and dismounts got out of the vehicle to cover to our east as we turned our crew-served weapons to the west. Down an alley I saw a man in black running toward us with an AK-47; I opened fire with my MK19 and saw the man fall from the blast. I could only see half of the man's body as the other half was hidden by a building, but he lay there without movement. It was a strange mix of emotions seeing the body of someone I had just killed at about thirty yards. My adrenaline was pumping, and there was fear, excitement, satisfaction, anger, sadness, and joy all at once. The fear was for my own life and the lives of my friends, the excitement and satisfaction were from doing exactly what I was trained to do, the anger was for having to be there and from these people attacking us, the sadness for having taken a life, and joy for having come out alive at the moment. The negative feelings would not become prominent until later as I reflected upon the moment, but they seemed to be there still as I fought to survive.

My hands were shaking as we moved on to the city center, but that would prove to be the last real contact we received for the rest of the day. It was hours until our relief came, and as time went people slowly started coming out of their houses. Few dared to cross the main road that we were sitting at, and then a car came out on the road and started coming toward us. I asked my truck commander (TC) if I should open fire, and he approved. I then told him that I was going to fire a warning shot with my MK19 first. Shooting a warning shot with an MK19 is a difficult task as it is an area weapon that has a fifteen-meter blast radius, but I was confident in my ability. I shot, and it landed just outside of the blast radius directly in front of the oncoming vehicle, which caused the car to make a ninety-degree turn onto a side road. The few soldiers that were standing and I all burst into loud laughter, as none of us had ever seen a car turn so quickly and sharply. It was shortly after this that our relief came and we returned to base.

It was upon our return and as I was lying in my bunk that the guilt would begin to flood my mind, which is another aspect of the PTS that I live with today. Protevi links this to the protoempathic identification that was not completely bypassed by the neural conditioning that I had received throughout my time in the military.[24] The guilt I felt was a mixture of thoughts and feelings. First and foremost I wondered about this man that

I had killed earlier in the day. I wondered if he had a family, and thought that he would never see them again. Secondly, I was angry that I had been put into that situation, as I was supposed to be out of the military a month earlier, but because of our deployment I had been stop-lossed. I wanted to throw down my weapon and tell my command, "Fuck off," "Do what you will," and, "Take me to jail." I knew this would accomplish nothing, however. I knew that I would feel like I was abandoning my brothers in arms who had my back, and I knew I had to be there for them. Lastly, there was the emotional drain of having been in an intense situation for nearly twelve hours; I was mentally, emotionally, and physically drained. I lay on my bunk, unable to sleep, feeling sick to my stomach, shaking and crying. For years after my deployment, I would dream about this day and wake up in a sweat. Furthermore, one of the side effects that would come from my PTS would be my weak early morning stomach, as I would often vomit up my breakfast if I walked too quickly in the morning. It still happens occasionally, but only when I am stressed.

These examples, which all come in the form of PTS, are excesses of war and docility. The life of a person in the military is filled with this disciplinary training upon the body, which is effectively physiological and psychological; in a sense this is masculinizing, feminizing, and infantilizing the soldier all at once. This is done in order to maintain the ability to do the job required of a soldier, which is often to kill but only to kill those whom they are told to kill and when they are told to kill. Upon leaving the military, the neurons reroute and the soldier is forced to face those memories without the blanket of disciplinary thinking that shields the morality of warfare and maintains the distinct boundaries of their identity. Soldiers are expected to be docile in relation to their chain of command, and when a soldier is traumatized by war that docility becomes dislodged and the excesses of masculinity come through if not properly maintained, controlled, and regulated. That trained docility runs counter to the ideal of masculinity, since docility is often thought to be a feminine trait. The disciplinary lifestyle within the military can sometimes not be enough to maintain the "military bearing" as soldiers sometimes crack, and the boundaries of reality began to blur, which is why you see some soldiers crack while still in the military. This leads to problems that vary in intensity, from subtle ones like driving erratically or not socializing well outside of the military, to more intense and dangerous issues like domestic violence or murder, which have become all too common on and around military bases across the country.

Transitions II

We had left from Germany on Valentine's Day in 2004 and returned on Valentine's Day 2005. It seems that the irony of this was not lost on the military, as the day that was meant for love was transformed into fear, but was again transformed back into a day of rejoicing as we returned to celebrate with our loved ones. While there was no sweetheart waiting for me upon my return, I was deeply looking forward to seeing my friends at P. J. O'Shea's, which was a double-edged sword because I knew the drunkenness that would ensue, but this too was something I was looking forward to. The next three months would be spent in some stage of non-sobriety, as I endeavored to forget the past year. Our base butted up against a firing range, so at night I would often hear the booms of tanks, which would cause me to jump out of bed in a panic as I searched for the weapon that was no longer constantly by my side.

Two weeks after we returned we were given a month leave, and I decided that I would go on a trip by myself. I bought a Eurail pass and headed north. While crossing a bridge into Sweden, listening to my MP3 player, Pink Floyd came on, "The Gunner's Dream." I hadn't heard a lot of the music on my MP3 player in a long time, and as I listened to this song I was taken into the memories of the past year, as the sounds of bombs, helicopters, and bullets resonate throughout the song. As the song progressed, waves of emotions washed over me, from disgust when the singer says, "You never hear their standard issue kicking in your door," to an immense sadness when he sings, "And no one kills the children anymore."[25] As the tears streamed down my face a searing anger rose up within. I wanted to hurt someone, not an innocent random person but whoever was responsible for causing me this pain. I wanted to fight, but I had no idea where to point my rage. My time in Iraq had been an injustice, and I felt a need to correct this injustice. I wasn't sure how I would do this, but it was at this point that I became determined to do something. The song remains an emotional trigger for me, as I still get emotional whenever I hear it.

The rest of the trip was pure debauchery. I was drunk nearly every day and every night, and also often took mushrooms, snorted cocaine, and slept with random women, all in an attempt to numb those feelings and emotions, while not caring about the consequences. While I was determined to make some sort of change, I could not face those memories yet. It wasn't until I returned to Germany weeks later and went to see an independent counselor that I would attempt to address some of this anger. While the counselor helped, it would be years before I considered myself at some point of normalcy—if there is such a thing—but what he taught me was that speaking about my experience made me feel better. Being able to tell my story was liberating and healing, as it was an opportunity to release much of the hate, anger, and fear that seemed to be strangling me from within.

I got out of the military on May 31, 2005, and was flown back to Denver. It was one of the best feelings I had ever had, as if a huge boulder had been removed from my back. But my return had not brought all good news as I soon learned that my grandmother was not doing well. The day after my twenty-fifth birthday, a week and a half after I had returned, she died. I was very close to her throughout my life, but for some reason I was completely devoid of all emotion. While everyone around me was profusely sad, I could not sympathize with their pain; it seemed that they were dealing with a small cut, while I was facing the Grand Canyon. To cope with all of it, I was attempting to deal with my emotions in a very unhealthy way, as drugs and alcohol filled much of my time.

Garett and Jeff got out of the military on the same day I did, and while Jeff went to Bulgaria to spend time with his future wife, Garett headed to Washington, DC. He too seemed bent on creating change as he teamed up with Bobby Muller, who was a Vietnam veteran, activist, and winner of a Nobel Peace Prize. Garett would become one of the "poster boys" for the veteran peace movement, working with the organizations Vietnam Veterans of America and Iraq Veterans Against the War. Garett was the first active-duty soldier to become a member of IVAW, and upon our return from the military he encouraged Jeff and me to join, which we did. IVAW became an outlet for me to release my anger in positive ways, from protests to hanging out and venting with like-minded individuals who were just as pissed off as me. It was therapeutic. It also hooked me into a number of other healing organizations such as Vets 4 Vets (a peer counseling group) and the Warrior Writers Project (which taught us to make poetry and art from our experiences, also the focus of chapter 7).

While IVAW had helped me before—and is the focus of the next chapter—I still felt like something was missing. Late one night while lying on my mom's couch, flipping through the channels, I stopped on a PBS special highlighting the classical sociologists; that night the episode was about Karl Marx. I became entranced, as everything that was being said seemed to make sense. So much so that the next day I went to the local library and checked out *Das Kapital*. The next night the show highlighted

Max Weber, and the next night Durkheim. I fell in love with sociology, and decided that I would go back to school and study both political science and sociology in order to best understand my experience. The transition into school was tough, especially interactions with the students who were fresh out of high school, who seemed to know nothing. They seemed to worry about the dumbest stuff and complain about everything, but this view was really my own selfishness, as I tried to quantify my pain.

I kept myself as busy as possible with school activities, homework, and activism, as these helped me to avoid the mental and emotional pain I was experiencing. It took close to three years for my VA claim to finally be processed, so I found my own ways to cope with the stress and PTS. Even after I was receiving VA benefits, I used my own means of coping since I did not like the antidepressants that they tried to keep me on. They made me feel number than I already felt, which was disturbing to me. I often returned to drugs and alcohol, but I had gotten over my dependency on them and my constant need to escape. My activism branched out from war-related issues to social justice issues, as I began to understand more about race, class, gender, and sexuality. I began to see the connections between these issues and militarism and realized that it was a multifaceted front that I must fight.

One of my professors at the time invited me to apply for the ethnic studies graduate program. The same professor, Eric Ishiwata, would encourage me to get my PhD where he did, in the Political Science Department at the University of Hawai'i at Mānoa. Following in his footsteps, I sought to become a professor, and I too hope to be "infectious" with my thought, like he once told me was his goal. I hope to teach a new generation about the dangers of militarism, racism, class inequity, sexism, and hypermasculinity. I fight to make a difference in every person I meet, and all the while atone for the wrongs I have perpetuated.

Moving Forward

So, what can be drawn from this story? Not only is the violent process of militarization highlighted but so are the ways in which it is embedded within a racist, sexist, hypermasculine discourse that perpetuates certain hierarchies of power. It is a testament to the atrocities of war and the ways in which war affects soldiers. It examines the biopolitical excesses of war, as veterans must fight to remake sense of their lives with little to no help or understanding.

But most importantly, it is my story, my truth, and hopefully an insightful lesson to you the reader as a call to arms, a call to fight injustice with me.

The story places me within my larger project of examining veteran activism, exploring the new politics that is arising from veterans' experiences, examining violence in peace, and showing how my understanding and relationship to both the Social and Soldiers' Contracts was formed. This is not a project of self-affirmation, as I too got out of the military and became a social justice advocate; rather, this is a project about a body politic of veterans' discourse that says something more significant about hegemony and neoliberalism. The following chapters will explore the narratives of veteran activists all around the country, as I sought out veterans who specifically considered themselves social justice advocates. I met a wide range of people, all dedicated to their service in the military and all passionate about their current activism. I will explore the discourse of American culture around many of these issues, and what these veterans are doing to try to influence and shape this discourse.

2

Forged in War, Battling for Peace

A soulja has put down their rifles and has picked up their souls.
Instead of bullets, a soulja has their words.
Instead of Dogma, a soulja listens to their heart.
Instead of secret codes, a soulja reflects their feelings and their thoughts.
Instead of stealing land, a soulja expands their intellect.
Instead of taking aim, a soulja takes reason.
Instead of building fortifications that divide,
a soulja grows with unity for all humankind.[1]

—Hart Viges (Iraq War Veteran)

The US government's global war on terrorism (GWOT) is said to be aimed at making the world safe for democracy. It has instead perpetuated a number of other problems, including violations of human rights, environmental degradation, racism, and sexism, thus bringing more violence in the name of security. The activist organization Iraq Veterans Against the War (IVAW) is comprised of military veterans who have fought in the GWOT. IVAW seeks to resist the continuous war that has been taking place since 9/11, through a number of tactics, i.e., going AWOL, occupying public spaces, and conducting war reenactments. One of the ways in which resistance is made is through the act of what Michel Foucault calls parrhesia. This translates as "frankness" or "telling all," but Foucault expands this definition to encompass a technique whereby a "moral attitude or ethos" creates an indisputable truth, ". . . so that at a given moment the person whom is speaking finds himself in a situation in which he no longer needs the other's discourse."[2] The truth that is exercised through parrhesia acts as "a weapon to be used for a partisan victory," as it "deciphers the discourse that perpetuates the permanent presence of war in society."[3]

A good example of parrhesia (which will be the focus of the second half of this chapter) is a series of testimonies by IVAW in 2008, called the Winter Soldier project. In these testimonies, veterans of war revealed the atrocities they had witnessed and participated in while on active duty. The veterans' acts of parrhesia worked to counter the narrative and effects of the government's "war on terror" by exposing the racism, sexism, lack of care for life, environmental degradation, and fiscal irresponsibility. This chapter will first provide a historical background of IVAW, as well as explore my personal experiences as a member, and then examine the concept of parrhesia as performed by IVAW members at Winter Soldier and in other forums.[4] Not only are these acts a form of resistance, but they also provide for an alternative discourse to the current GWOT literature and a form of healing for the mental and emotional trauma caused by war.

Iraq Veterans Against the War

IVAW is rooted in the activist group Veterans for Peace (VFP), and was modeled after the similarly named Vietnam Veterans Against the War (VVAW).[5] At the 2004 VFP annual convention, a group of recently returned veterans of the Iraq War participated in a panel. Participants Kelly Dougherty, Michael Hoffman, Alex Rybov, Isaiah Pallos, Diana Morrison, Tim Goodrich, and Jimmy Massey came together to start IVAW on July 24, 2004.[6] Kelly Dougherty, who would later go on to become the executive director of IVAW from 2006 to 2009, started the first chapter in Colorado Springs.

I first heard of IVAW in the spring of 2005 when Garett decided to join the group, becoming the first active-duty member of IVAW. While still in Iraq, we had blogged about our experiences there with a critical voice; we were likely some of the first soldiers to do so.[7] I decided to wait until we exited the military to join IVAW. I waited because we had run into some problems with our chain of command while blogging, and I didn't want to cause more disruption than I already had. Garett, however, was determined to rock the boat as much as possible, which often painted a target on his back while he was in the military. Once we were out of the military, however, we were able to fully engage in IVAW, without repercussions.

IVAW was founded upon three principles/goals: "An immediate, unconditional withdrawal of all occupying forces from Iraq; Health care and other benefits for all veterans and service members; [and] Reparations to the Iraqi people."[8] These goals would become the foundation of the organization's message and actions over the years. The group first received national attention in 2005, as veterans of IVAW joined the activist Cindy Sheehan, the mother of a soldier who died in Iraq. Garett and Jeff joined other IVAW members helping to provide security and solidarity with Sheehan outside President Bush's vacation home in Crawford, Texas.[9] The group followed with a bus tour called "Bring Them Home Now," making stops at military bases and college campuses across the country, hoping to bring the realities of war to those who had not experienced it, and showing those who had that it is possible to resist.[10] These two events not only helped to spread IVAW's message, but also acted as an initial recruitment drive.

As previously mentioned, in 2006 the first official chapter of IVAW formed in Colorado Springs, Colorado, and the national office was established in Philadelphia.[11] This was convenient for me as I was just a two-hour drive north, in Fort Collins, Colorado. Jeff was living in Colorado Springs and Garett often visited his mother, who also lived there, so I drove down for many of those first meetings. While 2006 was fairly quiet for IVAW, the organization was focused on building up its foundations and membership; by the end of the year there were ten chapters across the country. In 2007 IVAW tripled its chapters—thirty-one by year's end—and continued to participate in leading actions, like the April 17 March on the Pentagon, which drew tens of thousands of protestors.[12] At the time, I was in Washington, DC, and as we marched from nearby the Vietnam War Memorial to the Pentagon, antiwar chants rang through the air, which was a very powerful experience for everyone involved. Garett was one of the march leaders, as well as one of the main speakers. I realized then that he had become one of the "poster boys" of the antiwar movement. This was very inspiring to me, but it also gave me a reason to make fun of him.

In the following months IVAW began implementing a tactic called Operation First Casualty, stating that "the first casualty of war, is the truth."[13] Operation First Casualty used guerrilla street theater to simulate the tactics used by soldiers in Iraq and Afghanistan.[14] The group VVAW had done the same thing in the 1960s, mimicking combat patrols through towns while carrying rubber rifles. Now, IVAW—like VVAW before it—made street theater a regular tactic, repeating the simulations at events all across the country. The first time I participated in an Operation First Casualty event, in Denver, I found it very charging. We started early in the morning, making sure everyone was on the same page. We brought in a number of local activists to play the part of the Iraqis and Afghans. Meanwhile, we were dressed in our own desert combat uniforms to play the role of the soldiers.

We discussed carrying rubber rifles like the ones used by VVAW decades before, but we decided against it for fear that the police may mistake them for real rifles and shoot one of us. Instead, we used our hands, miming how the rifles would be held. Even though we were not wearing the full combat load carried by active-combat soldiers, it was still physically demanding as the day drew on and the temperature rose.

Our route started at the Colorado Capitol, wound down the always-busy 16th Street Mall, then cut over to the Denver Military Entrance Processing Station (MEPS), where we held a press conference highlighting the lies that were told to us by recruiters when we had enlisted into the military. Afterward, we worked our way back to the Capitol, and ended in Veterans Park. The actual operation was fairly simple; we walked in a staggered formation as we did in the military during combat patrols. The activists who were playing the part of "the enemy" walked ahead of us, chanting slogans like, "US go home!" We then approached the individuals who seemed to be leading the chants, physically extracted them from the larger group along with anyone else who resisted, threw them on the ground, put a bag over their heads, and zip-tied their hands behind their back. While we were gentler with our actors than we had been with the Iraqi and Afghans we dealt with on our deployments, many of the actors left the day bruised and cut. One of activists told me he was shocked by the brutality and violence, as we not only physically threw them down but we often screamed obscenities at them. A veteran friend who had participated said that he felt like he was back in Iraq when he threw down one of the activists, as he felt the same hate, fear, and anger arise during the action. We conducted this simulation over and over throughout the day, handing out fliers explaining what was going on to curious onlookers. Some watched in horror (I remember one old lady crying); some kept on walking, indifferent to what was going on; a few folks stopped and thanked us for our message; one gentleman called us traitors as he walked off, seemingly disgusted. It was a very powerful tactic, as it affects not only those to whom the message is targeted, but also the veterans and activists participating. For me, the event was mentally, emotionally, and physically draining, yet it left me inspired and yearning to do more.[15]

The purpose of this kind of action is, as much as possible, to bring the war home, as it simulates the embodied violence and brutality that occurs every day in a war zone. The shock of this violence in public spaces that would normally be spaces of peace is meant to trigger a visceral reaction that forces the viewer to think about what it would be like to be in

Iraq or Afghanistan. The fact that the actors speak English and look like a majority of the onlookers forces the viewer to empathize with the actor as he or she seeks to repel the soldiers, who are not only out of place but also perpetuating violence upon the actor, who again looks just like those who are watching. The aim is to create a space of empathy for those in Iraq and Afghanistan who are the targets of US violence. The action is a visceral reflection of the violent reality of war, which many Americans may or may not be aware of or acknowledge. Being forced to face these truths pushes the onlookers to examine their relationship to the violence that is being perpetuated by their government, in their name. Furthermore, it is a direct expression of the current construction of the Soldiers' Contract that is being portrayed for the onlooker. While many protests seek to raise awareness about particular issues, these guerrilla street theater tactics create an experience of violence in a nonviolent way, an effective (and affective) embodied tactic that IVAW would continue to use.

As John Protevi points out, encounters between two bodies—in this case the by-standing viewer and the veteran—can have a mutually empowering affect. Protevi calls this a somatic "affection," where a psychological and physiological change can be felt.[16] For the veteran it is the "flashback," the feeling of being back in Iraq or Afghanistan; for the activist and the onlooking viewer, it is the visceral feeling of sickness in the gut, or the tears formed from experiencing the horrors of what these veterans were re-creating. Furthermore, this re-experiencing of the tactics of war, in a different context, works to shift the way that the veteran relates to his or her past experiences, thus lessening the trauma. This is similar to the way in which the military is using virtual reality simulators bringing soldiers back to the sites of their traumas, in order to reprogram the trauma they relive through their flashbacks.[17]

For IVAW 2008 was a pivotal year, as it held three major events and grew in membership and chapters. By the end of the year, there were fifty-seven active chapters, including the Fort Collins, Colorado, chapter that I founded and served as president of. The first major event of 2008 for IVAW—held March 13–16 at the National Labor College in Silver Spring, Maryland—was a re-creation of a VVAW event called Winter Soldier.[18] More than 225 veterans, Iraqi civilians, and military families testified at the event, which was broadcast live online.[19] There were numerous panels, but the main themes included: Breakdown of the Military, Civilian Testimony, Corporate Pillaging, Cost of War at Home, Crisis in Veterans Healthcare, Future of GI Resistance, Gender and Sexuality, Legacy of GI Resistance,

Racism and War, Response to DoD, and Rules of Engagement.[20] While the
2008 Winter Soldier was largely ignored by the mainstream media (similar
to VVAW's Winter Soldier), the progressive media picked it up in full
force. The event provided a forum for healing for many veterans, making
it a success. While I was invited to speak, I wasn't ready at that time to tell
my story. I was still keeping it locked within, and not sure how to tell it
or how to face the shame of the things I had seen and done. I will return
to Winter Soldier in the next section of this chapter.

The next two major events of 2008 revolved around the Democratic
and Republican National Conventions. The planning for these events began
early in 2008 on an IVAW camping retreat at the Crags outside of Colorado
Springs. Members from the headquarters team in Philadelphia joined the
Colorado chapter to outline a plan for the coming months. There were many
disagreements over tactics. Some of the more radical members wanted more
drastic actions such as simulating Iraq by using burning cars and mimicking military convoy operations, which could have caused a media frenzy;
while moderate members preferred the tactics we were already engaging
with, such as guerrilla street theater. In the end, a good compromise was
found on most points of disagreement. The DNC in Denver proved quite
fruitful for IVAW. We performed numerous guerrilla street theater actions,
as well as conducted a "tower guard" (a tactic in which scaffolding is set
up and veterans emulate a guard post, symbolically protecting their nation
and honoring their oath of enlistment). In addition, IVAW organized a
free concert for the public featuring the bands Rage Against the Machine,
MC8, the Coup, the Flobots, and many others, all emceed by famous punk
rocker and Dead Kennedys front man Jello Biafra. Rage Against the Machine
had not played a show in many years, and people were excited to see the
group play together. The energy from the show was amazing, and at the
end of the performance, Rage told the more than ten thousand people in
attendance to turn to the streets to march from the Denver Coliseum to
the Pepsi Center, where the DNC was taking place.

The unpermitted march was the biggest activist event during the DNC,
spanning more than a mile long. As previously mentioned, there had been a
lot of conflict leading up to the march between IVAW members, who also
argued over the route we planned to use. Again, the more radical members
called for something more drastic; they wanted to march on to Interstate
70 and Interstate 25, effectively shutting down the city of Denver, while
others thought a more prudent route was in order. Since we did not have
a permit for the march, we feared the police reaction. However, just hours

before the concert began a Denver police officer called one of our coordinators to offer a compromise. They would help support a route from the Denver Coliseum to the Pepsi Center's "free speech zone."[21]

The march primarily comprised attendees of the concert, meaning most were between eighteen and forty years old. Members of IVAW marched in the front, wearing uniforms and marching in formation as we did when we were in the military. Just behind the veterans were the bands that performed, carrying a big yellow banner that read, "Support GI Resistance." Behind them was the large crowd of people marching. I was driving the support van that followed the march, carrying water for those who needed it and picking up any veterans who were not able to physically complete the march. As we made our way from the Denver Coliseum to the Pepsi Center, police lined the sidewalks, and I could see the hate and anger in some of their eyes. I distinctly remember one of the policemen angrily staring at the marchers and pounding his baton in his hand, longing to use it. We had been told that when the police were briefed, they had been warned to expect violence and that protestors would be throwing rocks and condoms filled with feces, which made us all laugh.

Once we arrived downtown at the Pepsi Center, I parked the van and joined the other veterans who had been corralled into the "free speech zone" that had been set up for protests. After standing at the free speech zone for an hour, we were instructed to disperse, with the warning that if we did not, they would shoot tear gas into the crowd and make arrests. We did leave the free speech zone, but rather than disperse we just moved to another gate at the DNC where a standoff ensued between police and veterans.

We were determined to come to some sort of resolution, and as I looked across toward the cops who faced us I saw a mix of emotions, from some who were angry and ready to fight to one cop in tears, not wanting to fight recently returned veterans. Fearing a repeat of the 1968 DNC, representatives of the Obama campaign sent a delegate who met with a couple of our members and promised an open dialogue with IVAW over the coming months. The message we delivered to the delegate included all three pillars of IVAW's mission, but most pertinent was the withdrawal of troops from Iraq. As our members emerged from that initial contact with the delegate and informed us of future meetings with the Obama campaign, it felt like a success, as if we had finally made some ground. Months later, I heard that IVAW was invited to meetings with President-elect Obama's office, but the leadership of IVAW blew off the meetings. Many members, including myself, were discouraged and bitter in light of the progress we seemed to have made.

The RNC a few weeks later in Minneapolis was not as successful, as police cracked down on nearly all the protests and actions by IVAW members. Even the free concert by Rage Against the Machine was shut down by the local police force, leaving the band to sing to the crowd through loudspeaker microphones. Knowing that the Republican Party would not back down from their support of the war, IVAW focused instead on its second goal: providing care for veterans upon their return home. This shift in tactics was made evident by IVAW member Adam Kokesh's infiltration of the RNC, where he disrupted Senator John McCain's acceptance speech holding a sign that read, "McCAIN VOTES AGAINST VETS," in order to highlight the senator's poor voting record on veterans' issues.[22]

With the election of Barack Obama as president, there seemed to be a shift in American political activism. Many who came out to protest against the policies of George W. Bush stopped demonstrating as the promise of "hope and change" ruled the dominant discourse. Many thought that Obama would end the wars immediately, so IVAW shifted gears to focus instead on Afghanistan. The first order of business for 2009 was to take a stance on the war in Afghanistan. There was a slight divide within IVAW, since some saw the reasons for going into Afghanistan as honorable, due to the events of 9/11. Many others, however, saw the war in Afghanistan as a continuation of an imperial project that benefited no one but the war profiteers, a project warned against by so many throughout our history, from Maj. Gen. Smedley Butler to President Eisenhower. Since its inception, IVAW accepted veterans from the Afghan war; the basic requirement for membership was to have served in any branch of the military, post-9/11. It was proposed that the same three tenets that were made toward the Iraq war would be carried over for the Afghan war: immediate withdrawal, reparations to Afghans, and provision of care to soldiers upon their return.[23] The proposal passed. With a more inclusive membership, and a broader vision, 2009 marked a new chapter of IVAW history. The organization continued to organize and hold small-scale events, like local Winter Soldiers, as well as supporting GI coffeehouses and leading peace marches. However, as mentioned earlier, it became difficult organizing and attracting civilian volunteers due to new presidential leadership.[24]

In 2010 the growing number of suicides in the military prompted IVAW to roll out a new program called Operation Recovery. Armed with growing knowledge about the traumatic effects of war, IVAW targeted military base commanders, as well as the broader community, in order to shed light on issues of PTS, traumatic brain injury (TBI), military sexual trauma (MST), and combat stress.[25] This spotlight on veterans' health has been the primary focus of IVAW in the past two years, shedding light on the unsustainability of the wars and the serious deficiencies in the Veterans Administration that need to be addressed immediately.

There are three other major events that happened between 2012 and 2014 that have not had a major impact but are worth mentioning. These include the advocacy for the release of Chelsea Manning (which I will return to), a protest of the NATO summit in Chicago, and an alliance with the Occupy Wall Street movement (which is the focus of the next chapter). The protest of the NATO summit attempted to re-create the powerful effect of a VVAW event during the Vietnam War, when veterans lined up and threw their medals away during a protest called Operation Dewey Canyon III.[26] While the event was indeed powerful, and even healing for some veterans, it failed to capture the nation the way Operation Dewey Canyon III had, as the original became iconic to Vietnam War protests. Instead, the event drew the attention of the FBI, and crackdowns on the groups participating in the event followed, showing how threatened the state feels by these voices.[27] In May 2014, IVAW released what they referred to as "The Ft. Hood Report," a nearly five-hundred-page document consisting of testimony of veterans and an analysis of the treatment of soldiers returning to Fort Hood. Much like Winter Soldier, the report aimed at exposing the ineptitude of the US military in dealing with the effects of the traumas of war.[28] In the past year there have been no nationwide IVAW events apart from their annual national conference, but the organization remains active and focused on advocating for veterans' care, reparations for the Iraqi and Afghan people, and immediate withdrawal of all forces—including private contractors—from Iraq and Afghanistan.

From 2013 to 2017, there has been much debate within the organization about changing the name so that it was more inclusive of veterans of other conflicts; and with the "ending" of major combat operations in Iraq, IVAW needed to rebrand. In 2016 the membership voted to change the name of IVAW to About Face: Veterans Against War. The name became official after the 2017 annual IVAW National Convention. While the organization will always have ties to the name IVAW, they are hoping the rebranding will breathe new life into it. With the rebrand, they have also begun to focus on more local issues such as fighting US militarism and social inequity (such as showing up to help at the Standing Rock Dakota Access Pipeline protests and supporting organizations such as Black Lives Matter), thus further highlighting the imbrication of the Social Contract and Soldiers' Contract.

Winter Soldier, Parrhesia, and Chelsea Manning

As described earlier, Winter Soldier took place March 13–16 at the National Labor College in Silver Spring, Maryland. More than 225 veterans, Iraqi civilians, and military families testified to the horrors of war. Many of their stories contained accounts that could be defined as war crimes. Instead, the events have been labeled "collateral damage," and no actions have been taken to prevent such atrocities. The stories relate more than the expected tragedies that come with war; they expose the systemic nature of these crimes and the manner in which the soldiers committing these atrocities become victims of the violence as well. The veterans who testified at Winter Soldier told their truths and bared their hearts for all to see, relating things such as the killing of innocent civilians to the torture of "enemy combatants." The executive director of IVAW, Kelly Dougherty, describes the reason for Winter Soldier as follows:

> We organized Winter Soldier Iraq and Afghanistan in part because our members see the history and day-to-day narration of the Iraq occupation being told and remembered by politicians, generals, pundits, and corporate media. The voices, experiences, and opinions of those most affected, the Iraqis, the servicemembers, and military families, are often marginalized or ignored. IVAW members seek to challenge the assumption that only those with wealth or power can write history or lend crucial insight to the life-and-death issues that affect us all.[29]

This statement highlights that testimonies were much more than just emotional tales of war; telling their stories act as a tool to fight oppression, and it can be seen as the basis of what Michel Foucault called parrhesia. While Foucault focused on the use of parrhesia in ancient Greek philosophy, there are many parallels that can be drawn to the events of today that demonstrate the power and importance of Winter Soldier.

There are four primary attributes that are necessary for parrhesia to be present within speech. First and foremost, it must be rooted within a democratic tradition that upholds this radical speech.[30] The democratic tradition described by Foucault is similar to our current focus on the freedom of speech protected by the First Amendment of the US Constitution. Foucault states that there is a reciprocal nature between parrhesia and the democratic ideal of free speech—one cannot exist without the other. Because parrhesia is intimately tied to our Western democratic ideals, it is always political speech in nature—though not all political speech qualifies as parrhesia.[31] This democratic tradition is one of the main reasons why many members within IVAW do what they do, as many still feel that they are defending their oaths of service and protecting the democracy they fought for overseas by speaking up at home. Furthermore, most all whistleblowers have used the argument that their actions are tied to this free speech that is meant to perpetuate democratic ideals, from Daniel Ellsberg who released the Pentagon Papers that undermined the Vietnam War, to current whistleblowers Chelsea Manning and Edward Snowden, who seek to undermine the current narrative for the global war on terrorism.[32]

The second attribute needed for parrhesia to be present is for it to be "connected to a situation of injustice, and which, far from the right exercised by the powerful over his fellow citizens in order to guide them, is instead the cry of the powerless against someone who misuses his own strength."[33] The testimonies heard at Winter Soldier look to expose the violence and trauma caused by the war on terror, exposing the abuses of power that caused death, destruction, and constant violence upon an entire population. The truth that is exercised through parrhesia acts as "a weapon to be used for a partisan victory," as it "deciphers the discourse that perpetuates the permanent presence of war in society."[34] So the testimonies of veterans who experienced and participated in acts of brutality undermine the narratives of war perpetuated by the government, and they help to create a new regime of truth that combats the narrative of the current global war on terror. For example, the current narrative of Guantanamo Bay examines legalities of indefinite incarceration without a trial; however, the testimony of US Army specialist Christopher Arendt, a guard at Guantanamo Bay, seeks to shift the narrative as he states:

> The temperature of the interrogation room was maybe 10 or 20
> degrees, with loud music playing. Sometimes that detainee would
> stay there for my entire 12- to 14-hour shift. He was shackled
> to the floor by his hands and his feet, with nothing to sit on,
> loud music playing, in the freezing cold . . .[35]

Arendt went on to describe the tactics of Guantanamo Bay's Quick Reaction Force, which regularly used pepper spray and physical force for any reason possible.[36] These stories contribute to a moral human rights narrative, which maintains that governmental bodies can only be legitimate so long as they comply with moral standards of human dignity; thus, torture is an act of delegitimization. This shift to a moral human rights narrative, as well as Arendt's testimony, becomes an additional tool for activist groups who seek to shut down military facilities like Guantanamo Bay.

Another example of this shift to a moral human rights narrative—that is similar to Foucault's second attribute of parrhesia—is often seen in veterans' stories about the "rules of engagement" (ROE). The current international relations literature that looks at "rules of war" examines the importance of how ROE policies are formed, how they are disseminated, and how they are interpreted. However, they often fall short in discussing the implementation and practice of rules of engagement.[37] The testimonies provided at Winter Soldier show soldiers sometimes had no idea what the established ROE was, how it was constantly shifting, or that it was frequently circumnavigated. As Corporal Sergio Kochergin testified:

> The third day after we arrived, our company commander, our first lieutenant, and one of our NCOs all got killed by an IED. As time went on, and as the casualties grew in number, the Rules became lenient. Because we saw our friends getting blown up and killed every day, we didn't really question them. We were angry. We just wanted to do our job and come back.
>
> We used "drop weapons" . . . given to us by our chain of command in case we killed somebody without weapons so that we would not get into trouble. We would carry an AK-47 and if the person that was shot did not have the weapon, the AK-47 would be placed at his corpse. Then, when the unit would come back to the base they would turn it in to identify the shot man as an enemy combatant. . . . After our own casualties mounted the Rules changed. We were allowed to engage anyone with a weapon without calling in and asking permission [to engage an enemy combatant]. . . . Two months into our deployment our Rules were to engage any person with a heavy bag and a shovel at intersections or on the roads . . .[38]

It is from this testimony, as well as the other similar ones at Winter Soldier, that a narrative emerges that challenges the standard literature on rules of engagement. The literature discusses the importance and legal nature of an ROE; however, when a contradicting testimony is introduced into the narrative, the importance of an ROE that changes at the whims and emotions of those who make it is clear. The constantly shifting ROE not only provides an alternative narrative to the security studies literature, but also chips away at the neoliberal rationalization/justification of security within the current global war on terrorism.[39]

The third attribute of parrhesia is that it is tied to "a game of ascendency." In other words, there are differences in the power relations between those who are speaking and those who are receiving the message.[40] It was within this "game of ascendency" that Foucault constantly shifted his gaze as he looked at the parrhesia relationships between philosophers to kings, advisors to kings, philosophers to students, a war hero to a senate forum, and many others. Within these different power relations, Foucault found a number of "regimes of truth" that took on different truth-telling practices, which is a large part of what he termed "veridiction." These truth-telling practices, or veridiction, are acts where the person speaking binds himself to his truth.[41] The power exerted over the person speaking his truth is "juridical, political, institutional, and historical."[42] In relation, these veterans were testifying not only to the general public, amplified through modern media, but to the official congressional record. Therefore, these veteran testimonies had an effect on power relations at several levels depending on the mode of delivery.

The final attribute is courage in the face of danger. For parrhesia to be present, the speaker must risk him- or herself through veridiction, as different power relations present different truth-telling practices and different levels of risk ranging from bodily harm to exile and even death.[43] This "courage in the face of danger" is already an attribute associated with soldiers, as they are expected to be warriors who fight in wars, the very wars that these veterans are testifying against. In many ways though, this parrhesiatic courage pushes against the masculine, war-fighting courage that one associates with soldiers.[44] The nature of the testimonies by the veterans at Winter Soldier speaks to a game of risk, as the veterans testify to war crimes that they have seen, participated in, and committed. First and foremost, the risk they face comes from those they served with, because while these veterans believe what they did was wrong, many of the people they served with may not feel the same. They then could become stigmatized by those they consider family, labeled as traitors or, to borrow a term from Brianne Gallagher, "PTSD pussies."[45] Furthermore, they risk hatred and contempt from the audience, they risk legal action from the military and world courts, and they face possible physical or legal retribution from the victims who may be watching, as well as punishment from governmental organizations such as the FBI, CIA, and NSA, who may find what they are saying to be a threat to national security. The threat to national security has become the basis for prosecution of whistleblowers such as Chelsea Manning.[46] One of the most important documents released by Manning was a video of US military helicopter pilots indiscriminately killing Iraqi citizens, which later became known as the "collateral murder" video.[47]

Derek Sweetman discusses the danger that the collateral murder video presents to the US government's neoliberal justification for the wars in Iraq and Afghanistan.[48] That justification is built upon a cost-benefit analysis that professes a particular "regime of truth." This regime of truth shows that the collateral damage of war is necessary; however, the video creates doubt in the necessity, thus making Manning's activism an act of parrhesia as it fits within the attributes described above. In a discussion of the US government's treatment of Chelsea Manning, Sweetman states:

> The particular threat that [Chelsea] Manning and Collateral Murder present is then, in a sense, existential. If the war effort is built on an appeal to truth and Manning is destabilizing that, then [her] treatment begins to be more understandable. Although Manning's treatment was not equivalent to that of those accused of terrorism and held in Guantanamo (where physical torture was an inarguable reality), it is possible to think of both Manning and the "terrorists" as sharing a similar position of enmity. Both attempted to undermine the claims of veracity upon which the existing neoliberal order is based.[49]

Therefore, acts like the release of the "collateral murder" video and testimonies like those of veterans who participated in Winter Soldier counter the cost-benefit truth regime that sustains and perpetuates war. It does so on moral grounds, by showing that a cost-benefit style of warfare is messy, bloody, and heartless. It takes the often-forgettable facts and numerical figures of war and replaces them with new facts, those of human faces, stories, and experiences, bringing them to the forefront of the people's minds. As Sweetman points out, these moral grounds assume that theorist Gene Sharp's conception of power is at work when one seeks to understand the US government's crucifixion of Manning; Sharp held that power is a relation of consent, and it cannot continue or perpetuate wars without the consent of the people.[50] To maintain consent the government sanitizes the image of war.

As Jean Baudrillard points out, technology has become a "virtual organ," where war is viewed through the multiple screens that render the enemy as an imaginary threat.[51] The simulacrum of violence creates an image of war that is sanitized, where the dead are erased from the image of war. The cleansing of war is primarily in response to previous wars, specifically Vietnam, where the atrocities like the My Lai massacre shocked the world and shifted the perception of war imagery toward the negative. In more recent wars, the dead are rarely available for viewing by the public, thereby preserving the "cleanliness" of war. For example, President George H. W. Bush banned the photographing of the returning caskets of fallen soldiers.[52] When atrocities such as the events of the "collateral murder" video are made available for viewing, the narrative that constructs the image of war shifts from a "clean" war to a "dirty" war, and public support begins to wane. However, as Joanna Tidy points out, the "collateral murder" video alone does not push the narrative from a clean war to a dirty one as it is an indiscriminate view from above; rather, it is the "view from the ground" and the testimony of soldiers like Ethan McCord—who was a soldier on the ground—that works to create this shift in narrative.[53]

So why the discrepancy between the treatment of the veterans who testified at Winter Soldier and the treatment of Chelsea Manning? Really there is none, besides the fact that one has become more publicized than the other; however, that publicity serves a particular purpose. This high publicity pushed the government to claim that the WikiLeaks release of documents constituted "aiding the enemy," though those charges were dropped due to a lack of evidence. By claiming that Manning was trying to provide aid to the enemy—the key factor needed to charge her with treason—it reiterates the narrative that patriotism, duty, and honor are tied to silence. If that silence is broken, those who speak against power will be charged with treason—an act punishable by death. While everyone who testified at Winter Soldier was not imprisoned and charged with treason like Manning, antiwar activists—especially those who are a part of Iraq Veterans Against the War—have been the target of the military and the FBI in their twenty-first-century version of COINTELPRO.[54] The attention given by the mass media to the "collateral murder" video made the Manning case a high-profile one, which worked both to her benefit and detriment. This video showed US Army Apache helicopters open fire on unarmed civilians. While there are many narratives that explain what the pilots saw and why they shot, the video provides a startling experience of war, one that is not filtered and "cleaned" by the media, but rather is footage of a raw or "dirty" war. Thus, the actions of

Manning, IVAW, and veteran testimonies work to de-sanitize the image of
the war and delegitimize the violence perpetuated by the US government.

Another difference between the narratives surrounding the Manning
case and the Winter Soldier veterans is that the "collateral murder" video
allows the viewer to experience the deaths more intimately—nearly firsthand
as there is an embodied feeling (similar to the way in which the guerrilla
theater action Operation First Casualty, described above, works to create an
intimate experience with the viewer and war), whereas the testimonies of
the veterans evoke more of a secondhand experience. The point of view of
the "collateral murder" video is that of the pilot or as Tidy states, a "view
from above," where the viewer not only experiences what the pilot sees
and hears, but can also see the crosshairs of the weapon, the flying bullets,
and the bodies being torn apart, target after target making it a sort of war
porn.[55] This creates the effect of actually being there—partially shifting the
narrative from a clean war to a dirty one. Leaked videos can be much more
dangerous because the ability to see the deaths becomes much more accessible and immediate, but, as stated above, it does not shift until a soldier's
view from the ground is added. For all of the differences between the narratives, there are some similarities; both the testimony and the video seek
to challenge the power and truth regime held by the US government. The
same holds true for the Edward Snowden/NSA whistleblower controversy
that is still playing out today. As Sweetman points out:

> The real danger that Manning poses is not the exposure of infor-
> mation—the release of what was classified—that we see in cases
> of traditional espionage. Instead, it is the production of doubt.
> This production of doubt is much more threatening than either
> the promotion of interest (in the traditional social movement
> sense, as embodied by the traditional anti-war movement) or the
> transfer of information from one state to another (as in cases of
> espionage). Seen from this perspective, the release of Collateral
> Murder can be viewed as the largest activist threat, and there-
> fore, according to neoliberal rationality, the one necessitating the
> most severe response. It also, though, points to the possibility
> of new approaches to activism under neoliberalism aimed not
> at converting or persuading, but at undermining the particular
> relationships of systems of power to truth. Manning's treatment,
> then, can be seen by activists as perversely hopeful, since it would
> seem to highlight the extent to which truth-oriented challenges

(those focused on destabilizing, not replacing truth-claims) are feared within the neoliberal system.[56]

This points to other similarities between Winter Soldier and the Manning case, which cut at the truth regime constructed by the US government not by exposing information but rather by creating doubt. As mentioned earlier in the description of the guerrilla street theater tactic Operation First Casualty, these truths push onlookers to examine their relationship to the violence that is being perpetuated by their government, in their name. Therefore, these practices of parrhesia are dangerous as they work to shift the narratives of war. This shift makes the original statements and justifications for war seem like forms of deception, which is why many people, especially veterans who fought in Iraq, often feel like they were lied to. Parrhesia becomes a function meant shift the balance of power away from forms of hierarchical violent militarism to more transparent forms of democracy, which is dangerous to the current order of power. Former chairman of the board of IVAW Camilo Mejìa neatly sums up the danger of this parrhesia when he states:

> We have become a dangerous group of people not because of our military training, but because we have dared to challenge the official story. We are dangerous because we have dared to share our experiences, to think for ourselves, to analyze and be critical, to follow our conscience, and because we have dared to go beyond patriotism to embrace humanity.[57]

Conclusion

Because the global war on terror has been presented as a never-ending process that is occurring everywhere, at all times, IVAW provides a counter-narrative that seeks to oppose and undermine the normative view. Accepting the idea of perpetual war not only creates quiescence in response to oppressive regimes of power, but also minimizes the theorization and actualization of peace. Many of the members in Iraq Veterans Against the War, who were once part of the destructive neoliberal forces within the global war on terror machine, now work to perpetuate peace. While these veterans are not perfect, and their activism can sometimes militarize the peace movements they are a part of, and their voices are often put above others—as highlighted by Joanna Tidy and in the intro—there is a process of reflexivity within parrhesia.[58] This reflexivity is to create a critique that is not only able to transform the state, but that is also a transformation of the self.[59] Therefore, these veterans are seeking systematic change while also seeking to demilitarize themselves, as they work to become less reliant upon the military and its culture, which is what Enloe points out in the process of demilitarizing oneself.[60] This transformative process can best be seen in the comments of reporter Aaron Glantz, who reported from Iraq and later helped to put together the *Winter Soldier* book, when he states:

> As I reported these stories, my heart filled with rage at these Americans and I felt myself going through the same process of dehumanization the veterans described at Winter Soldier. If I had a weapon instead of a microphone, I don't know what I would have done. I understood the motivations of the fighters who fired on the American soldiers as they rolled their tanks and Humvees through civilian neighborhoods. I returned home with a rage toward these soldiers and toward my country, a rage that has only subsided after I've had the opportunity to meet these same soldiers now that they're veterans and have had the chance to take off their uniforms and put down their weapons. I've understood through these personal interactions that in war it is not the "other side" that is the enemy but the war itself and the leaders who started it.
>
> This is why I think Winter Soldier is so important. These brave veterans, by coming forward en masse and in public, give us the opportunity to begin an important conversation about the nature of war and the effect on the human condition.[61]

Such testimonies and acts of parrhesia have the power not only of self-reflexivity, but they also serve to push others into spaces of self-reflexivity, and hopefully into spaces of parrhesia. Furthermore, members of IVAW are working to show that their view of the Social Contract is different than what is being enacted by the state, by exposing their role within the Soldiers' Contract through acts of parrhesia. Groups like IVAW are theory in action, and we, as academics, need to create a reciprocal relationship to these activist communities. The next chapter will expand this concept of theory in action by examining veterans' relationships to the Occupy movement as they fight internal state violence. Furthermore, we will move away from my personal experiences and begin hearing the narratives of other veteran activists.

3

Occupy Veterans

I, Benjamin Schrader, do solemnly swear that I will support and defend the Constitution of the United States against all enemies, foreign and domestic; that I will bear true faith and allegiance to the same; and that I will obey the orders of the President of the United States and the orders of the officers appointed over me, according to regulations and the Uniform Code of Military Justice. So help me God.[1]

On July 14, 2001, I took this oath, and it is in this oath that a number of other military veterans—including myself—have found validation in their activism.[2] The oath is meant to show loyalty to the nation, and many veterans still feel it is their duty to uphold that oath long after their time in the military is over. Because the oath states that they are to defend the Constitution against "all enemies, foreign and domestic," it is easy to see how many veterans could translate this into many different forms of activism today. For many, this oath is the basis of the Soldiers' Contract and their relationship to the Social Contract.

One example of veterans utilizing this oath within their activism can be seen in those veterans' involvement in the Occupy Wall Street (OWS) movement. OWS is a movement that has often been labeled as unpatriotic or even un-American by conservative pundits, as it confronts the structural violence that has been perpetuated through neoliberalism by the global financial system.[3] It is through this interaction that a thought-provoking dialogue takes place between service to one's country and protesting for the betterment of the nation, which is the soldier's critique of the Social Contract. The discourse of military veterans offers an alternative view of how the Occupy movement might be viewed as these veterans utilize activism to challenge the neoliberal policies of Western liberal democracy that in turn affect the communities that their identities are intimately tied to.

To do so, I examine state violence primarily through three different narratives, while still deploying the analytical framework of critical military studies. The narratives I will be using are: the story of YouTube sensation Sgt. Shamar Thomas, who has constantly publicly denounced state violence and is currently working to raise consciousness through community organizing; the attack on Occupy Oakland protestors and the subsequent injury of veteran Scott Olsen; and Iraq Veterans Against the War's statement of support for the Occupy Movement.

Shamar Thomas

When Shamar Thomas was two years old, his father died as a result of gun violence. In order to support her family, Shamar's mother joined the US Army. Being in the military offered a steady income, but the cost of living was still highly prohibitive, especially for a single mother. Because of this, Shamar often lived in some of the more "rough" neighborhoods near military bases.[4] After attending twelve different schools all across the country, Shamar graduated high school at his mother's urging. But because he had moved around so much, he was constantly the target of bullying, and it was in the brotherhood of gangs that he found reprieve.

Many of the other gang members Shamar knew had come from similar backgrounds, many were also the target of bullying, many grew up without a father, and many longed for a stable sense of family.[5] However, being in a gang gave him a sense of family, where the "OGs" ("original gangsters," or older ones that were still a part of the gang) acted as the father figures and the other members were like brothers. These children experienced not only a sense of belonging but also a sense of responsibility that they had never before had, not only to each other as they would depend on one another to stay safe, but they also were given guns, money, and drugs to be responsible for. However, the longer Shamar was in the gang, the more dangerous the streets became.

Shamar saw the military as an escape hatch, as it was an opportunity to get out of the game that was putting his life at risk on a daily basis. It was shortly after 9/11 that he joined the US Marines. He knew that by joining the Marines he would still be at risk of danger, but it was a different kind of danger, he felt, more controlled, and he would be better trained to handle the violence he would face. He found interesting similarities to gang life within the military, as it was also founded on brotherhood and camaraderie, and he was given specific responsibilities such as maintaining and operating multimillion-dollar weapon systems—in contrast to the guns, drugs, and money he was responsible for while in a gang.

While in the military, Shamar was deployed to Iraq and fought in the 2004 battle of Fallujah. While there were many horrific stories to come out of that battle, Shamar said that his unit fought honorably, and he did not witness any of the war crimes that many others attested to. While Shamar went on many local foot patrol missions, his primary job while in Iraq was watching Iraqi prisoners. Again, he reiterated that his unit treated people with decency, and that he witnessed nothing like the torture and abuse of Iraqi prisoners at Abu Ghraib, which had become news around the same time that he was in Iraq.

Upon Shamar's exit from the military, he enrolled at St. Francis College in Brooklyn and then transferred to Syracuse University. However, the compensation he received from the military (GI Bill) was not enough to live on and he soon became homeless, living in a veterans' homeless shelter.[6] Shamar left college and returned to the streets of Long Island to begin community organizing around gangs and youth. He knew he wanted to give back to his community and to help kids understand that they had options beyond gangs, but at the time he wasn't sure how to get involved. While sitting on the couch one day watching the local news he saw a report on the Occupy Wall Street movement; curious, he decided to go down and check it out. After his first trip to Zuccotti Park in Lower Manhattan, and seeing the ways in which the police were treating the protestors, he knew he needed to return. He liked what he heard from the Occupiers but was disgusted by the police behavior that he observed; he viewed their escalation of violence as not only unnecessary but also brutal and oppressive. It was on his second trip there that he would become famous with the Occupy movement, and infamous with the police and others who disagreed with the movement.

On October 15, 2011, the New York Police Department ordered a crackdown on the Occupy Wall Street Times Square protest, which became violent as police tried to break up the demonstration. The most memorable aspect of the evening for many, though, occurred a block away from the violence as Sgt. Shamar Thomas faced off with about thirty police officers. The result of the confrontation was telling, as the six-foot-four, three-hundred-pound veteran yelled at police while wearing his Marine uniform after seeing protestors being attacked by the NYPD. As he yelled at the police, he asked a number of questions, none of which the NYPD was willing to

answer. Shamar questioned: "Why are you doing this? Why are you hurt-
ing US citizens? Aren't you supposed to be protecting these people?"[7] These
questions highlighted his view that the police were in violation of their own
Soldiers' Contract, as he believed they were violating their oath to protect
and serve. Both his physical presence and the fact that Shamar Thomas was
a war veteran seemed to intimidate the NYPD, as the confrontation dragged
on for more than five minutes. While he would eventually peacefully leave
the scene, Shamar's act of parrhesia was recorded and put online, becoming a YouTube sensation, and currently has more than 25.3 million views.[8]

It is in this scene that an interesting intersection takes place. Sgt.
Shamar Thomas, an ex-gang member, a war veteran, living in poverty, peacefully protesting, and witnessing violence at the hands of the state he swore
to protect. Violence is evident not only by the state toward the protestors,
but also in Shamar's multifaceted position of having fought in a war and
fighting on the streets in poverty, as well as currently and previously as a
gang member. In describing this violence by the state, Eugene Holland states:

> In one case, the violence is spectacularly noisy and direct—the
> modern state is indeed typically defined in terms of its absolute
> monopoly on legitimate or legitimated violence: on command,
> make war; disobey, and you answer to the police. In the other
> case, the violence is hidden, as it were, and indirect: Marx refers
> to the "silent compulsion of market relations" that makes the
> labor contract essentially involuntary; he also reveals that the
> "secret" of "so-called primitive accumulation" is that it more
> fundamentally means primitive destitution, that is, forcing people
> into abject dependence on capital for their very survival.[9]

This passage highlights the two types of violence that are perpetuated
by the neoliberal state not only against Shamar but against many of the
impoverished in the US, which is known as structural violence.[10] The first
form of violence is direct and somatic, and relates to the violence used by
the police and the military. This form of violence is legitimated in order
to protect and maintain the systems and powers in place, like Wall Street.
The other type of violence is structural. This form of violence is caused by
systems like Wall Street, which the state seeks to protect through direct
violence, thus putting direct violence and structural violence in a cyclical
relationship. The poverty that comes from these capitalist institutions forces
the state to choose between increasing capital versus the good of the people,

in which the state chooses the former through a private centralization of the means of production, which in turn perpetuates poverty.[11] As Johan Galtung states, "Violence is present when human beings are being influenced so that their actual somatic and mental realizations are below their potential realizations."[12] In other words, due to decision of the state-finance nexus to choose capital over the protection of the people, which leads to somatic and mental realizations below their potential realizations, violence is being inflicted. However, here the violence is correlated with capitalism, as it is a function of the state to protect those who profit by any means necessary, even while violence is being produced by corporate entities against those whom the police are sworn to protect. It is because of this violence that Shamar Thomas stands up and fights, stating:

> This is a chance to voice our issues—police brutality, economic injustice, foreclosed homes. . . . I'm a warrior, I don't have any fear in the streets. So how do I sit on a couch and watch people fight for our freedom and not do anything about it? That's cowardice. This is about my freedom and the freedom of my people.[13]

It is not only at events like Occupy Wall Street that Shamar Thomas has worked to expose these problems; rather it is his other organizing since Occupy that needs to be examined. After the confrontation with police, Shamar Thomas worked to start two organizations: the first was Occupy Gangbangers[14] and the second was Global Veterans of the 99%, which was coordinated with Iraq Veterans Against the War. The latter group would eventually become a subcommittee within the New York IVAW chapter, and the group would also organize with others such as Veterans for Peace, OccupyMARINES, Occupy Navy, Occupy Airforce, Occupy Coast Guard, and Occupy Military Families.[15] Beyond Occupy, he became involved with an organization called GMACC (Gangsters Making Astronomical Change in the Community).[16] His goal in engaging with the different organizations was:

> . . . to engage gangsters and former soldiers in Occupy, trans-forming the destructive violence bred within warrior communi-ties into a positive, unified power that challenges the corporate state actors who have victimized those communities—by sending them to fight in illegal manufactured wars, disenfranchising the inner-city poor, and failing to offer economic futures to either.[17]

The organizing done by Shamar Thomas is evidenced in various ways. The first is that it can be seen as a uniting of the "deprived and the dispossessed."[18] Since Shamar Thomas comes from these groups—veterans and gang members—it makes his ability to organize the deprived and dispossessed more attainable, making him what Antonio Gramsci calls an "organic intellectual."[19] Therefore, what Shamar is doing is organizing with gang members who have grown up in violence perpetuated by these systems and organizing with veterans who have been exploited by the state-financial nexus, and teaching both groups who their enemy should be. Then instead of fighting themselves, they understand where their oppression is rooted, and can thus work to fight the system that holds them down.

Shamar Thomas's focus is in his message, as he often asks the gang members, "How are you a gangster when you're killing your own people in your neighborhood, your own army, somebody who's poor just like you?"[20] In this message, he aims to direct their rage toward the state and the corporate interests that are exploiting their communities.[21] Shamar's work reverses the value of poor blacks, particularly gang members who are often seen as a problem within society who drain community resources due to the cost of policing them; thus, he transforms them into a positive force that seeks revolutionary change. As for his message to veterans, he states:

> They're robbing veterans first-hand. . . . How do you consciously give an eighteen-year-old $1,500 a month to fight a war where he's on the front lines, so he can't even save up enough money to get his own place when he gets out? We talk about supporting our troops and "honoring our veterans," but how are veterans going to send their kids to college or even buy a car on the pensions they're paid? We all know in our hearts that there is one thing, or many things, wrong. . . . Would you fight for freedom?[22]

The violence that veterans are asked to perpetuate in the name of freedom comes at a high cost to the veteran, mentally, emotionally, and physically, as shown in previous sections. This is a part of the Soldiers' Contract. All the while there is little compensation for the trauma that comes with the wars they are asked to fight in. This not only damages veterans to the point of injury but also perpetuates into future generations, often leaving veterans and their families destitute. It is this destitution that often leads youth to join gangs, feeding into the cyclical process that Shamar Thomas aims to break. He goes on to state:

> We have a powerful weapon: our voice, we're getting veterans
> and gangsters around the country together into the movement—
> understanding why we're here, why we're oppressed. We make
> them question who they are and help them to look at Wall
> Street—these are the people we need to fight against. Once we
> take money out of politics, we can take back our communities.[23]

It is within this message that the ties between the state-finance nexus culminates, exemplifying the different levels of violence—at home and abroad—that are perpetuated by those on Wall Street, those who send our troops to war, and the state apparatus that protects capitalism.

It is the functions of capitalism that are in part the reason Shamar Thomas was in a gang, joined the military, was sent to war, and became homeless upon his return. Shamar is engaging capitalism and state violence on multiple levels as he attempts to draw the parallels between the war on the streets and the wars abroad. It is the immorality toward our citizens that he fights against as the neoliberal Western democratic system that perpetuates violence upon the people and upon the veterans it sends off to war. Shamar Thomas seeks to change this by exposing the injustices and organizing others to stand up, speak out, and fight. This is evidenced in the quote above as he proclaims the power of one's voice and the ways in which it can be a powerful, invaluable weapon—which is very similar to how parrhesia is described in the previous chapter. Furthermore, the critique is a clear statement on the state of the Social Contract brought forth by a former upholder of that contract, the soldier.

It is Shamar Thomas's firsthand experience in gangs, in the military, and on the streets that gives him the ability to be an effective organizer against state violence. Shamar does this as he makes clear the relationships between war and poverty, which facilitates the disruption of the neoliberal Western democracy. As Foucault points out, these acts of parrhesia undermine the power structure of neoliberal Western democracy through the exposure of the ties between war and poverty.

Scott Olsen

Scott Olsen's background is almost the exact opposite of Shamar Thomas's, and yet they end up coming to nearly the same positionality but on opposite sides of the country. Scott grew up in Onalaska, Wisconsin, didn't really move around, had a stable family with not much of a military history, and enjoyed computers growing up. He joined the Marines after 9/11 fearing the country was "facing an existential threat."[24] But while in the military he began to realize that what he was told and believed didn't match what he was seeing on the ground. With eight months left on his contract, and after two deployments to Iraq, he was given an administrative discharge tied to his disdain for what he found in the military.[25]

His first experience with activism and the formation of his class-consciousness came with protests against Wisconsin governor Scott Walker's attack on unions, and further developed when he became a member of Iraq Veterans Against the War.[26] He then moved to San Francisco to work for a software company. When the Occupy movement began, he decided to join the Oakland group and became a permanent resident at the Occupy Oakland encampment, working his job during the day and occupying at night.[27] On October 25, 2011, in Oakland, California—just over a month into the Occupy movement—Olsen was peacefully protesting when police decided to break up the protest by means of force. In the melee that ensued, Olsen was shot in the head with a tear gas canister. The canister fractured his skull, and he was taken to the hospital for surgery to relieve the swelling in his brain. The irony of the event is that Olsen was twice sent to Iraq and returned both times physically unharmed, yet when he came home and attempted to exercise the First Amendment rights that he had fought for, he was critically injured by the state.

The Scott Olsen incident represents what Alain Badiou calls a "spark that 'lights a prairie fire.'"[28] That fire can be seen in the resulting vandalism and riots that took place in the weeks following the attack on Olsen, as many marched in support of him, especially those who support the veteran community. Badiou continues, "Just as uniformly, the government and its police not only categorically refuse to accept the slightest responsibility for the whole affair, but use the riot as a pretext for reinforcing the arsenal of the police and criminal justice system."[29] Similarly, the police denied that they were responsible for Olsen's injuries and continued to use violent military tactics to combat the protestors.[30]

On state violence, Badiou further points out:

To believe that the intolerable crime is to burn a few cars and rob some shops, whereas to kill a young man is trivial, is typically in keeping with what Marx regarded as the principle alienation of capitalism: the primacy of things over existence, of commodities over life and machines over workers, which he encapsulates in the formula: "Le mort saisit le vif."[31]

While Olsen was not killed, as the quote above outlines, a similar line of thought can be drawn in the protection of capital with an utter disrespect for life. The police often claim that their tactics are not lethal and are meant to protect the people, but had Olsen not gone to a hospital, he very well could have died from his brain swelling. The incident has subsequently left him with some brain damage.[32] Furthermore, who is it that the police are trying to protect? It is clearly not the protestors, as the violence seems to act as a form of repression, while Wall Street continues to profit from those who have been violated. Therefore, it is protection for the profiteers of violence, not the people whom the police are sworn to protect, as the "non-lethal" weapons used against such protestors can, in fact, often be lethal.[33] This ties directly to Charles Tilly's claim that war making and state making are intimately connected as a type of criminal protection racket.[34] In Tilly's essay, he highlights the way in which the state maintains the legitimacy to utilize violence in order to protect the functions of capitalism that support the state.[35]

The protests that intensified across the nation after Olsen was shot brought more attention to the Occupy movement. Interestingly, RT News interviewed Shamar Thomas to get his thoughts on the event. In response to a question about veteran participation in Occupy, Shamar stated:

> I do believe that all veterans have a reasonability to protect these people because, like myself and Scott, we fought in foreign wars for you know, the idea of peace and that we're there to ensure freedom and our way of life in America, and so to come back to America and to not stand up for the people that are here, that you fought for, is an injustice to yourself and what your values are.[36]

In this way, Shamar Thomas is working to push against the alienation of capital by reinscribing patriotism and the soldier's oath to protect the American people, by putting people and values before capital and highlighting this violence as injustice; this is the ideal of the Soldiers' Contract. On the other hand, Scott Olsen's body and positionality is being privileged as it is within this idea of a fallen soldier that an attempt to create a resonant narrative is being made by those at Occupy. If successful, the fallen soldier who was a part of the military, which many accept as a legitimate form of violence due to years of state propaganda, has now fallen due to state violence. While both forms of violence can be claimed as legitimate, many will have a dissonant reaction to violence toward the fallen soldier.

The violence that is created by the state-finance nexus is a concern to veterans and to all those involved in the Occupy Wall Street movement.[37] It is because of the events that happened to Scott Olsen that IVAW decided to release a statement about the Occupy movement, which succinctly ties together the themes of this chapter.

Veterans Are Part of the 99 Percent

The first part of IVAW's statement of solidarity with the Occupy movement helps explain the ways in which veterans are affected, directly and personally, by this violence. It reads:

> Most of our military is made up of the 99%. We join the military for many reasons. Some join because of family tradition or a sense of patriotism. Others join for citizenship, education or to escape poverty or violence in our homes and neighborhoods. Many service members realize the wars we fight contribute to poverty and violence in Iraq and Afghanistan communities. We are coming home to a broken economy where veterans have higher unemployment, incarceration, suicide and homelessness than the national average.[38]

This passage highlights a number of interesting notions. First and foremost is the idea that the military is primarily comprised of the 99 percent.[39] This is the thread that holds the rest of the passage together, as those who join are almost always of lower socioeconomic classes. Furthermore, immigrants who have come to this country and joined the military seeking citizenship are usually coming to the US because of the imaginary that the United States is the "land of opportunity" (which is the focus of chapter 6). Those who join the military to get an education do so because they cannot afford it otherwise; and escaping poverty is an obvious link to the 99 percent, and violence in one's home and neighborhood is almost solely tied to lower socioeconomic classes. Even the idea of joining the military because of family tradition can be tied to class issues, as soldiers from the lower and working classes have been the ones who have primarily fought previous wars.[40]

Another rationale for joining the military, the idea of patriotism, ties to the opening vignette of this chapter. It is often patriotism that leads soldiers to believe in the oath of service they take before, during, and after their time in the service. Furthermore, the oath of service is the basis of the Soldiers' Contract. Within the oath is the order to defend "the Constitution, against all enemies, foreign and domestic," and it is within the Constitution that a violation by the 1 percent can be found. The preamble of the Constitution states:

> We the People of the United States, in Order to form a more perfect Union, establish Justice, insure domestic Tranquility, provide for the common defense, promote the general Welfare, and secure the Blessings of Liberty to ourselves and our Posterity, do ordain and establish this Constitution for the United States of America.[41]

It is in violation of the establishment of justice, the lack of domestic tranquility, and of general welfare—in other words in violation of the Social Contract—that these veterans find the domestic enemy and stand in solidarity with the Occupy movement. As they point out, "We are coming home to a broken economy where veterans have higher unemployment, incarceration, suicide and homelessness than the national average." To look at the numbers on two of those issues, "the VA estimates that on any given night there are 200,000 veterans living on the streets and nearly 400,000 experience homelessness over the course of a year."[42] The VA also reports that there are an average of eighteen veteran suicides a day.[43] So it is not just the people these vets are defending, but also the veterans themselves who are being violated by this same systemic enemy, as social programs, including the VA, are stripped of funds in exchange for higher corporate profits/lower corporate taxation.

The second section of IVAW's statement states:

> Our nation's leaders have betrayed us. We have been asked to risk our lives and mental health for the defense of our country and the well-being of foreign allies. The causes for military conflict have proven false while corporations profit. The military

industrial complex continues to grow in wealth while the rest of
the world pays for it in dollars and blood. Instead of increasing
programs to attempt to repair damages, many schools, hospitals,
and social services are shutting down. Programs for veterans are
inadequate and are leaving us physically, mentally, and emotionally bankrupt.[44]

This section highlights a number of issues, but first and foremost it returns
to the idea of being violated by the state in the name of profitability. A
2011 report by the Project on Government Oversight (POGO) found that
private contractors made 1.83 times more than federal workers who did
the same job.[45] Similarly, critics charge that there is at least $20 billion
(perhaps upwards of $50 billion[46]) worth of waste by military contractors
in which that money is basically going into the pockets of the CEOs of
these private contracting companies.[47] While this is nothing new, as the
military-industrial complex thrived from World War I through the Cold
War, and especially during the Reagan years, it has boomed again with the
current war on terror and the wars in Iraq and Afghanistan. What's clear
is that war is a profitable business that is supported by the state and that
is just as responsible for the economic woes facing the nation.

The second important aspect highlighted in the passage above concerns
the negligence by the US government in treating wounded soldiers, which can
be seen as a silent function of the state in perpetuating violence. Although
profits are high for those in the private sector of the military-industrial
complex, veterans are coming home and having to fight for benefits. While
it is becoming easier to cash in on programs like the Post-9/11 GI Bill with
liaisons at nearly all college campuses, it is still a long and arduous process
for those seeking treatment for physical and mental problems that occurred
as a result of one's military service. Because of the two recent wars, the VA
system is extremely underfunded and overstretched. This raises the question:
If those who are supposedly the "heroes" and "protectors of freedom" are
treated this way by the state, then what does it matter in giving benefits
and health services to the everyday citizen? It would seem that there is
no priority for ensuring that the everyday citizen is taken care of, which
makes one question the processes of Western liberal democracy. Instead of
the promotion of a "general welfare," the Fortune 500 companies on Wall
Street are winning; it is now a promotion of profits and the bottom line,
and the state will use any means to protect those profits.

The third section of IVAW's statement of solidarity with the Occupy movement is subtitled "Veterans have a history of effective grassroots organizing." It reads:

> IVAW has been a voice for veterans and their grievances since our founding in 2004. We understand that change comes about when people speak up, organize, and demand justice. Veterans and active-duty service members have a history of organizing, from the Bonus March to the Vietnam War. Iraq and Afghanistan veterans have an important contribution to make to this movement.[48]

This passage exemplifies the ways in which veterans have been and continue to play important roles in activism for social justice. It is evident that IVAW is working toward issues beyond those concerning veterans, as their mission statement seeks reparations for the Iraqi people. Similarly, the havoc reaped upon the American people by the neoliberal state is similar to the violation that the veterans have experienced in their encounter with war. This violation—as discussed in the earlier section on state violence—is tightly linked to the state-finance nexus.

IVAW's letter of solidarity closes by stating:

> As service members we are told that we fight for human rights and democratic freedoms. However, these rights seem to be continually denied at protests across the nation, often times by police using excessive force and violent tactics. We support our members, fellow veterans and members of this movement who have been subjected to this gross contradiction, and who have refused to remain silent.[49]

The activism expressed by veterans and by participants of Occupy as a whole works to push against the state-finance nexus that seeks to legitimize state violence. As Tilly points out, "popular resistance to war making and state making made a difference. When ordinary people resisted vigorously, authorities made concessions: guarantees of rights, representative institutions, courts of appeal. Those concessions, in their turn, constrained the later paths of war making and state making."[50] But popular resistance sometimes needs sparks to action, and while there were many leading up to the Occupy movement, and many within it, the attack on Scott Olsen also acted as one.

It is in the wake of the Scott Olsen incident that the IVAW statement was forged, as the violence that was perpetrated on him exemplifies a
denial of the "democratic freedoms" that he and other veterans so adamantly
fought for. Furthermore, it is this denial of rights that pushes the veterans
of IVAW to organize and resist the state-corporate nexus that continues to
profit at the expense of the people.

Conclusion

The participation of military veterans within the Occupy Wall Street movement creates an alternative narrative of the ways in which the movement can
be examined. With groups like IVAW and individuals like Scott Olsen and
Shamar Thomas working within the Occupy movement, a broader understanding of the state-financial nexus can be seen in relation to the extent of
violence that stems from the neoliberal Western democratic system, especially
violence perpetuated by the state. The enactment of the Soldiers' Contract
by veterans participating in the Occupy movement disrupts this violence,
as they have sworn to protect the very people that the state is violating.
Paradoxically, it is then the state itself that can be seen as the very enemy
that the veterans must fight, as it is in violation of the Social Contract by
not establishing justice, nor ensuring domestic tranquility, by neglecting the
common defense, and by neither promoting the general welfare nor securing
liberty for ourselves or our posterity. Furthermore, the state is egregiously
violating the First Amendment—which guarantees the right to free speech
and peaceful assembly. Therefore, there is an interesting, multilayered relationship between the Soldiers' Contract and the Social Contract: the tension
between soldiers' loyalty to their country and their opposition to the way
the state acts, and the tension between truth and power.

Furthermore, in these veterans' fight against state violence, they seek
to raise a new kind of class-consciousness that creates a condition of possibility in which a radically egalitarian, anti-capitalist, co-revolutionary space
can be formed. Their activism is a crucial component in making change,
and groups like IVAW, along with veterans like Sgt. Shamar Thomas, can
participate in these roles, as they are able to reach across multiple levels
of subjugation. Once on the front lines of battle in Iraq and Afghanistan,
they now come home to fight on the front lines in the battle for America,
continuing to honor their oath to the nation.

4

Enviro-Warriors

> But the love of wilderness is more than a hunger for what is always
> beyond reach; it is also an expression of loyalty to the earth, the earth
> which bore us and sustains us, the only home we shall ever know, the
> only paradise we ever need—if only we had the eyes to see. Original
> sin, the true original sin, is the blind destruction for the sake of greed
> of this natural paradise which lies all around us—if only we were
> worthy of it.
>
> —Edward Abbey, *Down the River*

Growing up in Colorado afforded me many outdoor opportunities, from
backcountry skiing to numerous camping trips. The summer before I joined
the military I was a river raft guide on the Colorado River. I have always
had a deep love and respect for nature, which made the outdoor elements of
my time in the military easier for me than it was for many others who had
not spent as much time outdoors as I had. In basic training, I remember
hearing the kids from the big cities like LA and Miami complain about
having to sit out in the cold rainy hills of Kentucky. Being Cavalry Scouts
meant that we would be spending a lot of time out in the wilderness. In
Germany, we spent countless weeks training in the woods of Grafenwöhr.
In rain or snow, we were constantly training. We traveled to the high hills
of the Czech Republic where we found "Wham-Fuck-Hill," a hill that we
snuck across in the middle of the night where you couldn't walk five feet
along the steep and thickly wooded terrain without hearing the "wham"
of a falling body followed by the soldier yelling "Fuck!" Our subsequent
deployment in Kosovo allowed us a lot of time in the countryside and
mountains there. After that we would go to Hohenfels in three feet of snow
to train for the hot deserts of Iraq, where we would spend a large portion

of our time patrolling not only the dense cities but the vast farmland and empty barren lands as well. While some within my platoon would see these missions as boring and monotonous, I found the solitude of the wilderness exciting, and I valued it as an escape.

My love for the outdoors has become ingrained in my personality, as it is something I need, and I can now see the power of nature. This power comes in many forms—from the literal sense, in the power generated by alternative sustainable energy, to the healing powers of spending time in the woods communing with nature. This power can be seen as a demilitarizing force as it works to not only help veterans deprogram from the traumas of war and the military, but it also pushes against the neoliberal model of militarism by maintaining that sustainability is better for national security, rather than resource extraction from unwilling countries.[1] Furthermore, scholars recently have often framed the environment as a part of the Social Contract; I would agree, and many of the veterans doing environmental work would say that the natural beauty of the nation is a part of what they were fighting for.[2] This chapter will explore some of the veterans' organizations that seek to harness and preserve this power, such as Veterans Green Jobs, Vet Voice Foundation, and Operation FREE.

Garett Reppenhagen

Garett was born at Fort Bliss Army Base in Texas, in 1975, the son of a Vietnam veteran, and the grandson of a World War II veteran. Military roots run deep in Garett's family. Because his father was in the military, his family moved around a lot when Garett was a child, but they eventually settled in Colorado Springs, Colorado, one of the most conservative evangelical Christian strongholds in the country. Garett grew up hating the military, as he bore the brunt of his father's discipline as a child, but another part of him held it in high regard, as it was all he knew at a young age. When his father died of complications tied to his service in Vietnam, he felt freed from his father's discipline, and his rebellious nature was able to run wild. He, his mother, and two brothers lived in a small ranch house on the side of a mountain in Green Mountain Falls, Colorado. It was here that he discovered his initial passion for the outdoors, as he was able to walk out his back door and climb mountains, hike, and camp anytime he wished. He dropped out of high school, and, after a few run-ins with the law, moved to Grand Junction, Colorado, where his older brother was attending college at Mesa State. It was here that we met, through mutual friends, and would eventually decide to join the military together, as highlighted in chapter 1.

It was through Garett that I also met Jeff, who would join us on the buddy program. The three of us went through boot camp together and were stationed together afterward. There were some deviations throughout our time in military, such as during our deployment to Kosovo. There, Jeff was not a part of the scout platoon but rather the driver for our battalion's command sergeant major, and while in Iraq he would become the brigade command sergeant major's gunner. When preparing for Iraq, our platoon sergeant asked if I was interested in becoming part of the battalion's sniper section, but since my time in the military ended halfway through our deployment to Iraq, I thought that if I did there was no way I would get out in time, not knowing we would be stop-lossed regardless. Garett on the other hand had no illusions and figured we would be there no matter what, and being one of the best shots in the platoon decided to go to the United Nations sniper interdiction course in Stetten, Germany. He thought it would be a unique opportunity to learn a new skill, and the training, which included sneaking around in the woods, reminded him of his childhood wandering around the mountains. So while the three of us were in different platoons, we remained close and usually saw each other on a daily basis.

As time went on, we all began to become more and more disillusioned with the mission in Iraq. Jeff had always been suspicious and resentful of the mission, but Garett's breaking point was the release of photos from Abu Ghraib, as it represented a betrayal of the reasons we were supposed to be in Iraq. His missions as a sniper didn't help either, as they revealed that we were more of an occupying force instilling fear rather than hope. Garett began speaking out against the war, at first just among us, and then to others in his sniper team. In a personal disagreement with the section sergeant about the politics of their deployment, Garett was removed from the sniper platoon and put on the battalion commander's personal security detachment. One afternoon a call came in that the town of Khalis's governor was under attack. The colonel was nearby and decided to respond to the call. They arrived on the scene and there was nothing really going on, but the truck commander saw a couple of men outside the governor's house with AK-47s and assumed they were the ones who were supposedly attacking the governor. He yelled at Garett, telling him to open fire, which Garett did under the assumption that the sergeant had more information than he did. It turned out the information they had was not correct. It wasn't that the governor was under attack but rather under threat of attack, and the men

standing outside the house were off-duty police officers who were protecting
the governor. The bullets cut through one of the men as the other dove
for cover. Once the chaos ended and Garett found out what he had done,
he understood that he couldn't limit his perspective to those around him.

We all had been writing about our experiences, but Garett and Jeff
formally started a blog called *Fight to Survive*, which we all contributed to.
We also sent emails to a band we had met, the Bouncing Souls, who were
posting our writings on their website on a link called "Letters from Iraq."[3]
Something Garett wrote caught the attention of our chain of command,
and Garett was called in for a formal meeting about the things he was writing. Our 1st sergeant wanted to throw the book at Garett, the colonel was
undecided, but our command sergeant major—who had Jeff as his driver
while in Kosovo, so he knew us and our views fairly well—was the deciding
factor. Sgt. Maj. Bartoszek was known as a hard ass, and he didn't agree
with our stance, but his feeling was that as long as we were not violating
operational security, which could put other soldiers in danger, we (of all the
people, since we were out putting our lives on the line daily) had the right
to say what we wanted to say. From that day forward, Garett felt that he
had been given freedom, but he understood that there were also people who
were out to get him. He then became the first active-duty member of IVAW
and started on his path of activism. Three months after our deployment in
Iraq ended, we left the military and headed back to the US.

Upon our exit from the military, I went to school, Jeff explored the
world playing music along the way, and Garett jumped head first into
activism. Garett was initially hired by Nobel laureate Bobby Muller to work
at his organization, Vietnam Veterans of America (VVA).[4] He was given
enough leeway to also be able to be on the board of directors for Iraq
Veterans Against the War. Since he was stationed in Washington, DC, he
spent a lot of time on Capitol Hill advocating for veterans. Garett would
eventually leave VVA in order to get back to Colorado, where he became
the director of veterans programs for the nonprofit organization Veterans
Green Jobs (VGJ). This opportunity opened many doors not only for him
but also for other veterans to get connected with the different programs
that help to get veterans outdoors. While the mission of VGJ was to retrain
veterans into the green economy, there were many other programs to which
Garett had access. For example, Garett, eight other veterans, and I went
on a weeklong rafting trip on the Yampa and Green rivers in northwestern
Colorado to work with BLM to clear tamarisk trees from the river.[5] The
trip would become not just a week of work and fun, but also a space in

which we could reflect upon the military, the environment, and the things that tied them together. In general, the focus for VGJ was on the micro-political level as it sought to train veterans in the green industries, which affect not only their personal lives but the communities in which they work, to create global change.[6]

VGJ's main mission was to help veterans gain employment after their military service. While many veterans attempt to utilize their education benefits after their service, it is often difficult for them to integrate into college life.[7] This is primarily due to class-related issues, since many come from lower socioeconomic backgrounds and are first-generation students.[8] VGJ gives these veterans an opportunity to learn—with fellow veterans—new skill sets that will make them successful in their transition to civilian life. As they say on their website:

> We are working to reverse the high unemployment trend among
> military veterans by linking them with training and employment
> opportunities in the green sector. By equipping our nation's
> former servicemen and women with transferable skills, tools
> and resources and connecting them with meaningful employ-
> ment, we believe we will help veterans to maintain their sense
> of service, give back to their communities and environment,
> and contribute to a healthy, sustainable and secure future for
> people and the planet.[9]

The mission of VGJ exposes the excess within the military apparatus produced by the neoliberal economy that veterans encounter upon their exit from the military. The military is often seen as a way out, since it provides educational opportunities and job skill training, though all too often their job skills do not transfer to the civilian world. The training that VGJ provides is similar to military training and can be seen as Foucault's disciplinary power, as VGJ seeks to retrain the body through work. While the training that they do is in no way as intensive or repetitive as the military, it is a lesser form of disciplinary power in that "every disciplinary system tends to be an occupation of the individual's time, life, and body."[10] The work and tactics deployed by VGJ are similar to those deployed by the military, from the use of camaraderie to using the outdoor skills learned in the military, as those seem to be more easily transferable than the "job skills" they learned. Thus, in many ways they are reproducing the militarized body and utilizing militarized tactics to re-socialize these veterans into non-militarized life.[11]

For example, VGJ would do training sessions in remote locations of the Colorado Mountains where the veterans would be broken up into squads in which they were to complete specific objectives as a team. Each squad had a team leader, similar to the military. This hierarchization is essential within disciplinary systems as the supervision ensures that transformation into the prescribed body occurs.[12] In this case it is a transformation into a productive member of society who has the skills to work within the "green economy." As mentioned earlier, many of the skills learned within the military are not translatable to civilian jobs, thus causing many veterans to have a difficult time transitioning into college life after their service. This has led to high levels of unemployment and high levels of homelessness among veterans, which can again be seen as excess within the neoliberal Western democratic state.[13] The excess produced—the veterans who are now skill-less and unemployed—by the security dispositif must find new skills to survive, which is where VGJ sought to be useful. This is why, as Paul Higate points out, many turn to military contracting jobs, because it is the one place their skills are useful. However, for those who do not wish to return to military life, options like VGJ—where their skills are transformed—are more suitable options.[14]

Michael Dillon and Luis Lobo-Guerrero state that within a security dispositif there is a certain paradox whereas "[s]uch biopolitical intercourse simultaneously both sustains and undermines itself."[15] Therefore, there is excess and a lack within the security dispositif, and as I describe in the final chapter, a constant need to try and fill the hole that war creates. War in general, and dispositifs in general, are never satisfied, as they constantly require resources and bodies to fulfill them. Because as Foucault points out, a dispositif is a "thoroughly heterogeneous set consisting of discourses, institutions, architectural forms, regulatory decisions, laws, administrative measures, scientific statements, philosophical, moral and philanthropic propositions—in short, the said as much as the unsaid."[16] Therefore, the security dispositif is a continual cycle, constantly growing, giving, taking, and destroying; those who are in the military are a part of the dispositif, and once they leave, they are no longer needed for the continuance of the dispositif, thus they are the excess. Which is where the many organizations come in, to pick up and reuse that excess.

Sadly, Veterans Green Jobs closed in 2014 due to the director's inexperience with managing nonprofits, which meant Garett had to look for a new job. The skills he gained with VGJ, though, were valuable, and he soon joined the nonprofit organization Vet Voice Foundation as its Rocky

Mountain director. His role there was similar to the work he did with VGJ in terms of getting veterans involved in outdoor activities; however, he then would organize those veterans to advocate for different policy issues in the state and nationally. For example, he would take veterans on outdoor experiences in areas like Brown Canyon, Colorado, and then he would take them to Washington, DC, and have them leverage their position as veterans to advocate for Brown Canyon to become a National Park. They would leverage their position by telling legislators about their experiences in these places and how they could feel the ways in which these spaces had the ability to heal the wounds of war. In the case of Brown Canyon, they were successful. This tactic became valuable, especially toward the end of President Obama's second term when he was looking to protect different open spaces. Garett worked to make sure veterans' voices were being heard by politicians who were shaping environmental policy. In this way, it could be said that the Vet Voice Foundation's primary goal is about the reciprocal relationship between the Social Contract and the Soldiers' Contract, as the organization works to highlight and advocate for the interests of those affected by both contracts. I will return to Garett and the Vet Voice Foundation toward the end of this chapter.

Jon Gensler

Another veterans' organization working to shape environmental policy is the nonprofit group Operation FREE (OpFree), which is a subsidiary of the Truman Foundation. In 2009, I hosted and moderated a panel of veterans who were touring the United States speaking for OpFree. While both VGJ and OpFree see global warming as a major risk not only to the planet but also to "national security," each group has a different focus as to their goals.

The strategy pushed by OpFree became clearer in my interview with one of its members, Jon Gensler.[17] Our interview took place at his office on the sixteenth floor in the downtown Manhattan offices of Cambridge Leadership Associates, where he was currently working. Jon was born in the southern part of West Virginia and was one of the only kids in his town to escape the local coal mines by going to West Point. A couple of months after 9/11 he was deployed to Kuwait as a part of an advanced tank battalion that could deploy anywhere in the Middle East in response to the attacks. But he would not go to war until a few weeks after the initial push into Iraq in 2003, where he was attached to a mortar platoon.

While there, he not only did regular patrols, acting as a "stabilizing force," but he was also charged with "retraining the local Iraqi police force." In the first few months his battalion had lost a few soldiers, including a close friend he had played football with at West Point, which had a deep impact on him. His platoon would then be sent back to Baghdad where he was promoted to captain and became the night tactical operations commander for his battalion.

Jon's battalion returned to the US in 2004, and he was transferred to Fort Carson, Colorado. It was here that he decided he needed to get away from the military to clear his head. While sitting at his desk looking at the world map on his wall he decided to go as far away from everything as possible; he saw New Zealand sitting down at the bottom corner of the map. He soon got out of the military and immediately headed to the airport. During his first couple of months in New Zealand he worked as a bouncer at a local bar in the south, but the hours bothered him and he soon quit to work for a landscaping company. He did this for about six months and then decided to quit and spend the next two months floating around two different wilderness areas. On the second day of this trip, Jon was kayaking in an area called Doubtful Sound when he had "some sort of epiphany." As he describes it:

> It's about a mile wide, and the cliffs are covered with green vegeta-
> tion and waterfalls, there's dolphins and they're swimming beside
> us . . . and I'd been struggling with my experiences in combat
> thinking at that point, I had lost, my battalion had lost a few
> people. I had lost a good friend of mine that I played football
> with at west point, who died in the very early weeks of the war.
> Just kind of struggling with the purpose of it all. And in this
> fjord kayaking, in the midst of all this massive grandeur. . . . I
> felt extremely connected to the world as a system, as a thing,
> and felt myself disappear into the rest of the connection. And
> it all kind of made sense to me. The reasons I went to fight,
> not that they were justified, but it made sense to me, how the
> system that we're in forced our hand to fight over resources. It
> was rooted in us not understanding what we're doing in the
> system of the world. It was a very crude understanding at the
> time. I decided at that time to act on that. If I could see the
> system, then I could act on it and make a change for the better,
> to prevent future resource wars. . . .[18]

Jon then left New Zealand and got a job with Lutron Electronics, where he would begin to learn the terrain of the green economy. He helped to establish a green council for the city of Bethlehem, Pennsylvania, and in 2007 moved to Boston to attend graduate school at MIT. There he became involved in issues of sustainability rather than energy, feeling that he was still too emotionally close to the issue of energy, due to coming from a coal state and serving in Iraq. But then the "perfect storm" arrived, pushing him into energy issues. Tragically, two more of his close friends died from advanced improvised explosive devices that were primarily funded by Iranian oil money. That, coupled with a recent 2006 mine explosion in West Virginia that killed twenty-five miners and a recent email from the newly formed group Operation FREE, inspired him to jump into the energy fight.[19] The trauma and violence of war and neoliberalism is what inspired him as he decided to be a productive force seeking to push against the current dispositif.

Jon was one of the first one hundred veterans to advocate with OpFree, as they brought 100 veterans to Washington, DC, two from each state, to talk to Congress. While the bill that the vets were advocating was tabled and eventually dismissed, Jon became intrigued on the policy activism front that OpFree was doing. OpFree is focused on more of a systemic level as they aim to shift the doctrine of American policy. OpFree's mission statement reads more like a risk assessment than a nonprofit mission statement highlighting values and goals. For example, within it they state:

> America's billion-dollar-a-day dependence on oil from hostile nations directly funds our most dangerous enemies, putting guns and bullets into the hands of our enemies. The Department of Defense has also stated that climate change poses a threat as well, destabilizing weak and failed states—the breeding grounds and safe havens for terrorist organizations like al Qaeda and the Taliban. With new, clean sources of energy to power our economy and fuel our military, we will no longer be forced to pay and protect regimes that support terrorism.[20]

The shift in focus from the "contentious" environmental threat to one of national security is intentional. While Republicans often deny global warming, they cannot deny national security, which is a rallying point for both Democrats and Republicans. Furthermore, OpFree uses military veterans to deliver the message in hopes that the message of national security coming from the mouths of veterans like Jon who were fighting terrorism will carry more weight on both sides of the political spectrum. This has a dual effect; not only does it create credibility for the movement, but it also frames global warming as a threat to the species. This focus on global warming as a threat to the species is a biopolitical maneuver that can best be explained through Foucault's inversion of Carl von Clausewitz's aphorism, to which Foucault states, ". . . politics is the continuation of war by other means."[21]

The constant shifts, flows, and evolutions of biopolitics take place in order to make life live, and as Foucault points out:

> One technique is disciplinary; it centers on the body, produces individualizing effects, and manipulates the body as a source of forces that have to be rendered both useful and docile. And we also have a second technology which is centered not upon the body but upon life: a technology which brings together the mass effects characteristics of a population, which tries to control the series of random events that can occur in a living mass, a technology which tries to predict the probability of those events (by modifying it, if necessary), or at least to compensate for their effects. This is a technology which aims to establish a homeostasis, not by training individuals, but by achieving an overall equilibrium that protects the security of the whole from internal dangers.

Biopolitics is therefore focused on the betterment of the species (or, in other words, producing more productive members of society), and that which does not transform within the dispositif is discarded as excess, and thus it is allowed to "let die."

As Brad Evans explains, the Western liberal wars of the twentieth and twenty-first centuries have been focused upon the betterment of the species by attacking those who seek to hinder progress or threaten stability.[22] Each new threat produces a new war, which leads to new policies and politics, in hopes of making new liberal societies that accept the biopolitical prescription that is being forced upon them.[23] Evans states:

> While liberals have therefore been at pains to offer a more humane recovery to the overt failures of military excess in current theatres of operation, warfare has not in any way been removed from

the species. Instead, humanized in the name of local sensitivities, doing what is necessary out of global species necessity now implies that war effectively takes place by *every means*.[24]

Therefore, the framing of environmental issues as national security issues shows that the aim is not peace but rather the protection of the species by any means necessary, a crucial part of the Social Contract. However, the species should not be viewed as the human species as a whole, but rather as the population within the biopolitical system working to maintain itself, in this case the Western liberal democracies in general, and more specifically, the United States. Thus while environmental issues are of global concern, these issues are being framed in such a way that those within America are meant to fear a loss of their American ways and identity if change does not occur. While OpFree's mission statement puts energy independence from Arab oil at center stage, through stories like Jon's, they are much more focused on pushing any green initiative legislation that comes to Congress. Furthermore, OpFree has been specifically focused on "greening the military," promoting a more sustainable military force.[25] This not only shifts the military apparatus within the security dispositif, but also has the ability for more sustainable wars that can last longer for less cost. While there is the promotion of less violence because terrorism will be defunded with a move away from oil, and less people will be displaced by inclement weather patterns, there will still be the ability for *perpetual war*. This tactic therefore embraces the risk of terrorism but seeks to avert the risk of climate change. Thus, discourses of "greening the military" still problematically sustain the need and usefulness of war. Finally, the push for energy independence does not address other forms of environmental violence that occur, including the use of depleted uranium and the destruction of foreign forests and wetlands, which affects wildlife as well.[26]

After Jon's initial work with OpFree in 2008, he spent the next two years bouncing between Washington, DC, West Virginia, and Boston as he looked for new ways to educate the public and policymakers about the ties binding national security, foreign oil, and the military. He helped with a documentary called *The Burden*, which highlights these issues, and participated on panels by telling his story.[27] At the time he had also started a job with a solar company that was working with the Department of Defense; however, with the 2011 sequester deal that loomed on the horizon, their work with the DoD came to a halt. This brought him to Cambridge Leadership Associates, a consulting firm that grew out of Harvard University's John F. Kennedy School of Government. The group works to bridge the stakeholders in different communities, including but not limited to politicians, policy writers, activists, community members, and businesses. It was this bridging of the civil-military spheres that placed environmental and national security issues at the forefront that attracted Jon, as he saw a disconnect between the different communities that needed to be in touch with one another.[28]

After my interview with Jon, I was invited to a panel that he had organized titled "Mission Critical: Clean Energy and the US Military," which was to take place in the law offices of Simpson Thacher & Bartlett. Scheduled to appear were Richard G. Kidd IV (deputy assistant secretary of the US Army Energy and Sustainability office), Colonel Russell LaChance (professor at West Point and deputy head of its Chemistry and Living Sciences Department, as well as chair of the West Point Energy Counsel), Scott Sklar (president of the Stella Group, Ltd.), and Kitt Kennedy (president of the National Resources Defense Council). The panel was for an organization called E2 (Environmental Entrepreneurs) that had hired Jon as a consultant. As it was scheduled for a couple of hours after my interview, I walked over to the building in which it was being held.

The law offices of Simpson Thacher & Bartlett were in a skyscraper adjacent to Grand Central Station. There were multiple points of security, and I had to show my ID at the entrance to the building and on the floor where the panel was being held. I felt drastically underdressed for this more formal event, as most everyone was wearing business suits, and while I was wearing a button-down shirt, my jeans stood out like a sore thumb. Needless to say, this panel was not for just anybody who might be interested in the topic, which was obvious by the three confirmation emails that I had to send at different points over the previous month, as well as the thick security getting into the building. The crowd seemed to mostly be CEOs, business owners, and presidents or VPs of a number of different organizations. The stories Jon had told me hours earlier of being chained to bulldozers in West Virginia seemed to include a very different crowd of activists than the suit-and-tie crowd here, who made change with their pocketbooks and phone calls. It seemed that this was the type of crossover Jon had in mind in connecting different groups of people and ideas.

The panel brought to light a number of interesting points about the current push to green the military. The first speaker, Richard Kidd, explained how the US Army is the largest utility consumer in the United States. It consumes $1.7 billion worth of natural gas, electricity, steam, and water annually; it uses more than 65½ trillion BTUs of energy, which is more energy in a year than is used by Jamaica and Iceland combined, with a bit extra left over; it manages as much land as the area of Massachusetts, Connecticut, and Vermont combined; it consumes enough water to fill 53,000 Olympic-sized swimming pools per year; and finally, the US Army spends $3.5 billion a year on liquid fuel.[29] According to Kidd, all this means that the army has a responsibility to lessen three types of risk: its financial risk, its "representational risk," or in other words, its impact on the communities it is around, and its "mission risk," which is the national security argument highlighted above. Thus, Kidd in theory is working to make the military less of a presence. Furthermore, he discussed ways in which the army is working to make "NetZero" bases, which produce as much energy as they consume. It is doing this not only by implementing the technology but also through institutionalizing this doctrine through policies and guidelines in their official memos and documents. The shift has been a challenge due to the sequester that froze federal funding in 2013, which meant, according to Kidd, that more than $250 million that would have gone to the green industry was lost in the first month. Kidd closed his comments by returning to Jon's story, which Jon had told as an introduction to the panel:

> [Jon's story] represents an opportunity, because it exposes a collective memory that can be leveraged, anyone who has been there (Iraq) for a year or two can tell you a similar story, we want to leverage that experience in order to make change. . . . We want every bullet to hit its target. . . . Same with energy . . . we want energy to become a consideration in everything we do . . . so that we can change the way we build our doctrine.[30]

This returns to the idea of veterans leveraging their identity to get a specific message out, particularly playing on the nationalism and patriotism of Congress, in other words, those who send soldiers to war. Similarly, the other panelists also spoke of shifting the dialogue from the "Al Gore" environmentalism debate—which had obviously become a scandalous position to take, especially among Republicans—to one of national security and a pro-business capitalist argument, as it is the private sector that will aid this greening of the military, thus benefiting all. By the end of the panel I concluded that its aim was to educate business executives about the progress the military had made in "greening" itself and to promote the future opportunities to work with the Department of Defense, so long as the sequester ends. It also seemed to be suggested that these business leaders could contact Congress and to try to end the sequester.

"This Is What I Fought For!"

While many of the veterans I interviewed were focused on trying to make changes to help the environment, many others were intent upon using the environment as a tool to help themselves and other veterans heal from the trauma and violence of war. Furthermore, most of the veterans I talked with who work on issues of sustainability and the environment all had stories similar to Jon's, as they often found a future purpose and an activist cause while in nature. Some found it on the water, some in the woods, and some on a mountain. While veterans may discover this inner impulse on their own, there are a number of organizations working to help returning war veterans with issues such as PTS that use nature as a medium to reach these veterans. These organizations often have duel missions: one is to help veterans to heal, and the other is to expose them to the issues facing the environmental movement, with the hope that they may become voices to aid the movement. Organizations like the Vet Voice Foundation, where Garett currently works, have had much success on both fronts, as they connect veterans to a number of these different organizations, and, as mentioned earlier, take veterans to Washington, DC, in order to lobby Congress about these environmental issues.

While Vet Voice Foundation is not solely focused on environmental issues, it is a big part of their mission. The board of directors and advisors is comprised of a number of veterans, and as I have heard Garett explain many times, they all feel that it is their duty to take care of the land that they swore to defend. These beautiful natural parts of America are what many veterans claim they were fighting for when they went to war, making it a part of their Soldiers' Contract. This sentiment is not exclusive to the vets of the Vet Voice Foundation. As friend and colleague Stacy Bare describes about a time when he and a couple of vets were standing on a mountain looking into the scenic vistas of the Rocky Mountains in Colorado, one of the veterans declared, "This is what I was fighting for!"[31] Furthermore, the same discussion was had at a veterans' retreat that I attended in the mountains in the summer of 2014, as we felt that it was these beautiful parts of America that make it so great.[32] The interesting thing about this common theme of fighting for nature is that it often comes in contrast to the hustle and bustle of the city. It is not that veterans feel like the happenings of the city are less important, but rather that it is the beauty and grandeur of wilderness that moves and inspires them. Also, as was discussed in many of my interviews and in other veteran circles I have been a part of, one of the difficulties many veterans have in returning from war is readjusting to everyday society.[33] From the stresses of dealing with a busy parking lot to the seemingly petty issues of the people around them, the stresses of war seem monumental in comparison. Every veteran who has been to war that I have talked to—in and outside of these interviews—has expressed something along these lines: the reintegration into daily life is very difficult, and this often makes veterans angry. For example, one veteran I interviewed named Brock stated:

> . . . everyone was just so obsessed with their little trivial problems and their lives, and I was like I just came from a place where every day there is some baby that is brought into our base because it fell on the fire, cause they heat their homes with brush that they gather out in the desert and they have fires in their homes and babies fall in them. And little girls getting beat by their fathers, or have acid thrown on them, or little boys that have to work to be able to raise money for their families getting their fingers chopped off in tractors and people dying and getting shot, I don't understand why you guys are complaining about these things. . . .[34]

In nature, the veterans do not have to deal with these issues: there are no questions from ignorant civilians, there is no rush to be anywhere—there is only you and the wild. Though, as Garett once said, "It's not the wilderness that is wild and crazy, it's the city."

The healing occurs by not only getting away from the stresses of everyday life, but also due to a number of other factors. First, exercise has shown to be valuable in helping to reduce stress for many veterans, which nature and hikes are good at providing.[35] This exercise does not necessarily have to be done in nature; however, when in nature one is usually getting some sort of exercise. The second factor comes from just being present in nature and/or the woods. Over the past fifteen years the Japanese have been studying what they call *shinrin-yoku*, or forest bathing. One study shows the effects of taking walks through forests, and while cortisol levels in the brain rise whenever one goes for a walk, the cortisol levels drop and sustain lower levels when walking in a forest.[36] They have even found that hospital patients who can merely see trees from their rooms will have lower levels of stress than those who cannot.[37] Finally walking through the woods enacts eye movement desensitization and reprocessing (EMDR),[38] which has become a therapy treatment used by psychologists across the country to help veterans with PTS. Oddly enough, Dr. Francine Shapiro discovered this in 1987 while walking through the forest.[39] When walking by the trees, the eyes constantly catch new targets to focus on, which makes the eyes move rapidly and allows the brain to take the traumatic experience a veteran is dealing with and re-associate it with something less traumatic—especially when walking as a part of a veteran group focused on dealing with personal experiences of war.[40] While the actual therapeutic process used by psychiatrists is much more involved—in that the therapist is getting the person to focus on the traumatic experience and is doing cognitive work with the trauma directly—walking through the woods enacts that same eye movement. As inferred above, participating in a group specifically focused on dealing with these traumas benefits the veterans because they are more than likely thinking about those experiences that they had while in the military.

I personally experienced this during a recent retreat in the mountains of Colorado with a group called Huts for Vets. The mission of the organization is simple: "To help veterans adjust to and enjoy civilian life by gaining tools for enhancing mental, physical, spiritual and emotional health."[41] These trips typically comprise around nine veterans, one psychologist, two group facilitators, and four volunteer assistants. There are also gender-specific retreats, in case a veteran's trauma is tied to military sexual trauma. The retreat began with a dinner and a night in an expensive ski home donated to the group in Snowmass, Colorado, where we all got to initially know one another. The next morning, we got up early and headed to the trailhead. We spent the day hiking just under seven miles, gaining around 3,500 feet of elevation. In the weeks leading up to the trip, the main facilitator sent out a number of emails encouraging participants to do the readings and to exercise in preparation for the hike. Having lived in the mountains for most of my life, the elevation change was not a huge issue for me, but I definitely could have been in better shape, as the steady climb was a long difficult trek. Those from lower elevations definitely struggled a bit more; however, everyone went at their own pace. We clumped into small groups and supported each other up the mountain.

The cabin we stayed at was 11,300 feet above elevation. It was originally a hut used by the Army's 10th Mountain Division, which was a special high-altitude ski unit trained to fight in the alps of Germany during World War II. In the 1970s, former Secretary of Defense Robert McNamara and his wife frequented these huts and decided to refurbish them. The hut we stayed in was named after his wife: Margy's Hut. I found a certain amount of irony in the idea that our refuge for healing was the same as that of the architect of the Vietnam War. At the same time, there was also a certain poetry to it, in his asking for forgiveness and his shift in thinking, and the parallels to what we sought in those high mountains.

Each day we had a number of readings tied to what we were doing, where we would sit around and discuss the material in relation to our experiences. The readings ranged from quotes and poems about the wilderness to an account of a Jewish survivor of a German concentration camp during World War II. Each reading had a purpose, whether it was to get us to reflect on the fragility of life or to understanding the grandeur of nature. The facilitators guided us through the readings as we discussed the meaning and content of each. Two of the sessions were guided by the psychologist, who worked to teach us tips and tricks on how to deal with some of these traumas on our own; this included a sort of in-depth journaling and a self-Socratic conversation that forces one to interrogate oneself. The latter evokes Foucault's idea of constantly turning in on oneself, asking why, and digging deeper to make one's own truth clearer. In a seminar discussing a history of how the self has been situated philosophically and in religion, Foucault states, "Often the discussion gravitates around and is phrased in terms of the Delphic principle, 'Know yourself.' To take care of oneself consists of knowing oneself. Knowing oneself becomes the object of the quest of concern for self. Being occupied with oneself and political activities are linked."[42] Therefore the purpose of this turning in on oneself is not only to understand one's truth, but this reflexiveness is political, as the veterans come to understand how their truth fits into a larger picture.

On the third day we began our descent back to the trailhead. Everybody went at their own pace, at times walking with others, but oftentimes walking alone, reflecting. These hours of reflection were calming, helping to soothe the anger and depression that had been building within my own personal life over the past few months before the retreat. This is something that I have dealt with regularly since my departure from the military, as my emotions have ebbed and flowed due to my PTS. My time spent in nature healing from the traumas of war has been much more helpful than anything that the VA has provided. Everyone from the group praised the trip and the healing nature that it provided, and leaving was difficult. We had formed a bond, and some said that it almost felt tighter than the bond they had with those they served with. The bonds formed in the military, as outlined in chapter one, become longed for outside of the military. Often veterans feel more comfortable talking and working with other veterans, who have been through similar situations and are less likely to judge them for things they may be ashamed of or things they would have to explain because a civilian may not understand. The healing power of nature, coupled with the forming of these bonds, works exponentially to heal the trauma and violence of war. These experiences not only show the power of the environment to heal, but they also become yet another reason for us to protect and advocate for the environment, as VA clinics fall short on helping returning veterans.

Conclusion

There is a long history of veteran activism on behalf of the environment, from President Theodore Roosevelt's creation of the National Park System to David Brower's founding of the Sierra Club. However, there seems to be a massive resurgence in the movement to protect the environment in the wake of 9/11. Perhaps it is a sign of the times, with the rise of information and "debate" about global warming.[43] More likely, it has become resurgent due to the motives of the most recent wars, which have been for and about resources, primarily maintaining and managing the global oil supply. The attempt to shift away from these "resource wars" forces the security dispositif to alter not only the debate but also the tactics of war itself, thus attempting to lessen the military's presence. This can clearly be seen with the huge shift of dialogue within the military around global warming, as it is now seen as a "threat to national security," thus making it an issue that falls under the Social Contract. There has been a response and a change within the military as it attempts to shift from the world's largest polluter to a sustainable, responsible steward of the land, although this stewardship is limited to bases in the United States. The foreign lands on which the military fights are often abandoned and treated as wasteland—contaminated with many different toxins, most commonly depleted uranium. While there is still a long way to go for the military to actually achieve a NetZero status, there seems to be a shift that goes against the currents of the military-industrial complex of the twentieth century and the current neoliberal forces that seek massive environmental deregulations, even though environmentalism often works in favor of neoliberal ideals as it is more cost effective. Furthermore, while this seems to be a positive and responsible shift, there appear to be dangerous possible side effects of a fully sustainable military, from a perpetual war apparatus to machines of war that no longer require human interface.[44] While these dangers seem imminent, the growing veterans' movement on behalf of the environment is inspiring, though the military as an institution has a long way to go before it can really be considered green and no longer a presence that is harmful to the environment.

From veterans organizing for local issues, like the Montana Wilderness Association—which attempts to create more protected state and national parks in Montana—to national groups like Vet Voice Foundation—which works to put a spotlight on these local groups and helps to lobby for these issues in Washington, DC—getting outdoors and protecting nature has become an important veterans' issue within the Soldiers' Contract. The neoliberal discourse of "less government involvement and regulation," which allows for businesses to exploit the land, is being contested by veterans who see their telluric bond as a motivating factor of what they swore to protect as soldiers. Furthermore, they see the land as a site of healing. Therefore, there is a positive feedback loop within their activism as the change they aim to make helps the environment, which in turn gives them more opportunities to heal.

With the lack of resources for the VA, primarily due to neoliberal cuts, programs like Huts for Vets, Veteran Expeditions, the Sierra Club's Military Outings program, and many others act as an alternative form of care that veterans can engage in to help combat issues like PTS. Finally, this push for environmentalism acts as a site of resistance within the US neoliberal discourse that positions environmentalists as radicals or "eco-terrorists," and instead uses the patriotism and reputation of veterans as tools to shift the framing of land stewardship into something that should be a social respon-sibility. While the other forms of activism that were examined in earlier chapters often focused upon a broader general knowledge connecting the public to veterans, these veterans' environmental activism is focused upon policy and congressional action. The advocacy of these policy shifts, which work on a macropolitical level, can be directly connected to the health of these veterans, who are working on a micropolitical level as they utilize these shifts to heal from the environment they are protecting.

> The old Lakota was wise. He knew that a man's heart away from Nature becomes hard; he knew that lack of respect for growing, living things soon lead to a lack of respect for humans too.
>
> —Luther Standing Bear (1868–1939, Oglala Sioux Chief)

Fighting Violence in the Ranks

Kirby Dick's 2012 documentary, *The Invisible War*, shocked much of the United States as to the epidemic level of sexual violence within the armed forces.[1] While this was not surprising to most demilitarization activists and academics who have for years pointed to the high levels of sexual violence in and around military bases, it definitely shocked the general public and those within the government.[2] Weeks before its release the film was screened by Defense Secretary Leon Panetta, who two days later would call for a change in policy when dealing specifically with sexual assaults.[3] *The Invisible War* would win more than a dozen awards and was nominated for an Academy Award for best documentary, gaining national acclaim.[4]

The documentary highlights the story of a number of women who had been the subject of sexual violence while in the military. Most of the women were not only raped but also physically beaten by men who were often their superior officers within their chain of command. The trauma continues to follow many of the participants of the documentary in the wake of their tragedy as they try to pick up the pieces, and as they move forward in their lawsuit against the military. The film also highlights the numerous military sex scandals that have happened over the past twenty years, including the 1991 Navy Tailhook scandal, the 1996 Army Aberdeen scandal, and the 2003 Air Force Academy scandal. These scandals show that this is not a recent phenomenon but something that has long existed within the military. In an age of heroization of the military, it was a shock for many that this was such a systemic problem, creating a surge of activism calling for change within the military. However, any changes that have occurred in the military's procedures dealing with these incidents have been minimal. For many activists, the main issue is the removal of decision making from the chain of command, which has not yet been addressed. This has been the focal point of most activists' calls for change. By keeping the commanders in the loop of the reporting process, many assault survivors fear retribution from their chain of command, as often the perpetrator is of a higher rank than the survivor. This causes a variety of possible conflicts of interest, from the command choosing to protect fellow officers and friends, to not wanting their command to be tarnished with allegations of sexual assault, which would be a reflection of their leadership. As one veteran told me in an interview, "Adding impartiality is a necessity because the conflict of interest is too great even for the good ones. Because sometimes even those who want to do the right thing are caught between a rock and a hard place."[5] Furthermore, not only are the investigations pursued within the direct chain of command of those who are accused, that same command also decides the punishment. This is why one in three convicted military sex offenders stays in the military; more often than not they are barely punished.[6]

Jessica Kenyon

One woman who has been fighting to make a change in these policies while also working to help survivors is Jessica Kenyon, the founder of the website militarysexualtrauma.org. I first came across her website, which was filled with useful information as well as art and writing from survivors of military sexual trauma (MST), when I was investigating veterans who were working with survivors of sexual trauma. I had been living in Upstate New York at the time, and after months of emailing, Jessica and I finally settled on a date to meet in the small Rust Belt city of Bethlehem, Pennsylvania. We met in a coffee shop on warm fall day, just before the weather was slowly shifting to winter.

Jessica had always wanted to join the military, as it was a family tradition. Her grandfather served in World War II, and her father was in Special Forces during Vietnam, so as soon as she was old enough she tried to enlist; however, her entry would be delayed until she could get health waiver for a heart murmur that was detected during her initial enlistment physical. In 2005 Jessica was finally able to join the Army as an Apache helicopter crew chief. She loved basic training, but only three days into her advanced training she began to be constantly sexually harassed by one of her training instructors. After reporting the incidents, she was treated as a pariah by her chain of command, and nothing came of her report. Once she went to her first duty station, the harassment intensified, as others had heard of her reporting the incidents while at training. She was stigmatized for this past report, which made her wary of reporting future incidents to her chain of command. Her hell would intensify as she not only faced discrimination but was sexually harassed again, as well as sexually assaulted while in Korea. As Jessica describes:

> So, this rumor mill had followed me all the way to Korea. You know, it's always wonderful to be seen as the new girl who is already seen as making problems, and you just reported all their favorite teachers, so I felt ostracized. Two more incidents happened there too because I was being ostracized, another because I had reached out, because you're a million miles away and feeling alone, no family, you don't speak the language if you leave the base, and only one of the incidents got reported. After being sick, I found out I was pregnant, which they then reprimanded me [for]. The only reason I wasn't charged with adultery was because my divorce papers had been filed.[7]

The sexual assault would leave her pregnant with her perpetrator's baby, while her command threatened to reprimand her rather than her offender. Only after telling them her story, and after they conducted a lie detector test on the perpetrator, which he failed, did they determine that her story was true. While they sided with her and did not punish her, they only gave him a slight reduction in rank and forty-five days of extra duty.[8] This worked out in his favor, however, as he wished to retire early and the reduction in rank allowed him to do so.

Jessica wanted to stay in the military, but as she states, "they pressured me out of the military, with the pregnancy. I didn't initially want to get out, but the pressure, stress, and depression led me to do it. I got a general medical discharge."[9] Upon her exit from the military, she started her website in order to help other soldiers navigate the processes within the military for reporting sexual assault. She has worked with the Service Women's Action Network (SWAN) and Sen. Kirsten Gillibrand (D-NY) on some of the suggestions for changes to policy, as Jessica's firsthand knowledge of the system was beneficial for forming a more comprehensive policy. SWAN has also referred survivors of sexual assault to her in order for them to find help with how to deal with their cases, as she has become a sort of private case manager for these issues. Most recently she has had to take a break from activism because the stresses have become too great and she has needed to take time to practice self-care, as she had decided to move to Japan with her husband. She also is working on her own case with the military as she seeks to upgrade her discharge status from a general medical discharge to an honorable discharge, and she is also trying to navigate the VA system to get help and reparations for the MST that she endures as a result of her experiences.

Violence in the Ranks

The epidemic level of sexual violence is nothing new within the military, as rape culture has existed within and around militaries for a long time.[10] By rape culture, I mean an institutional space where rape and sexual assault are normalized. Furthermore, both rape and torture have been used as tactics of war both strategically and politically in order to exert, gain, and maintain power.[11] While sexual violence in war is often framed as sexual desire, Ruth Seifert moves it away from a biological framework to more of a social construct tied to issues of power. Seifert states:

> Wars, violent conflicts between people, as well as sexual attacks on women, are historical and social processes that are carried out collectively and, thus, must have collective meaning. They are not the sum total of a couple of hundred thousand genetic predispositions for aggressiveness. Biology cannot claim to have an immediate and privileged access to reality. On the contrary: Biology, itself, is a social construct that—like all other modes of knowing—can only become a way of knowing within a certain social context. Biology is a system of classifications which helps humans make sense of their experience.[12]

Therefore, knowing that the act of rape is not at all about sexuality but is rather an act of power, we see certain parallels between rape, torture, and war in general. Each is meant to dominate, humiliate, and destroy the enemy. Furthermore, these violent acts of power tie into a hierarchical system of patriarchy.[13]

Masculine identity is not just perpetuated inside the military but also throughout civil society. As many feminist scholars have discussed, the military is seen naturally as a masculine institution where feminine attributes are not only discouraged but also often punished.[14] Furthermore, the military is often seen as an institution that one joins to "find one's masculinity," especially in an age where the youth is often seen as an emasculated culture.[15] As V. Spike Peterson points out, though, within the military there are multiple competing masculinities, and these masculinities are hierarchal and patriarchal.[16] From my own observations while in the military, at the top you have the hypermasculine fields that encompass the combat arms occupations, and on the bottom you have the more feminized desk jobs; similarly, you have the same with branches of service, where the United States Army and Marines are seen as the most masculine, while the US Navy and Air Force are seen as more feminine.[17] With combat arms positions seen as the most valorized, there is a drive by those in other fields to try and compete with the combat arms fields. This drive is not just a personal competition trying to satisfy one's own ego, but it is also professionally driven, as those who have served in war are often promoted much more quickly than those who have not. Both the need to satisfy the ego and the opportunity for advancement are apparent on a daily basis, especially in daily banter and jokes. For example, those who are not combat arms soldiers are often called names by those who are, like POGS (person other than grunt), REMFS (rear echelon mother fuckers, for those who don't deploy), or FOBBITS (bases in the combat zone are called forward operating bases or FOBs, thus FOBBITS is a reference to J. R. R. Tolkien's mythical hobbits, who never leave home). Thus, there is a constant culture of attempting to "remasculate" oneself, which often happens through violence. Furthermore, women within this hierarchy are almost always positioned at the lower rungs, so that even when they are in command positions they do not receive the same respect a man would receive. As Abby Hiser states in her Winter Soldier testimony:

> Once I was in a leadership position, it was difficult to gain the respect I deserved. . . . The mission became difficult after I reminded a lower-ranked male soldier what appropriate conduct was when speaking to a sergeant; he did not respond well. . . . When I deployed to Iraq, there were many opportunities to help other units, platoons with missions going outside the wire. I mentioned I wanted to join a few of these missions, yet I was immediately turned down due to my lack of time in Iraq. Yet there were men there just as long as I was or less, and they were allowed to go on these missions.[18]

In this way, Hiser was not only treated unfairly due to her gender, her ability to be promoted as quickly as her male counterparts was hindered due to their ability to participate in combat operations while she was barred.

The remasculating violence that takes place within this patriarchic military masculinity is a part of the presence, which resides on and around military bases, tied to issues like domestic violence and rape.[19] *The Invisible War* has given considerable attention to the problem of military sexual trauma (MST), and there has been a lot of news recently as to the statistics of sexual assaults within the military, as highlighted above.[20] The most recent stories have exposed perpetrators like Sgt. 1st Class Gregory McQueen, who was Fort Hood's sexual assault prevention coordinator, who was supposed to lead trainings for soldiers on the topic of sexual violence.[21] McQueen is accused of not only sexually assaulting a female subordinate, but also of running a prostitution ring, in which he was prostituting lower enlisted females to other male soldiers. McQueen was eventually sentenced to twenty-four months of confinement and a dishonorable discharge.[22] There was also the recent case of Air Force Lt. Col. Jeffrey Krusinski, who was in charge of the air force's sexual abuse prevention program, and who was charged with sexual assault for drunkenly groping women, though he was acquitted of any crime.[23] In both of these cases the men were not only high-ranking officials but were also in trusted positions, in which they were supposed to act as allies. And in both cases, they seemingly abused their powers; one even used his position as a tool for sex, which highlights the lack of agency that many in subordinate positions face within the military. Sadly, these are not isolated incidents, as this type of behavior has become the norm.[24]

This betrayal is not limited to the sexual assault of women. The stories of the sexual assault of men in the military may be becoming more prevalent, but they are not new, especially when we contextualize MST not as a gender-specific problem but rather as a systemic issue tied to power. Furthermore, MST can be seen as a violation of the Soldiers' Contract, as both the de jure and de facto contracts that are formed with soldiers have been broken—from not protecting these soldiers in the first place to subsequently not providing them justice under the Uniform Code of Military Justice (UCMJ). However, a large part of the activism that is taking place in relation to MST is specifically tied to reforming the codes and procedures in relation to sexual violence, which is what organizations like SWAN and people like Brian Lewis have long been focused on.

Brian Lewis

Brian Lewis grew up in a small town outside of Baltimore, Maryland. Raised by a single mother who worked for the Department of Defense, he was drawn to military culture at a young age. The middle school he attended had disciplinary issues with students, but his geography teacher—a naval petty officer—impressed upon him the values of structure that came with military life.[25] Brian soon became involved in the school's Junior Reserve Officers' Training Corps (JROTC) program. He would achieve many honors such as captain of the drill team, platoon commander, as well as unit commander of the JROTC program at Fort Meade. After high school Brian wanted to go to college but knew that his grades were not good enough to get into a good program, so he continued on the military track by enlisting in the Navy as a submarine fire patrol technician. He decided that he wanted to work on submarines due to the ways in which his recruiter had described it to him. His recruiter, "a surface type," said it was different, there is a certain level of intimacy and camaraderie that comes with working on a sub, which is what drew Brian to it. So in June of 1997, he shipped off to boot camp.

While the US Army and Marine boot camps focus on a more physical challenge, the US Navy and US Air Force are more mentally challenging. Brian, for example, was more focused on science and technology in training to be a crew member on a nuclear submarine. He spent time training in Florida and Connecticut and it was at his submarine training that he would really learn the value of what he described as a "brotherhood." This was primarily male bonding that he would encounter, as women were not allowed to serve on submarines at the time. The all-male social bonding is within a masculine environment, hence the "brotherhood"; however, the proximal closeness of one another and the life-or-death reliance upon everyone having to do their job effectively structured the hierarchies into nonviolent formations. It was as his recruiter described, a true family environment. He would carry this love for his job over to his first duty station in Hawaii, which gave him what he described as the Hawaiian term for this sort of working and cohesive family, *ohana*. While he would describe his commanders' leadership as lacking, he would also learn that leadership can come from below. As he describes life on a sub, "It was a brotherhood. It wasn't like how we say it in the masonic fraternity. No, these were my brothers! They are going to save your bacon or die with you."[26] But after a year, he would leave Hawaii and proceeded to Guam, "where I was to meet my fate."[27]

Brian knew a few people at his new duty station, which was comforting, but he was no longer on a sub and had lost his sense of community. There was a completely different culture, as he notes, "On a sub there is about 125 of us; in a surface community there is upward of five thousand, and you won't get the tight-knit exposure and camaraderie that you have on a sub. . . . After having that *ohana* it was hard being in a place that did not have that tight-knit feeling, especially if discipline fails."[28] It was at this new duty station that Brian was raped by a fellow soldier.

He went to a senior member of his command to report the incident and was ordered not to officially report it. From then on, his command worked to make him feel isolated, even going as far as ordering fellow soldiers—who were his friends and worried about his well-being due to recent erratic behavior—to not have further contact with him. This isolation not only felt like a betrayal but also as if he had been left behind—something he then swore he would never do to another person. According to Brian, he was the third or possibly fourth victim of his perpetrator, who would never face justice for his crimes.

After a couple of months of isolation, Brian felt he was coming apart at the seams, as no one would listen to or believe him. His command had him chemically sedated, restrained, and then medevaced to San Diego, which was his lowest point in the process as he "felt alone in the woods," only wanting a friend to stand beside him. Back in San Diego he was medically discharged, a "section 8," for a supposed multiple personality disorder.[29]

Male MST

While the stories of the sexual assaults of men are now becoming more common, they are not new.[30] One of the first stories about male MST to make it to the mass media was a 2014 *GQ* exposé on men who had been sexually assaulted in the military, highlighting veterans as far back as the 1960s.[31] The article opens by stating, "Sexual assault is alarmingly common in the U.S. military, and more than half of the victims are men. According to the Pentagon, thirty-eight military men are sexually assaulted every single day."[32] A 2014 DoD study showed that while women were almost 5 percent more likely to be sexually assaulted, it happens annually to more men due to the disproportionate amount of men in the military.[33] With the high number of male soldiers being sexually assaulted on a daily basis, it is a wonder that this had not come to light earlier. However, many of the men who are sexually assaulted do not report the incident for a number of reasons. First, they state that they were ashamed of what occurred.[34] Second, many of the assaults were perpetrated by a group of soldiers, and they often outranked the survivor.[35] Therefore, they not only feared for their lives, which were often threatened, but they also feared for their careers. Aaron Belkin's work *Bring Me Men* highlights similar stories of male rape throughout the military.[36] Some of the rapes were acts of masculinization, some were rituals approved by those in command in order to either punish soldiers or put them in their place.[37] While in the military, I witnessed something similar in what at the time I thought was a funny prank. One of the mechanics, often thought of as a "know-it-all," was tied down by fellow soldiers and was rectally penetrated with a banana. There were no repercussions for those who perpetrated this heinous assault, as many in our unit not only saw it as funny and as "boys being boys," but he was also victim-blamed, as many thought that the sergeant "had it coming to him."

A recent study shows that men and women who screen for MST have significantly high rates of suicide.[38] This, coupled with the high rates of suicide among soldiers and veterans due to war trauma, makes male survivors of sexual assault a particularly vulnerable population with possibly high rates of suicide. Studies point to a number of reasons for the high rates of suicide recently within and around the military, from the longer and more frequent deployments to the higher incidents of nonfatal trauma.[39] Sociologists Harold Braswell and Howard Kushner agree that these are factors; however, they also feel that the culture of the military embeds a "masculine fatalism" into soldiers. This masculine fatalism is in part of the process discussed in chapter 1, in which the individual is stripped down and the value of the group is elevated to supreme. Furthermore, this devaluation of the individual is tied to a particular kind of masculinity in which the value of life is lessened, and thus becomes expendable, whereas the group is assigned the higher value. Therefore, when individuals become a weak link within a unit, their trauma becomes feminized, and they become a target that must be toughened up. If the individuals are not able to become a part of the group again, a particular shame makes them feel ostracized, thus leading them to suicide.[40] Again, if we pair this conceptualization of a masculine fatalism among soldiers with sexual assault of male soldiers, there is the possibility of higher incidence of suicide.

The masculine fatalism concept relies on the social bonds created within the military. These bonds are often similar to and sometimes stronger than familial bonds. Thus, when Jessica told me in our interview that after sexual assaults there is often the deep feeling of betrayal, she compared this to the betrayal of a survivor of incest. In Judith Herman's extensive work on trauma, she looks at child incest survivors, and this sense of betrayal is aimed at the family, as the child often feels that both parents are complicit in the act of sexual assault.[41] One survivor that she interviews states, "I have so much anger, not so much about what went on at home, but that nobody would listen. . . . At the time nobody could admit it, they just let it happen. So I had to go and be crazy."[42] Similarly, in my interview with Jessica, she talks specifically about this betrayal when she states:

> Part of the problem is that nobody is on the victims' side, because if you support the victim your career is on the line because you are betraying the brotherhood. . . . I treat many of the survivors as incest survivors, because in basic training, they break you down and you are told this is your family, you listen to your commander more strictly than your parents, they are in charge of your food, your cloths, and well-being, and everything under the sun. So when an incident happens there is a high level of betrayal. And when that betrayal happens it is much closer to treating a case of incest than a regular case of sexual assault because the system broke down, like a family betrayal. This person was supposed to be a father figure, or a brother, and they have betrayed a level of trust not often found in the civilian world outside of the family. The betrayal is huge. Many times they will say that the sexual assault was bad but the betrayal was much worse, because they tried to get justice, help, or support, and they all falter. The betrayal is not just by the perpetrator, but also from the command, other soldiers, the whole system.[43]

While this feeling of betrayal is general to all survivors of MST, Jessica states that she feels this becomes even more intense for male survivors, as it is not only a violation of their body, but it is also a violation of their masculinity. Even the title of the *GQ* exposé highlights this stigma attached to male MST, "Son, Men Don't Get Raped."[44] While the idea of sexual assault being a "women's problem" is problematic in and of itself, it is not just a problem within the military but also a problem once these soldiers leave the military and seek help from the VA. As the exposé highlights:

Unfortunately for male victims, the VA's facilities for MST focus largely on women. In fact, the statute that establishes these programs makes mention only of female victims. Interviewees for this story indicate that the quality and availability of outpatient treatment for men is spotty at best. Some men report being denied care altogether.[45]

This sentiment was echoed by Brian, as a major part of his activism since getting out of the military has been focused on bringing attention to the disparities in the VA for care and research of male MST. While the care for women survivors of MST at the VA is not great, Brian claims that it is much better for women than it has been for male survivors of sexual assault, as this stigma of male MST carries over into the VA. However, the level of care varies greatly from VA facility to VA facility; some facilities have counselors on call, crisis centers, and often support groups (some do not), which is probably the most important part of the healing process for these veterans. This restoration of social bonds is important not only for survivors of sexual assault but also for veterans suffering from PTS, as these groups are able to relate stories and experiences that allow the veterans to know that they are not alone in the traumas that they have experienced.[46] I extend this group cohesion and healing to all veteran activist groups that I am looking at throughout this book. As Herman points out:

> When groups develop cohesion and intimacy, a complex mirroring process comes into play. As each participant extends herself to others, she becomes more capable of receiving the gifts that others have to offer. The tolerance, compassion, and love she grants to others begin to rebound upon herself. Though this type of mutually enhancing interaction can take place in any relationship, it occurs most powerfully in the context of a group.[47]

While Herman is discussing groups specifically geared toward healing, activist circles have many of the same elements involved, from a goal-oriented drive to the need for empowerment. There is also a parallel in the mirroring process describe above, in that when they heal, they better understand what the military is—they better understand the Soldiers' Contract—and what is needed in order to heal from war. There is a similarity between war and healing from war, a mirror of sorts, in that they not only have to face the traumas of war, but they can best address those traumas with their brothers and sisters in arms who are also trying to heal from traumatic experiences.

Male Sexual Trauma Activism

At the time that Brian got out of the military, he was living on the West Coast and quickly became involved in an abusive relationship, as he doubted his self-worth. His grandmother eventually talked him into returning to Baltimore to seek help from the VA. He was initially suspicious of seeking help because of the ways in which it was used to hurt him as they filled him with drugs, used his trauma against him, and constantly worked to discredit him. But between counseling, a supportive family, and meeting his current spouse, he began to recover. In 2011, his partner encouraged him to attend an event in Washington, DC, focused on MST put together by the organization Protect Our Defenders. He was one of three men who attended, though the event was overwhelmingly women. He was asked and accepted a position on Protect Our Defenders' advisory board, but he still felt that there was not enough being done to bring awareness to male survivors of MST. Brian became the face for the subject of male MST when he started the organization Mr. MST, in 2014.

Brian is a geocorporeal actor seeking to create more of a critical mass of survivors coming forward in order to raise awareness about the problem. As Basham states of the geocorporeal actor, "Such attempts to order bodies can affect how corporeality is experienced and 'the corporeal power or capacity' of differentially embodied soldiers 'to act in various ways,' and as ordering practices in the everyday lives of geocorporeal actors, gender, sexuality and race can also reinforce wider rationalities about who fights and for whom."[48] While Basham is discussing the way in which bodies are ordered within the military, the trauma of rape coupled with that militarized body, and the subsequent call to action through activism, makes their subjectivity an interesting cross section of understanding. One survivor who also embodies this geocorporality, Heath Phillips, has taken to multiple forums, from Twitter to YouTube, to expose his MST and to encourage other veterans to come forward. In one interview Phillips states:

> I'm speaking out now, partially because of how I was treated, also because I don't think that other people who have had this happen to them should stay hidden anymore. I think we

all need to speak out. There's unity in voices. We could move mountains together if we pushed. If we stay hidden, we're not going to get anywhere. Every single time I talk about this, I feel like I'm shedding a piece of skin off me that has been holding me in, and yeah it hurts, but afterwards the calm is so much better than that hurt.[49]

In this testimony, we see a couple of things: first and foremost, we see a call to arms for male survivors to come forward to try and make change. This is especially important since male MST is not commonly known about or thought of in the context of the sexual assault epidemic within the military. Brian's activism echoes this sentiment as he hopes to find his eventual replacement within the movement so that he can spend more time with his friends and family as well as focus on his law practice. At the same time, he also hopes that the increased exposure will allow for more funds and research to focus upon helping male survivors of MST. Secondly, we see a testament to the healing aspects of parrhesia discussed in chapter 2. If more men came out and spoke of their experiences with MST, perhaps we could see a reduction in suicide rates within the military. While I am not directly correlating the two, there seems to be some parallels, especially regarding the ways that survivors are treated by the military.

As far as results are concerned, it has been mixed bag. While there has been attention brought to the issue of MST, there has been little attention brought to male MST outside of a news story here and there. The attention to MST in general, though, has made the military at least attempt to address this systemic issue, as sexual assault trainings have become normalized within the military, which often brings speakers like Brian to come and discuss these issues with members in the military trying to make a de facto change in the culture. Legislatively, there have been two big attempts to make de jure systemic change. First was the Military Justice Improvement Act, which was meant to take the chain of command out of the decision-making process concerning sexual assaults, which failed due to the active opposition of high-ranking military officials who felt it undermined their authority. Second is the Protect Military Honor Act, which is currently in committee in both the US House and the Senate. This act aims to ensure that military members who were sexually assaulted will not be given "general" or "medical discharges," which can affect their ability to get help from the VA when they are out of the military, as well as the fact that any discharge that is not "honorable" is often looked down on in the civilian world. If this bill passes it will be a big win for the activists fighting the violence in the ranks.

Conclusion

The push to expose sexual trauma for men does a number of things. First and foremost, it shines a light on the rampant sexual trauma throughout the military, against both women and men. It also shows the inefficiencies that the military has in dealing with sexual assaults, both inside and outside the military. Finally, it works to shift the discourse of who gets raped. As Belkin points out:

> The prevailing frame of rape as a crime against women should be seen as both a cause and effect of a broader set of gendered discourses about sexual violence in the military and civilian culture. . . . Even the most subtle decisions about how to tabulate and report data can contribute to the framing of sexual violence in the military as a women's issue. Because affirmative male response rates to survey questions about sexual violence tend to be low, Pentagon studies can downplay and even erase the incidence of male-male rape by reporting percentages rather than absolute numbers of men and women who indicate that they have been victimized.[50]

Therefore, activists such as Jessica, Brian, and Heath Phillips are geocorporeal actors trying to push the sexual dispositif in the military by exposing those inefficiencies of military surveys. They do this while also trying to heal from traumas and the ways in which they were told to be certain types of subjects by the sexual dispositif of the military. Their activism also seeks to effect current and future military policy. The shifting of military policy has the potential to shift the gender/sexual dispositif within the military and renegotiate the Soldiers' Contract. The shift means that the way in which the military forms, controls, and maintains gender subjectivity is thus tempered. If the military's grip on gender subjectivity is tenuous, then there are less formations of hypermasculinity and therefore less need to prove one's masculinity. Furthermore, the ways in which women experience the military can be more equitable.

Their activism is also seeking more accountability within the military, effecting de jure aspects of the Soldiers' Contract. This accountability would lessen the hierarchical power within the military, thus creating space for truth to be heard and justice to be served. This would more than likely not just affect the gender/sexuality dispositif within the military (de facto aspects of the Soldiers' Contract), but all hierarchical aspects of the military, including racial hierarchies. Furthermore, this could allow the space for accountability around injustices such as war crimes, which has been an aim of groups like Iraq Veterans Against the War, in forums similar to the Winter Soldier testimony. Therefore, we see the importance of the activism of these activists who seek to shift the gender/sexuality dispositif of the military. However, it is important to remain vigilant in this fight against the patriarchy embedded within the military because as Cynthia Enloe points out, "[P]atriarchy has survived because of its facile adaptiveness, not because of its rigidity."[51]

Finally, the maintenance of the hypermasculine male within the military, which is created through this imbrication of masculine discourses and tactics, highlights the ways in which violence is used to maintain the neoliberal order. From using rape as a tool of war to the continuance of rape being swept under the rug, rape will continue to be accepted in the military unless a massive cultural overhaul takes place. But as of now, it is seemingly seen as too valuable of a culture to tear down as it protects the Western neoliberal democratic state and its ideals, which is why we still have not seen any change in military procedures concerning sexual violence.

6

Service, Citizenship,
and the American Dream

Since the dawn of the nation, immigrants have served within the US military in times of war. Craig Shagin points out, "Over a half-million served in the Union Army during the Civil War. Similarly, large numbers of foreign-born fought in World War I, World War II, and the Korean and Vietnam Wars."[1] Many immigrants came to America to become part of a new nation, many were leaving behind treacherous situations, and many were merely seeking a new life. While the reasons are myriad, there is often a common thought that many of these immigrants held: the idea that by joining the US military and serving the country they could become citizens of the United States of America. As of 2008, there were more than 65,000 immigrants currently serving in the armed forces, with about half of those naturalized due to their military service.[2]

A sizable amount of immigrants serve in times of war, and these soldiers are part of how war imaginaries interact with the concepts of service to one's country, citizenship, and the idea of the American Dream. To explore these intersections, I examine three personal narratives: that of Hector, a Mexican immigrant who honorably served in the US Army and was deported after committing a crime following his exit from the military; that of Jules, the grandson of a World War II Filipino veteran, who joined the army and later fled to Canada to become a war resister; and the story of Matt Zeller and his Afghan interpreter, Janis, as Matt fought to help Janis gain US citizenship.

What Is a War Imaginary?

The war imaginary has a multifaceted meaning.[3] The jumping off point here is from a larger concept, that of a "social imaginary." Manfred Steger poignantly frames the social imaginary as:

Constituting the macromapping of social and political space
through which we perceive, judge, and act in the world, this
deep-seated mode of understanding provides the most general
parameters within which people imaging their communal existence . . . the social imaginary is neither a theory nor an ideology,
but an implicit "background" that makes possible the communal
practices and a widely shared sense of their legitimacy.[4]

Charles Taylor, whom Steger is drawing from, goes on to explain that it is
"background" because "[I]t can never be adequately expressed in the form
of explicit doctrines because of its unlimited and indefinite nature."[5] With
this "unlimited and indefinite nature" in mind, the use of it here becomes
a bit more focused in relation to the US military.

There are a number of aspects to this imaginary, from the image of war
to the image of the military apparatus. Furthermore, there is a multiplicity
of war imaginaries that relate to and can be tied to the imaginary being
proposed here, i.e., the war on drugs, the war on women, the war on men,
the war on Christmas; the list is again unlimited and indefinite. However,
the scope here is focused on the war imaginary within and around the US
military apparatus, those who join the military, and the wars in which it
has historically and is currently engaged in.

The war imaginary can be seen as the chameleon skin of the US
security dispositif as it is a constantly shifting image meant to perpetuate
and maintain US militarism. The war imaginary has a reciprocal relationship
with the security dispositif as it is formed by and helps to shape the policies, institutions, practices, ideology, and discourse of the security dispositif.
However, there is not a singular war imaginary within the security dispositif,
as there is a multiplicity of imaginaries, though it is the security dispositif
that holds them all together. For example, within the military a soldier who
has a racist construction of the war imaginary, who fights so that he can kill
Muslims, can fight next to and be intimately bonded with a fellow soldier
who has a more liberal construction of the war imaginary, and who fights
to promote democracy and freedom. The differing war imaginaries are the
product of an unlimited number of variables, from personal experiences to
media constructions of war. Cynthia Weber's work, *Imagining America at War*,
attempts to capture the multiplicity of war imaginaries within the United
States, post-9/11. Weber focuses on film representations of society—primarily war movies—in order to examine the moral identity of and to find out
precisely who the "we" is in the American imaginary.[6] As Weber points out,

the films examined "were mobilized in post-9/11 cinema to construct US individual, national, and international subjectivities as well as diverse historical trajectories for 'becoming a moral American' and a 'moral America.'"[7] It is within the war imaginary that the position of soldiers in relation to the Social Contract becomes clear, as their understanding of what that contract is relates to why they joined the military and what that service means to them, thus forming their understanding of the Soldiers' Contract.

The subjects of this chapter further this variety of a war imaginary. Hector holds his service as the most honorable thing he has done in his life and would join again in a heartbeat. However, his crime and nationality push him outside the narrative of a US soldier "hero." Jules on the other hand saw the things he was doing in the military as dishonorable, which is what drove him to go AWOL and has now made him a criminal as he tries to stay in Canada. So, we already see here two similar yet very opposing views of veterans and their time in service. The story of Matt and Janis, however, is a bit more complicated in that while Janis was a contractor for the US Army in Afghanistan, his service to the soldiers created a sense that he was "one of us" and deserves US citizenship.

Hector Barajas

I initially met Hector Barajas through Facebook, in June of 2013, after hearing about a group of veterans who had been deported. They were calling themselves "Banished Veterans." I started following the group on Facebook and through their website, and when I was ready to start my research I began to reach out to the folks mentioned on the website and on Facebook. Hector was the first to get back to me and we promptly scheduled a Skype discussion.

At the time, Hector was running a veteran community house in Rosarito, Mexico. In that first conversation we ended up talking for a little over an hour as we discussed a number of different topics, from our military service to what it was like there in Mexico. The interview was emotionally heavy, and I began to realize how big of an issue this was as Hector highlighted not only all the deported vets that he had personally come in contact with, but also gave his estimates of how many others could be out there. While there are no official government figures or estimates, Hector believes the number of deported vets could be in the tens of thousands. In a *Playboy* article Hector is quoted as stating, "From my understanding, we have had more than 10 veterans in each detention center. There are about 250 centers in the United States. Let's say 16 years of deportations since 1996. Ten times 250 equals 2,500. Twenty-five hundred times 16 equals 40,000."[8] While this estimate seems very high, I can neither confirm nor deny these numbers, but Hector and I have both tried to get more solid numbers from the Department of Homeland Security, to no avail.

A few months later I would make the trip to Tijuana to do an in-person interview with Hector.[9] Over lunch he told me his story. Hector was born in Mexico but immigrated to the US as a child with his parents. He joined the military to gain citizenship, but also to try and escape the ghettos of Los Angeles. While in the military he was a part of the 82nd Airborne, and he was honorably discharged a month after 9/11. While he never served in combat, he still maintains that he would go to war for the US in a heartbeat. Since the events of 9/11, more than 3 million people have joined the military, with a large portion of them citing the events of 9/11 as a motivation for joining.[10] The perceived patriotism of those soldiers who joined after 9/11 perpetuates a particular war imaginary, as it creates a hero narrative in which the soldier is framed as the defender of freedom and fighter of injustice. This narrative was revived by the Bush administration borrowing from the World War II imagery of war and the military. Whereas soldiers were needed to fight the evils of Hitler's totalitarian Nazi regime, post-9/11 we were called to fight the evils of Osama bin Laden's terrorist assemblage, al-Qaeda. Because soldiers are perceived as sacrificing their lives for others' freedom, they are thus revered as the pinnacle of what it means to be American, which often carries down into multiple generations, making joining the military a family tradition.[11]

While patriotism and tradition provide a large justification for joining—especially between the years of 2001 and 2005[12]—another reason lies in the benefits provided to those who join the military. With as little as a general equivalency diploma (GED), a fairly clean criminal record, and no major health problems, anyone can join the military. If the military is behind on their quota for recruits, there are waivers that can supersede any deficiency a recruit may have. Upon joining the military, soldiers are paid a modest but steady salary with opportunity for advancement, given training to their field of work,[13] given the opportunity for higher education support, provided free health care for themselves and their family, given a stipend for food and housing, paid more depending on family status, and often given the opportunity to travel the world.[14] The recruitment process often glorifies these benefits as well as the patriotic aspects of the image of the military, while simultaneously downplaying the drawbacks and perils, thus reinstituting the clean war imaginary explained above. Furthermore, the multiple benefits the military provides can often be seen as a "way out" for many people who are in desperate situations. With the rising cost of education and an unstable economy, many have turned to the military to get out of dire socioeconomic situations.[15] Since the United States ended the draft in 1973 and transitioned into an "all-volunteer" military, many understand that the military now operates through a "poverty draft," often recruiting people from lower socioeconomic areas, which often has the largest impact on communities of color, though little is said by academia.[16]

For some, another benefit of joining the US military is the promised path to US citizenship, which is what Hector sought. As highlighted above, there is a long history of immigrants joining the military in order to gain US citizenship. This view of the military can be seen as a "way out," as many of the immigrants who have joined the military come from the working class and are looking for a way to take care of their families.[17] As immigration laws have become more stringent in "the land of opportunity," joining the military has become one of the few ways to become a citizen. The military has often offered a path to citizenship for those who serve a minimum of four years, but there is no guarantee, which leaves the path to citizenship as an imaginary view of the military.[18] This imaginary view is both "imaginary" in the ordinary sense of "made up, not true" and in the conceptual sense of Taylor and Steger, etc., because you have served four years there is no guarantee. It is seen as a reward for being a good soldier, which is part of the imaginary, but it is not guaranteed, which Hector would soon find out.

Upon his honorable discharge from the military, Hector returned to his hometown of Compton, California, which is often thought of as one of the rougher neighborhoods in the United States due to the prevalence of gang violence there. It was here that he met the woman who would become his daughter's mother, and where they still reside today. After returning to Compton, Hector began hanging out with his childhood friends and getting into the same kind of trouble that he tried to escape by joining the military. One night after having a few drinks and smoking a laced joint, he was driving around with some friends and thought that a car was following them. Hector, who was not afraid to stand up and fight, shot at the vehicle, which fled the area immediately and reported Hector and his friends to the police. Hector was arrested and charged with aggravated assault. While no one was hurt, the prosecution bumped the charges up to a felony, which is a common occurrence when dealing with immigrants.[19]

During the time he had served in the military, Hector was never counseled by his chain of command on the steps he would need to take to become a citizen, and upon his exit he was told to contact a VA center, with the statement that maybe they could help. However, when Hector left the military he had no idea that he could be deported, especially since he had been honorably discharged. In fact, since President Clinton's 1997 immigration reforms, more veterans have been deported for minor drug offences. While Hector's offense was not minor, and he was sent to prison for three years, upon his release from prison he was deported. He thought he would be free to go, having served his time in prison, like any other American citizen would have, but he was instead deported.

Shortly after his deportation, he was lucky enough to run into some other veterans who inspired him to do something about the injustice he saw. He stated many times throughout our time together, "I never asked for any of this; I'm not an activist by choice." But while he did not choose the life of activism, he goes about it with a restless and inspiring passion. Everything he does throughout the day is toward the goal of helping others in his situation and to help him become a better person. At the end of our lunch he said something that made me think for a while, "Those who fight for their country, they sacrifice a lot, for their families, for their brothers, for their friends' families, for everyone. . . . People should remember and know that." It's this sacrifice that I found time and time again, not only among veterans but among the activists who are fighting for a change, and while Hector may not have chosen this life of activism, he continues to sacrifice like he did when serving in the military. I see this in his daily work, as he constantly seeks out newly arrived deported veterans, none of whom he would ever turn away. His sacrifice for other veterans is what made the creation of Banished Veterans possible, as there was no one working with or helping this population of veterans.

The first few years after his deportation, Hector spent most of his time on the San Ysidro border crossing, which is one of the busiest in the country as it connects San Diego and Tijuana. Each city has an estimated population of 1.3 million, while the region in general has more than 4.9 million.[20] On an average day, a total of more than 74,000 people cross the border—around 165 buses a day, over 35,000 cars a day, and 20,000 people walking across every day.[21] The steady stream of cars and people leaves a large bottleneck, primarily on the Mexico side of the border, since the authorities care little about what goes into Mexico, but there is a high degree of scrutiny concerning what comes into the United States.

The crossing is broken up into a number of sectors. The farthest east is the walking entrance into Mexico. Then as you move west, there is the walking entrance into the US, then the driving entrance into the US, and finally, on the far west is the driving entrance into Mexico. There is a walking bridge on both sides of the border that goes over the roads. In the middle of the northbound (into the US) entrance, there is a small park where we stop before Hector gets down to business. At first I just watch Hector as he marches back and forth between the cars in his uniform, carrying one of his two handmade signs. This one reads, "! STOP DEPORTING US VETERANS." The other one reads, "I AM A US VETERAN DEPORTED." The second sign seems to get more attention when he switches after about an hour at the border. I start to follow him in order to get a closer look at everything. There are a number of vendors drifting in and out of the cars selling everything from trinkets to churros. At the front of the line stands Homeland Security officials, who walk through the cars with their M4A1 carbine assault rifles. I recognize the weapon immediately, since it is one of the same weapons I carried while in the military. This militarization of the border makes an interesting setting for the activism of a deported veteran. Hector is being kept out of the United States by the very militarization that is his claim to citizenship.

Many people listen to Hector's story as they wait in the seemingly endless line to get into the United States. He tells them of his service, his mistake once out of the military, the time he served in prison to repay his debt to society, his subsequent deportation, and of the other veterans who have been deported. He carries old leaflets that have information for his organization Banished Veterans and tells folks where they can find out more. The geocorporeal struggle is apparent as his uniform and sign play on the hearts and minds of those returning to the United States, playing on their patriotism and their constructions of the war imaginary as he attempts to spread awareness and shift the ways in which those who pass by think about veterans, citizenship, and migration.

We take a break back in the little park and talk for a bit. He tells me that what hurts the most are those who do not care about the sacrifice; he says that sometimes people say hurtful things and you just have to let it go, otherwise fights occur. All in all, Hector wishes that he was not so alone in his activism and that more deported veterans would become vocal. He knows and has dealt with many deported veterans, but many of them have become hopeless thinking there is nothing left that they can do. Many, he says, have turned to drugs and alcohol, a temptation he knows very well since it has also been his escape mechanism for a long time. "When out telling my story," he tells me, "you have to bare it all, it will affect people, you have to be honest, it will eventually tug at their heartstrings."

We continue to walk through the lines of cars for another hour. This is a short day for Hector, as he usually spends eight hours a day marching back and forth talking to people. He's thankful the day is cool, since some days the temperature easily surpasses 100 degrees. As we near the gate for me to return to the United States the tone turns somber, as we both are a bit saddened by my departure. We give each other a goodbye hug and promise to keep in touch.

I have visited Hector since this initial trip, and his progress has been phenomenal. He has been able to get the ball rolling on his own deportation case, and also on a number of other veterans' cases. He has appeared or will be appearing in a number of news stories and upcoming documentaries; and he has founded a safe house in Tijuana for deported veterans, where they can come to get resources to fight their deportation, and also to fight the dangerous streets of Tijuana. Hector has had some help from fellow veterans stateside, and from a number of lawyers who are working on his case pro bono; however, it is a very slow bureaucratic process that could take years. His advocacy gained the attention of media outlets and politicians across the US as he was visited by members of the Congressional Hispanic Caucus who used his story to push for immigration reform; his crimes were pardoned by the governor of California, which helped his case for a permanent visa; and his story was featured in an episode of the popular military criminal television drama *NCIS*. In May 2018, Hector's dreams were realized as he was granted citizenship and allowed to return to the United States. Even though he can now return home, he has promised to keep up the fight for deported veterans and will stay for one more year in the safe house to ensure its long-term stability. He then plans on continuing his fight from the US.

Jules Tindungan

Already an American citizen, Jules Tindungan is the grandson of a World War II Filipino war veteran. Many Filipinos were offered citizenship to fight for the US, yet very few were actually awarded it.[22] However, Jules's grandfather was one of the few to actually receive citizenship, which then allowed him to relocate his family to Southern California. Many members of the next two generations of Jules's family—including aunts, uncles, brothers, cousins, and his father—would also serve in the military. So it was a bit of a family tradition to serve, but Jules grew up listening to punk rock bands like NOFX, Bad Religion, and the Dead Kennedys, all of which carried an antiauthoritarian tone. Although he felt like an outcast, Jules still enlisted, mostly to escape his family and the "dead ends" he saw in Los Angeles, thinking that perhaps the military and offers like the GI Bill could help him find a secure and suitable future. While serving in Afghanistan, Jules's view of the military would shift due to the tactics he saw being used. Some of these tactics included "recon by fire," a highly dangerous and unreliable tactic of going into areas trying to draw fire from the enemy; raids on innocent people or going into homes and searching for evidence of a crime and usually taking all males of "fighting age" (usually anyone who appears over 16 years old) in for questioning, even though most raids are based on bad intelligence; and the dropping of bombs "with no eyes on target," which means there is no one to confirm who is being targeted, which often leaves the high probability of an innocent person being hurt or killed. Near the end of his deployment, Jules was injured by shrapnel from an IED, which tore through his hand. It took a week for him to get flown to a hospital, and until then he was assigned to stay in the tactical operations center (TOC). It was here that he got a real bad taste in his mouth as he "realized that it was all bullshit, since command was constantly sweeping things under the rug, not properly utilizing funds, paying people off with shovels and basic equipment." His image of the war and justification for fighting was totally and irrevocably altered.

The image of war within the current set of wars being fought is intimately linked to the events of 9/11, in which "we," being democratic nations who promote free trade and capitalism, are fighting against "them," being Islamic terrorist assemblages that were the aggressors on 9/11. The US maintains the constant backdrop of 9/11 in order to maintain the moral boundaries and justify its need for war, whether through the rhetoric of needing to get those responsible, or in the rhetoric of fear of another 9/11 happening. By fighting wars across the globe, the US maintains that it is safer here while it fights the enemy over there.[23]

These moral justifications within this image of war also work to erase certain parts of history. The US portrays itself as the innocent victim, with many asking, "Why do they hate us so much?" But those who ask this question are forgetting the years of US involvement and tampering with Middle Eastern politics, and ignoring the constant bombing and harassment of Islamic nations.[24] As Michael Shapiro points out:

. . . the legitimation narratives of state power that suppress the violence through which the territorial systems of states became virtually the only recognizable map. Without recognizing what this map has repressed, we cannot recover an important dimension of the history of warfare and therefore develop an effective ethical and political apprehension that engages peoples who are not easily coded within the dominant system of sovereignties. It is necessary, therefore, to elaborate the forgetfulness and repression that accompanied the production of the international imaginary, the dominant territorial moral geography.[25]

This passage highlights the ways in which histories—even atrocities—can be erased in the name of promoting a moral and righteous need for war, which brings the image of war full circle as it is thus cleansed of moral apprehension. This opens a multitude of justifications for people to join the military, thus creating an image of the military that is a morally justifiable organization whose sole function is to perpetuate democracy and freedom worldwide. But Jules's image of the war had shifted to one in which it was an unjustifiable war, in which the military no longer represented the innocent victims of 9/11, but were rather the aggressors in a war to mark the state's supremacy.

Jules returned stateside in 2006 and soon learned that his unit would be going back to Afghanistan the following year. Instead of suffering through another deployment fighting in a war he had lost all faith in—as well as dealing with the daily racism of the military—he instead decided to go AWOL and fled to Canada. This was not an easy decision as it evoked a "quiet shame" within his family. His mother continues to tell people at her church that he is still deployed, and they pray for him to return from "Afghanistan" weekly. She has been telling this story for the past seven years. At first his family thought he had left because of his PTS, but as Jules told me, while the PTS was a factor, in the end it was more an unwillingness to fight that war anymore.

We decided to meet at the Canadian United Steel Workers Union Hall building at noon, because the War Resisters office was based out of that building.[26] I arrived a bit early and waited for Jules to arrive. While waiting out front I saw a large male approaching me who appeared to be of Asian or Pacific Island descent. When I saw that he was wearing a US Army Afghanistan War Veteran hat, I knew that this was the guy I had been waiting for. Jules gave me a nod and a big smile, and we did the "handshake/hug." He asked how my trip was and apologized for being late. I was illegally parked, so we decided to cruise back to his place for a bit, since there was more parking by his house.

He described his place as kind of an "anarcho/commune-shared space," but said that those who lived in the space didn't really live by any particular dogmatic politics or guidelines. We climbed the cluttered and dirty stairway, which opened up to a big room. The first thing that caught my eye was a large skateboarding half-pipe in the middle of the room, and then the very stylish kitchen at the other end of the room. Known to the public as Soybomb, the space often hosted local bands, art events, activist events, and fundraisers.

In 2007, Jules went AWOL and arrived in Vancouver, Canada. He started living and working with a number of activist communities, from anarchists and communists to other war resisters. It was here that he met his future wife, Nicole, who was also engaged in a number of radical organizations. Nicole had duel US/Canadian citizenship since her father is Canadian, but she primarily grew up in Kansas and Illinois. It was in the Midwest that she found radical politics as she worked with a number of anarchist activists in her youth. When the wars began she moved to Vancouver to become a part of the antiwar movement. She currently works at a noodle shop while also trying to make money as an artist of political comic books; she also spends as much time as possible with the numerous activist organizations that both she and Jules put their time and energy into.

After going out to lunch, we returned to Soybomb to conduct a conference call with an organization they worked with called Frontlines International. The call would have a number of different folks from around the US and Canada, spanning different eras of activism. While waiting for everyone to get on the call, Jules and Nicole explained what Frontlines International was about. The basic idea was a collaborative space between the "occupier" and the "occupied," thus bringing together soldiers, activists, war resisters, refugees, and immigrants from many different countries. The group's mission statement reads:

> We envision this project to act as a shared "Toolkit" or "Clearing House" for our common interests. Largely through social media, resources can be shared and voices can be amplified. For this we will establish our central social media hubs. Once

established, these will lay the groundwork for an infinite amount
of focused sharing and organizing. This organizing could include
any number of public events, from film showings and book tours
to protests and vigils.[27]

The agenda for the day was to help one of the members with an upcoming
event and to discuss other issues members may have. The upcoming event
was a talk to be given at a coffee shop in Philadelphia by a female veteran
who was a drone operator in the military.

After the conference call we went to the Anarchist Book Fair in downtown Toronto. As we traveled to the book fair we talked about a number
of subjects, from the precariousness of Jules's citizenship status, to their
search for Canadian veterans who would speak out against the wars, both
of which were connected. He explained that he was an "illegal immigrant"
who was applying for citizenship through two different processes: first,
requesting political asylum and second, through his wife's citizenship. On
the same day that he received a letter saying that he had a case for citizenship through his wife's status as a citizen, he also received a letter stating
that his request for citizenship and asylum was denied due to him being
considered a criminal in the United States.

Part of the case that Jules was trying to make with the Canadian courts
relies on the fact that Canada does not prosecute those who refuse to go to
war; in fact, they only send those who volunteer within the military to war,
and if you do not want to go to war then you do not have to. Therefore,
being a war resister in Canada is not illegal, which was the basis that Jules
was arguing from. This geocorporeal subject position shows a lived precarity,
as the geopolitical policies affect his status of being legal, yet he is labeled
"illegal," as a criminal in the eyes of the US, ironically for something that
is legal in Canada, the country from which he seeks refuge. However, the
Canadian government decided that his case was invalid, so he now stays
in Canada, undocumented. Part of Jules and Nicole's current work seeks to
find Canadian veterans who resist, but they have not been very successful.
Furthermore, it has been difficult to find any veterans who speak out against
the government, since there have been recent issues around veterans who
speak out. They have had their benefits revoked, and, as stated above, only
those who wished to go to war went.[28]

As we said our goodbyes later that evening and I prepared to leave,
we made plans to stay in touch. In March I returned for a conference and
we met up after they attended one of my panels. At lunch they gave me an

update about one of the other war resisters, Kimberly Rivera. Kimberly is a mother of four and was pregnant with her fifth child when the Canadian government deported her.[29] She had been living in Canada since she fled the US in 2007 after having been deployed to Iraq for a year in 2006. The military police were waiting for her on the other side of the US-Canadian border, and she was promptly put into custody. After a swift trial she was sentenced to ten months in a military brig, where she gave birth to her child, Matthew Kaden. During her pregnancy she went through strenuous activities and chores put forth by the military command.[30] When she went into labor she was given substandard treatment, and her son was immediately taken away from her and sent home with her husband. She was not even allowed to breastfeed, but rather had to pump her milk during visiting hours.[31] Kimberly applied for a forty-five-day amnesty to be released early but was denied. Upon release, she and her husband moved to Texas, where they still reside and are both struggling to survive.[32]

As for Jules's case, he is in the process of an appeal and is still currently waiting to hear a decision. His lawyer and those familiar with the case do not seem hopeful, especially with the current conservative regime in power within the Canadian government. Though he thinks that the Rivera case served as a test for deporting war resisters, with the uproar and protests that occurred in the wake of her deportation, he thinks that his deportation could be delayed or abandoned. As of now he waits, not sure whether he will be swooped up in a raid by the Canadian Border Services Agency and deported. If so, he would surely be greeted by military police at the border. There is a complexity within his activism, where he must fight, but not be too visible because he could be deported. Loud so that others can hear and fight with him, but not so loud that he angers those who could deport him.

Matt Zeller

Matt Zeller's family has been in the United States since the eighteenth century and his family has fought in every major war since the Revolutionary War. Like his grandfather, who joined the military in the wake of Pearl Harbor, Matt joined in the wake of 9/11, with his ancestors' service in mind and a desire to serve his country for his children. Upon exiting boot camp for the Army National Guard, he decided to go to officer school, since he was almost finished with college. Upon completing his degree, he won a national security scholarship, which allowed him to learn a new language, Arabic, that was "critical to national security." Soon after he was recruited to work with the CIA and was then deployed to Afghanistan with his National Guard unit in 2008. His job was to train Afghan military and police, and he chose to be out on the front lines. Matt had a very patriotic view of the war and of his service, and he believed in why he was there.

Matt was deployed to Ghazni, Afghanistan, in January 2008 as a US Army intelligence officer sent to train Afghan police and military.[33] While out on patrol in the city of Wahgez, on April 28, his squad got lost. Their maps were more than twenty years old and they were trying to get back to their base. While going through a small town the squad was ambushed. The lead MRAP was hit by an IED leaving it inoperable; instead of abandoning it they were commanded to stay and protect it until a wrecker could come and take it back to base. The four men in the MRAP had severe concussions and they were tactically disadvantaged as they were on low ground with high hills all around them. It was a very hot day, and as Matt stepped out of the vehicle to go to his defensive position, another explosion went off, knocking him to the ground. An hour-long firefight then ensued, as the Taliban was firing mortars and shooting their AK-47s at the downed convoy. Low on ammo, they finally received reinforcements, which turned the attention of Matt toward the incoming support fire. Not paying attention to what was going on behind him, he heard AK-47 fire, and as he turned his head he saw his Afghani interpreter Janis firing at two armed Afghans who had been sneaking up on Matt. Had Janis not fired, Matt would surely have been killed. This event brought Janis and Matt together to become best friends. Matt would not leave base without Janis and would not allow anyone else to use Janis as an interpreter. They took care of each other throughout the deployment.

Upon Matt's unit leaving Afghanistan, Matt swore to bring Janis to the United States, which, at the time, Janis did not think was possible. When Matt returned he got involved with the CIA Afghanistan office in Washington, DC. This was unhealthy as he not only obsessed about the war but also was dealing with severe PTS and TBI, which caused him to self-medicate with alcohol. He initially went to the VA for help, but after receiving a bill from the VA he decided to turn to the bottle instead. In 2010 he decided to run for political office in his home area of Upstate New York, which forced him to sober up. After losing the election, however, he slipped back into alcohol. His wife at the time forced him to clean up and get help from the VA. While his marriage eventually came apart, he was able to sober up and deal with many of the emotional problems tied to his PTS.

During this whole time, Matt and Janis had stayed in touch via Facebook. In July 2012, Janis contacted Matt telling him he was in trouble. He had applied for a visa two years earlier, but there had been no progress. Because he was one of the few interpreters to work and fight without covering his face to protect his identity, he was recognized by the Taliban and received numerous death threats from them. In order to apply for a visa as an interpreter, one must meet two criteria: first, the interpreter has to have served at least one year "faithfully and honorably," and second, there must be an active and ongoing threat to his or her life. Both of these applied to Janis, and he went through a lot of different panels and hearings. At the final stage of his application process, there was a backlog due to the number of different agencies (the Departments of Homeland Security, Defense, and State, as well as the FBI and CIA) that all have to sign off on the application. Due to this bureaucratic mess, it is almost impossible to be granted this visa unless someone is vigorously advocating for the applicant. Janis made it to this stage, but the unit employing him then laid off all its interpreters. At the time, the unit and the Afghan military unit in the area did not trust the interpreters and saw them as "collaborators" with the Taliban. This raised a red flag for his application process.

He contacted Matt, who started reaching out to his political contacts. Matt contacted a friend at the Huffington Post who made a video and wrote an article to show others and try to gain support. The video appalled people, as they could not believe we were not helping people like Janis. This led Matt to an organization called the Iraq Refugee Assistance Program (IRAP), which was started by Iraq and Afghanistan veterans who are now going to law school; they offer pro bono legal services for interpreters trying to get US visas. The organization has more cases to work on than it can handle, primarily due to the bond that often occurs between interpreters and soldiers, since the interpreters are making similar sacrifices. In many ways this relationship between interpreters and soldiers complicates the war imaginary, as it transforms those who are seen as the enemy by most people into friends. Another interesting aspect is the geocorporeal connection between interpreters and the soldiers. The military creates the activism because the military has let them down on two fronts, first by not making the interpreters' country safe and secure, and second, by leaving them behind when they leave the unsecure country.

Matt had also started a Change.org petition. The day after the Huff-ington Post article came out the Change.org petition hit 100,000 signatures, causing the State Department to notify Janis that his visa was being granted. Janis then quit his job and sold his house in preparation to come to the United States when the embassy revoked his visa due to an anonymous call (most likely from the Taliban, according to Matt) identifying Janis as a national security threat. Matt immediately reached out to all of his media contacts and wrote an op-ed that went viral, trying to shame the State Department, because all the reports indicated that Janis was no threat.

With Matt receiving so much media attention, IRAP asked him to lobby Congress for a piece of legislation that held thousands of Iraqi and Afghan interpreters' lives in the balance. Matt then founded a 501c4 called No One Left Behind (NOLB), which he still runs to this day. On the eve of the 2013 government shutdown, Matt and his partners in NOLB went door to door on Capitol Hill lobbying for a ninety-day extension on the government program that acquires visas for interpreters. While on Capitol Hill he got a meeting with Rep. Jim McDermott (D-WA), who in turn called the undersecretary of state to advocate for Janis. He was then put back on the visa list. As Matt stated, "I won! I beat State [department]! They were so damn afraid of a media fiasco that I was causing that they caved. He was polygraphed two more times by the CIA, and now he will be here next Tuesday!" He was happy that he was able to get Janis here, but he realized that the system was still problematic and that there were thousands more interpreters left behind, including two other interpreters he worked with in Afghanistan, one of whom he says will never be able to come to the United States due to a failed security screening that caused him to get fired a few years earlier.

Matt and Janis continue to work with NOLB, telling their story to members of Congress, to community groups, and different policymakers. Another aspect of their work is to help the incoming interpreters adjust to life in the US, as they often arrive with only a single suitcase of belongings. As their website states:

> We provide furnished apartments, modest financial support to
> help cover the weeks it can take before their social service benefits
> (food, medical, etc.) begin, and assistance with seeking employ-
> ment. We also pair up newly arrived refugees with other Iraqis
> and Afghans who have successfully immigrated to the US—to
> help smooth the transition.[34]

The view of these interpreters is as fellow veterans, comrades, and brothers in arms. So much like the camaraderie that comes with soldiering, there is a level of camaraderie that is shared between interpreter and soldier. As Matt told me, "Many of these guys have done more for this country than most of the people in it, they deserve citizenship." As in Hector's story, there is a level of sacrifice and service, as they often risked their lives for the American mission, which is why Matt believes that these interpreters deserve citizenship. However, because of the current geopolitical climate around immigration, particularly from south of the US border, coupled with his crime, Hector has lost that "deservingness" of citizenship. It is Matt's tenacity and ardent advocacy that allows Janis's "deservedness" to come to light. Had Matt not advocated so passionately, Janis would definitely have become another victim of US bureaucracy and more likely than not, of Taliban violence as well. Furthermore, there is a shifting geocorporeal relationship at work here, from Matt's historical familial relationship as a soldier, to his going to Afghanistan and becoming intimately close with an Afghan. This led to Matt's return to the US and his shift into activism, as well as his becoming critical of the state because his brother had been left behind. This is similar to Hector's story, as he too feels left behind by the same government that left Janis behind. While Matt works to subvert the state, Hector does all he can to work with it. Their subject positions are constantly shifting as they encounter different parts of the security dispositif.

Conclusion

The nuances between these three stories are stark, as well as the differences. Both Hector and Jules are in precarious situations put forth by the neo-liberal state: while one fought to survive on the mean streets of Tijuana, longing to return to the United States, the other fights the bureaucracy of the Canadian judicial system in order to remain in Canada. On the other hand, Matt has been able to navigate the US bureaucracy to get Janis on a path to citizenship, most likely due to not only his tenacity but also possibly his own white privilege.

Hector and Jules both felt alone and rejected, but both clung to hope. All three fell into activism, and while there is much self-interest in their personal cases, they all fight not only for other veterans but also for other people who are disadvantaged and/or down on their luck. For Hector, there is a religious aspect to his activism, whereby he seeks penance for his sins, and through his good deeds and tribulations he hopes to be redeemed. I have often felt this myself through my own activism and it seemed to be a somewhat reoccurring theme throughout my interviews, as many veterans seek some sort of penance for their time in the military. Many veterans come home feeling that they have done wrong and seek to right those wrongs through social justice movements. This is clearly seen in both Hector's and Jules's stories—from Hector's work with his fellow homeless friends and his work to help other deported veterans, to Jules's work with indigenous populations and other war resisters. To this day, Matt still works with NOLB, but also works with organizations such as the Truman Foundation and Team Rubicon (a veteran organization that does disaster relief).[35]

Both Hector and Matt work to shift the narrative that defines "who is deserving" of citizenship. Hector's service does not supersede his "criminality" or his place of birth; however, he works to redefine his subject position so that his service to the country is seen as more important than anything else. Similarly, Matt has successfully made Janis into a "war hero" who may have only been a private contractor if not for Matt's efforts; the fact of his service has become the case for him winning his path to citizenship. Their vision of the Soldiers' Contract is that service is directly tied to citizenship. Jules on the other hand feels that the Soldiers' Contract has been violated, which is why he fled, so he now seeks refugee status and/or citizenship from the Canadian government; however, he has also been labeled a criminal by the US government for breaking his contract by having a conscience, and for refusing to fight, which is ironically a right given to Canadian soldiers, because their Soldiers' Contract is constructed differently.

These three stories exemplify how veteran activism can shift the narrative around the war imaginary. It can shift ideas about who serves, what is honorable, and what is not. They highlight a history of veterans' images of the military, from Jules's and Matt's family tradition of service, to Hector and Jules seeing service as an opportunity to escape from their current situations. While the success of their activism varies, they have all seen some victories in the face of difficulty. Their service acts as a hinge for their activism as they work to make change, not only for themselves but for those who face the same difficulties. Their activism collectively works to uphold many of the democratic ideals that this country was founded upon, as well as to shift the narrative about who is included in the American Dream, making it more inclusive. The current construction of the American Dream is set within neoliberal ideals, and these veterans' activism and these narratives work to disrupt this construction.

Furthermore, the military works to create specific subject positions, and these vets are working to shift their subject positions in relation to the subject position created by and in the military. Regarding his citizenship status, Hector, for example, works to make his service the main force of his subject identity, so that he can return to the United States. Matt works to shift the subject position of his interpreter, by attempting to manipulate and push the state. Jules seeks to shift his subject position within his status as an immigrant to Canada, though the military has labeled him as a criminal, making it difficult for him to shift his subjectivity.

7

Remaking Sense

Mad Lonely World

as I walk along and wonder
devour demons with my bare hands
thoughts exposed for a moment
feeling lonely
with people surrounding me
feeling lonely
hey yo Jonas, it's gonna be ok
feeling lonely still
reject the drawers for the pills
taking over, expand the blood vessels
controlled thoughts no longer random
imagination held at ransom
only to exist, through terror tantrums
exists in the deepest abyss of my expression
feeling lonely
the most high is overshadowed by dark thoughts
not allowed to succeed so easily
not without struggle
try to break away hesitation, no concentration
friends look at my face and think they know where I've been
but have no idea
they think they know where I've been
they think they know what I know, where I've been
they've been thinking, they know what I know
what I think, I think that I know
where I've been, I think that I know where I've been to know why
for a moment, I'm feeling lonely

—Lara Jonas

The trauma of war remains within our minds, bodies, and souls. Some memories are now old fading scars, while others remain scabs that we constantly pick at. All of the veterans I interviewed experienced some sort of difficulty in their return to civilian life. For some it was nearly impossible to integrate back in to daily life, for others it came more naturally. A recurring theme in the attempt to return to normalcy was the use of different crutches, from drugs and alcohol as many tried to forget, to art and activism as they tried to transform their experience into something positive. Art possesses a transformative quality that not only deals with the wounds of war but also can undermine militarism as it provides a more productive and peaceful way of being. There are two organizations engaged in this work that are intimately bonded, the Warrior Writers Project and the Combat Paper Project. The latter takes soldiers' uniforms and transforms them into paper, while the former allows veterans to transform their experiences into art, oftentimes on the paper constructed from their uniforms.

The Warrior Writers and Combat Paper Project Affair

Sometime in late 2007, while at a Vets 4 Vets peer group therapy session, I met Lovella Calica, and while she stands just less than five feet tall, her passion and courage makes her seem like a giant. At first, I remember thinking something like, "Who is this little girl in this room with all of us crazy ass combat vets. . . . She wants us to do what? Write poetry? What the fuck is this? This is a waste of my time!" Thus, exposing my own gendered perceptions of poetry, as I saw it as something women did, not battle-hardened men. As with most of the sessions that she would moderate, and still does moderate, she told us, "It doesn't matter what you write, it doesn't have to make sense, just write! Keep writing and writing until I tell you to stop. . . . It isn't about what you write, it is about getting the pen on the paper!" And so we wrote. I remember the first time I did this drill. By the time I was done I was bawling my eyes out. My tears flowed like the words on the page, uncontrollable, deep, passionate, and full of rage, sorrow, and regret. Like Odysseus, whose tears flowed on Calypso's island beach, I sought to heal from the moral injuries I had sustained while in the military.[1] I had come to realize the power of writing, and the gift being given to us by this sprite-like woman. The poetry worked to deprogram the hypermasculinity, the dehumanization, and trauma, as it shifted the way in which we looked at our time and experiences in the military.

Lovella continued the Warrior Writers Project, and to this day she travels the country leading workshops and currently has three books in print filled with veteran artwork, poetry, and short stories, with another book on the way.[2] It is not exclusive to Lovella, as she has trained many others on how to conduct Warrior Writers workshops, and there are many veteran writing workshops all across the country, many independent of Warrior Writers. But it was early in 2007 when Warrior Writers was initially conceived, and at their second ever event, in Burlington, Vermont, Lovella conducted a workshop at a small papermaking studio. Iraq War veteran Drew Cameron ran the studio at the time, and it was here that a collaborative vision was born, as the process of making paper out of uniforms could be coupled with using them for art and poetry. Cameron had been using art as a medium for channeling his experience for the past year, and Warrior Writers worked as a conduit that could help others as well.

The subsequent art show that ensued highlighted Lovella's photography, a couple of veterans' art and poetry, and a couple of exhibits by Drew. One of Drew's pieces was titled "Basic Combat Load," in which one of his storage trunks from Iraq was put on display. It contained "photographs, it was my knife, my dog tags, my Zippo, you know, the earplugs case, you know, rank leftovers, weird lighters that I had found, you know, like shit."[3] The piece was inspired by Tim O'Brian's book *The Things They Carried*. As Drew described O'Brian's book, he stated:

> That hit me fucking hard because Tim O'Brian wrote about this way of telling a war story, like he gave permission to be able to, because it's like he's showing his cards in that book . . . and gave permission to tell a story that evokes a truth . . . not sort of like this happened and so that's why this is true, but that you can tell a story that helps you realize a truth. And I don't know, I read that book and I felt like it gave me permission to do a bunch of shit.[4]

Tim O'Brian, a veteran of the Vietnam War, had found the power of healing through art and storytelling. Furthermore, his writings have aided in the transformative process of others, specifically veterans, to examine their experiences and transform them into art of their own. There is currently a debate within the veteran writing and art community about the idea of art as a form of healing and therapy versus art as purely art. While in San Francisco, I got into a discussion about this with Drew's business partner, as it was her contention that the art should be looked at and judged on its own merits and that to label the process and product as a form of therapy cheapens the art. I would again hear this argument from a veteran and founder of the Veteran Print Project, Yvette Pino. The Veteran Print Project couples artists with veterans, as the veterans tell their stories to the artists, who then create a piece of art; it sometimes takes hours, it sometimes takes months. The art is then showcased with the veteran's story. While both Yvette and Drew's business partner rejected the label of art therapy, all agreed that it was a transformative process and had the potential for healing and remaking sense of veterans' experiences, as I and many other veterans have attested.[5] Yvette told me how one of her first pieces had transformed her relationship with her father, as she was finally able to express her experience at war to her father in a way that she could previously not find the words for. So, whether or not one person may place hierarchical value on art over therapy, there is nonetheless an affectual impact of the art: on the veteran, on the artist if it is not the veteran, and on the viewer of the art.

These stories were primarily transformative for the veterans, but many times they were also aimed at working toward telling their stories to a broader audience; thus, aiming to be transformative for society. As Kathy Ferguson reminds us in her discussion of anarchist art and poetry, "[T]he state will never be in the clear if artistically-inspired shocks to thought allow events to travel, to take up new residences and do unanticipated work."[6] It is this Deluzean notion of art as a "shock to thought" that veterans seek, whether it be to inspire or to inform the viewer, it seeks to affect the viewer in a way in which critical thought is induced. Some of these art pieces expose either the atrocities or the banalities of war, each expressing a personal truth of the veteran, whether through poetry, paintings, short stories, or any number of other mediums. Protevi seems to look at this "shock to thought" as a form of affect tied to a shifting in one's political physiology; whereas the encounter between the art and the subject not only shifts the viewers' perspective on the art but also on their political understandings.[7] Furthermore, as Protevi describes Deleuze and Guattari's pedagogy of thought, he highlights that in order to properly think and understand, one must be pushed outside of one's comfort zone.[8]

As Cynthia Enloe states, "Militarization is the step-by-step process by which something becomes *controlled by, dependent on, or derives its value from* the military as an institution or militaristic criteria. What has been militarized can be demilitarized. What has been demilitarized can be remilitarized."[9] Similarly, many of these veterans aimed to demilitarize their selves, through a deconstruction of their experience and a reconstruction through art. This ontological shift from the militarized mind to more of a demilitarized mind is long and arduous. For myself, each time I retold my story or created a new poem, my perspective had changed, and I felt one step closer to being less militarized. One misconception of this line of thought may be the idea that demilitarization means an absolute void of militarization, but this is a flawed way of thinking. Rather, we should look at it as a "step-by-step process where we no longer are controlled by or dependent upon the military." From the mitigation of the symptoms of PTS to being able to tell our stories in nonthreatening ways, art creates this space. This is most clear in the process of papermaking, as exemplified by Drew Cameron and the Combat Paper Project.

Drew's longtime affair with papermaking began with his father, who was also an artist and a veteran and was the one who had taught him to make paper. Many of Drew's artistic abilities lay dormant during his time in the military, but when he returned to college in 2005, an art class allowed him to bridge the concepts he was learning about in his international relations courses with his own experiences. He soon became an apprentice at the above-mentioned papermaking studio, and then the manager. It was here that he really fell in love with the art and the process of making paper, especially since he majored in forestry. Drew's art encompassed a number of media—from the countless photos he took in Iraq to using the letters he wrote home from Iraq. Some of these appeared in the Warrior Writers books, and some appeared in places like Monica Haller's Veterans Book Project.[10] The reuse of his old photos and letters was transformative and healing for Drew, as he explains:

> It's like revisiting, returning, remaking sense. . . . To redefine, and transform those memories to your own, to have them, become, to embrace them more, and have them become more understood as a story. Instead of kind of a memory trap. A way of thinking about the same thing again, again, and again, but instead to kind of open it, take it apart, not even to necessarily put it back together but to just to kind of have it in another form. And that's been one of the most helpful things for me for sure. Being comfortable with the experience, and what to make of it, and who I am because of it.[11]

This quote is telling on a number of levels. The art is not only transformative of the memories and experiences, but it also acts as a source of subject formation. The art becomes an external source of reflection that is not only meant to impact the viewer but also affects the artist and perpetuates a constant state of becoming. Furthermore, as Paula Howie points out, "art can assist in turning implicit body memories into explicit conscious narratives leading to a transformed sense of self."[12]

The constant reflection and turning in on himself and his art brought about a very poignant insight that I found was a recurring theme throughout my interviews. Drew states:

> . . . that war is absolutely and totally unfulfilling and I think that
> feeds into this addictive nature of it. Cause there's never enough,
> you never feel that even when you come out in a twisted way
> like I came out on the other side, knowing that I never wanted
> to be a part of that again and I still wanted to go back.[13]

Many of the veterans that I interviewed described something similar to this; from the excitement and subsequent sorrow that came with rushes of adrenaline and power while in combat, to the need or desire to return to war. The reasons were always personal, but all carried a hint of something left unfulfilled in their experiences of war. In a TED Talk, war journalist Sebastian Junger discusses this desire to return. He states that we need to understand this desire for a number of reasons, so that we can reintegrate returning soldiers and so that we can end wars. For Junger, the problem is that there is not "a simple neat truth."[14] This complexity of war can be seen throughout our society, from soldiers' desire to return to our own enjoyment of war films as a society. Junger pushes to think of war not in moral but in neurological terms, as the adrenaline of war creates a high level of excitement. This affects people differently, often leaving veterans with multiple traumas. However, Junger goes on to hypothesize that what many of these veterans really miss is the brotherhood that came with these traumas; those who experienced similar traumas and who were there by their side daily are no longer there, leaving a large hole in their life and everyday experience. Art works to fill that hole, mend the trauma, and transform the pain. As Drew explains:

> . . . then so for me the art and poetry was a literal way that
> I could do it, I could talk about rejecting the idea of being
> assigned an enemy. Or I could talk about how fucked up it is
> that I loved my rifle like my girlfriend and I felt naked and

empty without it. And how that was sad. So it was a way that
I could begin to evoke a truth for me, just exploring one thing
and getting words out that could draw people in.[15]

As Drew makes clear in the above quote, the art also is meant to draw
people in so that they can empathize and understand some of the aspects of
the military, militarism, brotherhood, and war that they may not be able to
understand otherwise. It also helps them to understand the Soldiers' Contract.

One of the most important aspects of this transformative process is
the communal aspect. This is important in many of the different groups,
from papermaking to writing poems at a Warrior Writers workshop. In all
Warrior Writers workshops, veterans are encouraged to share what they wrote.
The voicing of these poems does a number of things. First and foremost, it
allows veterans to share their experiences and feelings, which creates a bond
between them. The shared experience is also an affirmation of their own
experiences; they are able to understand and realize that they are not the
only ones who have been through the things that they did, saw, felt, and
feel. The positive reinforcement of this bond is very similar to the bond
of camaraderie of the military. In fact, many of the veterans I interviewed
commented that the veteran organizations that they were involved with had
many similarities to the military, and the unity aspect was key. This reinforces
the brotherhood Junger described above, and highlights the complexity of
the interaction between these activist veterans and the military. Furthermore,
many vets stated that these groups were very helpful in their reintegration
process, because they were able to struggle and fight together, and, just like
in the military, they had each other's backs.

The place where most of the healing and transformation takes place
is within the group experience, from reading poetry with one another to
making paper. As Drew points out:

The process used to write . . . or the process used to make paper,
which was very communal for me. It was more important than
what came out, cause it's like your changing, certain pathways
in the process, and it doesn't matter if the paper that you make
is given all away; because it's been done, and your memory
and you were there in the moments that you shared with other
people, and that can never be taken back. That's another kind
of truth, or a remaking, a redefining, transforming, something
from its literal sense, removing how static it is, not irresponsible

but scary because it is compartmentalized in a memory and in
a static state of symbolism and then you open it up, there's no
way of telling where it's gonna go.[16]

Therefore, the group process affects the art, the poetry, and the individuals, as they interact with one another. The following section is a narrative
account of my experience at a Combat Paper workshop that I attended in
the fall of 2013.

Combat Paper

While traveling the country conducting interviews, I planned on stopping
in Philadelphia to visit one of my army buddies, Gordie. There happened
to be a national Warrior Writers Conference going on in Philly that week-
end as well, which happened to be within walking distance from Gordie's
house. I had done Warrior Writers many times in the past and knew that
I would enjoy sitting in on at least one session. Years of attending these
workshops have transformed my experiences; once they regularly evoked
tears and remorse, but they now bring excitement and energy as I look
to bond with my brothers. I tried to get Gordie to join, but for personal
reasons he declined to accompany me, mostly due to not wanting to deal
with and face some of the traumas he still carries. At the workshop I ran
into my friend Eli Wright.

I have known Eli since 2008, when we did actions at the 2008 DNC
protests in Denver with IVAW. Eli is one of the more prominent members
of IVAW because of his work with Combat Paper and from the popular
slam poet Andrea Gibson's poem "For Eli."[17] While at the Warrior Writers
workshop, Eli invited me to come to his Combat Paper site in Branchburg,
New Jersey, if I had time. I wanted to bring my colleague Brianne Gallagher
to the workshop, so he suggested that we come to the Friends, Family, and
Allies Workshop that they were having in the near future, though he told
me that there was always an open door for me to come and bring people
whenever I wanted.[18]

The event was held at a community printmaking studio, one of the
only open centers for papermaking in the Northeast. We arrived at the studio
promptly at noon, and there were a few people already milling about the
studio, including Eli. We all sat around and chatted for a few minutes as
people slowly trickled in. The large room/communal studio took up half

of the small three-story building. The basement housed the pounder and the storage area, while upstairs there were a few offices and smaller work spaces. In the large room we were in, there were tables that surrounded the border of the room, as well as large tables in the middle of the room. It was here that we would do the majority of the day's work.

That day the work would be the physically strenuous, labor-intensive part of the process, which was termed the "deconstruction" phase. Eli floated around the room answering questions and guiding people as to what they were supposed to do. Some people had done this before, for others it was their first time. More people came in, many bringing food, which sat on a table at the western wall of the studio. The "deconstruction" phase went as follows: we were to break the uniform down to its most basic elements. We were to remove all buttons, patches, zippers, and unnatural fabrics. Most of the camouflage uniforms—or battle dress uniforms (BDUs) and desert BDUs (also known as DCUs)—are made of 100 percent ripstop cotton. The uniform we chose to work on was a class A dress uniform. The outer part of the uniform is all cotton, while most of the inside has nylon and polyester. These needed to be separated because natural fibers make the best paper. Furthermore, all the seams needed to be separated. There were two ways to do this: one was with a knife as you cut each of the stiches that held two larger pieces together, or the way that I preferred to do it, with brute strength, tearing the two pieces apart with my bare hands. On some of the seams the latter did not work, and a knife was required, but for the most part I tried to use my bare hands as much as possible. Tearing the uniform to pieces with my hands felt good as I released my anger, hate, and resentment upon the uniform. I thought of all the things within the military that really made me mad, from my experiences in places like Iraq and Kosovo, to all the stupid uniform inspections we had to go through. I tore with fury, until my hands hurt; they would be sore for the following two days.

Once all the parts are separated, the different patches, buttons, and insignia get saved in a bucket for possible future use as part of the art, which can be glued to the paper. The nylon and polyester get thrown away. All the natural fibers are salvaged from the uniform and are then cut up into little pieces about the size of a stamp, which takes a bit of time as well.

Each uniform is separated into individual buckets, since each uniform represents each person's personal story and history. One of the participants at the workshop was an older lady who brought her late father's uniform that he wore in the Korean War. She told us about their relationship, about what the military meant to her, about what it meant to him, and about what this experience was like for her. The uniform that she cut up would be bagged and saved for the following week's workshop, where the uniform would be turned into pulp, put onto a screen to dry, and be pressed. The week after that it would be paper. The uniform we were working on was not my own, so it went into a general bucket that would be used by those who were not able to participate in the first step of the process. As Eli stated, "There is always more cutting to be done, it is a never-ending process."

As we worked, people weaved in and out of the different groups, introduced themselves, talked about who they were, and they were always genuinely curious as to who you were. There were a number of Vietnam-era veterans there, which was a great as we told stories about our experiences. I overheard one of the vets call out a name to another vet who replied; this caught my attention, as it seemed that Jan Barry was attending the workshop. Jan was one of the primary founders of Vietnam Veterans Against the War (VVAW), and according to Andrew Hunt, VVAW would not have formed had it not been for the dedication and hard work of Jan Barry.[19] As we chatted he said that he recognized me, to which we went back and forth trying to figure it out. Finally, we realized that we had met at the Warrior Writers workshop in Philly a few weeks prior, but we had never exchanged names then. In some ways, I felt in awe of someone who had such an impact on history, but this friendly elderly man was very humble and rather nonchalant about his past activism. He told me that most of his time was now spent making art, writing, and talking to different groups of people around the country. We talked for a bit and returned to our work of deconstruction.

I ended up talking to a number of different Vietnam-era veterans, which was probably one of the most rewarding aspects of the day for me. My interview with Drew Cameron from two months earlier kept popping into my head. I remember him saying something at lunch to the effect of all war stories are the same, no matter what generation of veteran it comes from. I realized this truth, as I saw a bond and brotherhood with these guys that parallels my bond with my war buddies. I also noticed the diversity of folks, from the more reserved to the loud and boisterous, which made me think of my crew of vets that I am close with. There are many similarities, and it felt all too familiar. In some ways this invigorated me, in some ways it saddened me. I am energized by the generations of activists, people who feel like I do, people who want the same things that I do. I am sad that we are still fighting unethical wars, that soldiers are still coming home and being not only forgotten but also ignored.

The day rolled on and we continue to cut, tear, and deconstruct the uniforms in front of us. As we did so, other parts of my interview with Drew Cameron started to come together. For example, as mentioned above, he said, "War is completely and absolutely unfulfilling" and later that "the process of making paper is a value-adding process." I did not realize it at the time, but these two statements are a part of each other; they complement one another, as they are two sides of the same coin. "War," as Cameron explained, "always leaves you yearning for more, you are never satisfied, even if you leave horrified by war and not wanting anything to do with it ever again, you still want to be in it, to go back, to experience it again and again." At the time, I completely agreed and understood what he was talking about when it came to the unfulfilling nature of war, but I did not completely understand the "value-adding" process of making paper because I had never done it. The experience of war becomes inscribed within the uniform, much the way it is inscribed into the mind and body. It comes to signify that experience—the horrors, the violence, the laughter, the camara-derie, the sadness, the fear, and the anger, all of it. It becomes embedded within the uniform as much as in our minds and bodies, as you can still see the blood and sweat within the uniform, the old dried-up tobacco leaves from cigarettes smoked long ago, the heavily uneven threads from patches sewn on by hand, ink from a pen, etc. They all remain in the uniform, and as we deconstruct the uniform that reinscription is brought out, the stories become fresh, the memories are relived. Questions begin to arise, and the stories as well as the uniform begin to be deconstructed. And when it is all torn apart, it is then cut down to the size of a stamp, mashed and beaten to its smallest fiber, and cleansed with water. It is then ready to be put back together; it is time to "re-make sense." The pulp is strained and put onto the screens where it dries as the fibers bind together; with pressure and time it coagulates into paper. We then write, draw, and paint our experiences on this paper. We "value-add," we fill the hole of the unfulfilling nature of war, through this deconstruction, through this examination, through the art and writing that we put onto the paper.

This deconstruction and value-adding process is an ontological shifting process as the nature and being of the uniform and all that has been inscribed into it is literally and symbolically broken down to its bare fundamentals and reconstructed into something new, with new meanings, ideas, thoughts, and memories. Thus, the process makes the uniform into a floating signifier. Even the Combat Paper website states:

> Coming home from war is a difficult thing. There is often much to account for as a survivor. A new language must be developed in order to express the magnitude and variety of the collective effect. Hand papermaking is the language of Combat Paper. By working in communities directly affected by warfare and using the uniforms and artifacts from their experiences, a transformation occurs, and our collective language is born.[20]

And through the process of cutting up, purifying through water, beating to a pulp, and rebonding into paper, all of this is possible. It is a new language, a new community, new meanings and articulations, all filling the unfulfilling nature of war. These new languages are an act of demilitarization as we took a part of the war and reinscribe it with a nonviolent action meant for healing and for art. The art is a new narrative in which the veteran has the agency to create who and what the self means within it, where they are the narrator.[21] Furthermore, as Christine Sylvester points out, by examining war and art we can redistribute "mourning and grief," which allows for a feminist politics of empathy and vulnerability to be present, for the self and for others.[22]

It was all this that I realized and was thinking about throughout the day. As we said our goodbyes, exchanged contact information, and gave departing hugs, a calm settled over the day. While we had spent most of the day cutting and destroying uniforms while thinking about the horrors of war, it was as if there was a feeling of contentment that spread throughout the participants. We had all learned a new language, all experienced a new bond, built a new community, and grown internally.

Conclusion

With an estimated 300,000 veterans returning with symptoms of TBI and PTS, there must be alternative forms of healing for veterans, especially in light of the twenty-two veterans, on average, who commit suicide every day.[23] Furthermore, many of these veterans who have committed suicide have already reached out for help. All too often the VA prescribes antidepressants, which do not interact well with alcohol, often the veterans' favorite escape mechanism.[24] With the continued stripping of benefits due to neoliberal ideals, the problem will only continue to get worse unless more alternatives like this are utilized.

As highlighted throughout this book, there are a number of issues that come about in the militarization process, from notions of masculinity to PTS. The military does a poor job dealing with these issues once a soldier comes home from combat, as there is little time to heal and no real attempt to deprogram a soldier from the training that is required to dehumanize and kill the perceived enemy.[25] There needs to be a space of demilitarization, where soldiers can heal and come home in a safe manner. Programs like Warrior Writers and Combat Paper fulfill that space as they disrupt the processes of militarization, and all that comes with it: racism, sexism, hypermasculinity, and dehumanization. While much of their work undermines the goals of the US security dispositif, by exposing the atrocities of war, it also helps those who have sacrificed a lot.

> Rags make paper, paper makes money, money makes banks, banks make loans, loans make beggars, beggars make rags.
>
> —Dard Hunter, *Papermaking:*
> *The History and Technique of an Ancient Craft*

Or, as I like to reframe it:

> Rags make paper, paper makes money, money makes banks, banks make countries, countries make wars, wars make rags . . .

Conclusion

The title of this book is *Fight to Live, Live to Fight: Veteran Activism after War*. The first half of that title was drawn from a song title of one of my favorite bands, the Bouncing Souls' "Fight to Live." The song and the band both have deep meanings for me, as my friends and I met the band just before we left for Iraq. After a couple of long nights of drinking (and smuggling someone across an international border for one of their shows), we all exchanged emails and they eventually gave us a forum to speak our minds to a larger audience; we wrote them letters and they would post those letters on their website.[1] They then took one of the posts by Garett and turned it into a song called "Letters from Iraq," which was about us writing to them. This cemented a tight personal bond that will last our lifetimes. The song "Fight to Live" is personal because it constantly reminds me of who I am, what I need to do, and who I want to be. It reminds me to never give up my quest for equity. As the Bouncing Souls say in the song, "Fight to live is the only fight, I got left in me." There were many dark and depressed nights that I would turn to the Bouncing Souls and their music, as every song seemed to relate to my life. I often feel that had I not had their music in my life, I would not be where I am today. I also feel that many other veterans are fighting to live in their everyday struggles, and it is through activism that they find that will to live, and thus live to fight.

While I looked primarily at social justice activists, there is a wide range of veterans coming home and getting involved in various forms of activism. This ranges from activism with traditional groups such as the American Legion and Veterans of Foreign Wars (VFW), to activism with radical right-wing groups such as the alt-right, the KKK, and other militias.[2] While I will likely look at these other forms of activism in future projects, my focus here was more congruent groups and veterans because in many ways this is my own act of parrhesia, and my own truth.

Much as the music of the Bouncing Souls kept me sane, my own activism, involvement, and fighting for social justice kept me driven and inspired. These were positive forces in my life that worked to shift the traumas I had experienced. The wins in activism left me soaring high, while the losses crashed me to desolate lows. This has led me to believe that the power of activism is very important for returning veterans, though it is a double-edged sword. While veterans are receiving the camaraderie and brotherhood that come with military service, there is still a sort of isolation that they battle on a daily basis. This became clear to me in two different instances. First was the recent suicide of three-tour Afghan war veteran and peace activist Jacob George. While I had only met him a couple of times, many of my friends were very close with him. While he struggled with his own experience, he was a very energetic activist as well as a talented songwriter. As he played his banjo and sang with his Arkansas twang, he rode across the country on a bicycle singing songs about farmers in Afghanistan and farmers in the US, and the absurdity that it was the farmers who were often sent to kill each other.[3] Many of my friends told me that his energy and passion were infectious, in a positive way. But in the fall of 2014, when the US began sending troops back into Iraq, Jacob was devastated, and he took his own life. The end of combat operations and the withdrawal of troops in Iraq felt like a win to many within IVAW and other peace movements, and to have soldiers sent back in felt like a crushing defeat. I feel that what has saved many of us from suffering the same fate as the twenty-two veterans a day who commit suicide is our activism as it has had a positive effect in shifting our subjectivities and demilitarizing our lives and minds.[4]

The second time I came to deeply understand this isolation I often felt was in a reading for one of my doctoral seminars, assigned by Jairus Grove. The reading was the French collective Tiqqun's This Is Not a Program. It is lengthy but worth reciting. Tiqqun writes:

> Contrary to what THEY have told us, the warrior is not a figure of plentitude, and certainly not of virile plentitude. The warrior is a figure of amputation. The warrior is a being who feels he exists only through combat, through confrontation with the Other, a being who is unable to obtain for himself the feeling of existing. . . . The warrior is in fact driven by a desire, and perhaps one sole desire: the desire to disappear. The warrior no longer wants to be, but wants his disappearance to have a certain style. He wants to *humanize* his vocation for death. That is why

he never really manages to mix with the rest of humankind: they are spontaneously wary of his movement toward Nothingness. In their admiration for the warrior can be measured the distance they impose between him and them. The warrior is thus condemned to be alone. This leaves him greatly dissatisfied, dissatisfied because he is unable to belong to any community other than the false community, the *terrible* community, of warriors who have only their solitude in common. Prestige, recognition, glory are less the prerogative of the warrior than the only form of relationship compatible with his solitude. His solitude is at once his salvation and his damnation.

The Warrior is a figure of anxiety and devastation. Because he isn't *present*, is only for-death, his immanence has become miserable, and he knows it. He has never gotten used to the world, so he has no attachment to it; he awaits its end. But there is also a tenderness, even a gentleness about the warrior, which is this silence, this half-presence. If he isn't present, it is often because otherwise he would only drag those around him into the abyss. That is how the warrior loves: by preserving others from the death he has at heart. Instead of the company of others, he thus often prefers to be alone, and this is more out of kindness than disgust. Or else he joins the grief-stricken pack of warriors who watch each other slide one by one towards death. Because such is their inclination.

In a sense, the society to which the warrior belongs cannot help but distrust him. It doesn't exclude him nor really include him; it excludes him through its inclusion and includes him through its exclusion. The ground of their mutual understanding is *recognition*. In according him prestige society keeps the warrior at a distance, attaching itself to him and by the same token condemning him. . . .[5]

Jacob George had a song that addressed this, talking about how he could no longer have a normal relationship, and that he didn't want to cause pain to those he loved. This is something almost every veteran I interviewed related to in one way or another, something that I relate to as well, as we all seem to try and reconnect with society upon our return. And while we struggle to make these connections, activism is a common space where the healing can begin. However, we are often the exception and not necessarily the rule.

While I was conducting interviews around the country, I had a very interesting encounter that I still often reflect upon, tied to this feeling of isolation. I was in New York, doing an interview with Jon Gensler about his environmental activism, and was then invited to the panel I discuss in chapter 4. I found myself with some time to waste so I walked around Grand Central Station, which was across the street from the offices I was going to. While walking through this iconic landmark I came across a man my age holding a sign that said, "Homeless Veteran, anything helps! God Bless!" I stopped to talk to him and he immediately realized I was a veteran, as if we could smell our own. As we talked we came to the realization that not only were we in Iraq at the same time, but also that we were in sister units. He was in 2/2 Infantry, in the same brigade as me, meaning he literally lived right across the street from me in Germany. We shared many of the same experiences, had been to many of the same places, and even knew some of the same people. It was times like this that the world truly felt small. As he told me his story, I couldn't help but think how easily I could have gone down his path. Upon his return, like most of us, he turned to the bottle. What hurt him the most was that he got pulled over multiple times for driving under the influence (DUI) tickets, which sent him to jail for a few months. This made it difficult for him to return to college, and ruined his chances of what he said was his dream, going to the police academy to become a cop. While he was living in his parents' basement, he felt isolated, and said he couldn't relate to any of his old friends. His parents tried to stage an intervention, but instead he left his Upstate New York home and headed for New York City. He had been there for a couple of months, mostly panhandling, but was trying to seek help and a job from the Veterans Administration. I gave him the phone numbers and email addresses of several activists I knew in the area, including my own, but to this day I have not heard from him. When I returned from Iraq I turned to drugs and alcohol, and many times drove under the influence, which I realize now was not smart to do, but had I been caught, I may have gone down the same road as this veteran, or maybe worse. In many ways I feel he has been let down by both the Soldiers' Contract as well as the Social Contract, as so many of our returning veterans have.

Stories like this make me say that activist veterans are the exception, not the rule. And while there is often too much, and yet not enough, written on the topic of veterans, they are able to articulate important political critiques that are not often heard. The encounter that takes place when veterans' narratives and theory are put together is interesting, as I have tried to show. Veterans have the opportunity to practice Foucault's concept of parrhesia, as they speak truth to power, shifting the hierarchies and power dynamics of the military dispositif that is to blame for the traumas they have experienced.

They confront these traumas by actually working for more peaceful solutions, for the sake of veterans, their families, their communities, and for the planet. No veteran I know wants a civilian to have to experience the things that they experienced. While they will honor the role of the soldier and the Soldiers' Contract, many are fighting for it to be the last time, the last conflict, the last war. Unfortunately, that is not beneficial for the security dispositif; because it seeks to maintain itself, it must continue to sustain a level of insecurity in order that it can thrive. While the world is a variety of shades of gray, the security dispositif continues to paint the world as black and white, good versus evil, much as it did with the current film sensation *American Sniper*, which is as much a part of the security dispositif and the war imaginary as the policies that the military sets forth. These veteran activists seek to shift these narratives in order to create what many of them consider a better world, whether that is a world without war, one that is more environmentally sustainable, or one that is more equitable in terms of race, class, gender, or sexual orientation.

Perhaps it was my experience at war and then as an activist that made me see the connections between war and politics, the messiness of it all, and how they work in a reciprocal fashion, always feeding one another. Or perhaps it was my academic track that led me to the conclusion, double majoring in political science and sociology, and then moving to an ethnic studies MA, and ending at a political science PhD, within a department heavily influenced by a wide range of critical theorists. I'm not 100 percent sure as to why the commingling of war and politics became such a fascination of mine. However, something in my gut knew that the tenets of this inversion held a lot of certainty for me within it. It forced me to perform a sort of self-reflexive examination of my own experiences as a combat veteran and as an activist. All that I had done had come into focus, and gave me a purpose to move forward. I wanted to continue to untangle the intricate webs of war and politics, and to complicate the simplistic aspects. It is because of this that I branched out to different people, experiences, activists, collectives, and organizations. As I stated earlier, the purpose of my work is not to solely understand my own experience, or myself, because I feel I have a personal understanding of those, as it is my truth. Rather, my aim has been to understand war through cutting and penetrating the layers of knowledge that hold the current conceptions of war together. In some ways I would say I also came to answer what Foucault sought to know when he said, "the last thing that I would like to study would be the problem of war and the institution of war in what one would call the military dimension of society . . . the question of military justice: what makes a Nation entitled to ask someone to die for it."[6] While I have not completely answered that question, I feel my work gets us that much closer to understanding it, and I think the key is in an exploration of what I am framing as the Soldiers' Contract.

While I am not looking at war directly, my project can be seen as one that examines the products of war—specifically soldiers and veterans—that were produced through violence and war. These veterans are able to locate and be located within grids of intelligibility in which violence, war, and politics are (re)produced and in which we find our current understanding of the present in the post-9/11, war on terror, neoliberal world. Throughout this book, I have looked at the multiple layers within the security dispositif. While my work will continue on after the completion of this book, I will continue to spin off and branch out into other areas of contention where war and politics meet, both as an academic and as an activist.

Two of the most interesting spinoffs I have been a part of recently were with the organization Vets Vs. Hate and as a participant at the Standing Rock protests to the Dakota Access Pipeline. Vets Vs. Hate is a coalition of veterans who have been standing up to rhetoric posed by candidate Trump, now President Trump. Here veterans used their subject position to directly counter the violent and racist rhetoric, especially around Muslims, highlighting the numerous Muslims in the armed forces, as well as the many that we know and have close and important relationships with abroad (for example Matt's interpreter, Janis, who was discussed in chapter 6). I also sit here having just read a report about the military and the white nationalist problem it currently has.[7] I must recognize this reality and vow to move forward to know, study, and understand these groups as well, as there are many veterans getting involved with white supremacist groups and other hate groups as we have seen at rallies across the US. Many veterans voted for, stand behind, and advocate for Trump, and while I may not agree with their stance, they must be heard, understood, and examined. They are saying something about our system as well. Many feel disenfranchised and left behind, many still seek the camaraderie of the brotherhood they lost once they left the military that these groups provide. While my activism is opposed to theirs, they are saying valuable things that we need to hear and understand, even if we do not agree with the message or the tactics used.

My participation at Standing Rock with other veterans (many from IVAW) cuts across many issues, from colonization, sovereignty, and issues of racism, to the US fighting for energy independence versus environmental impacts.[8] While much attention was brought to the protests once veterans showed up to stand on the front lines, halting the pipeline for a short while, their presence also seemed to be a distraction that would make people think that the issue was over once the pipeline had stopped—however, the pipeline continued to be built the once Trump took office. The nuances of these issues coupled with the growing interest in veterans' issues, show that not only do veterans have a lot to say and contribute to politics and activism, but that their perspectives are also informative to those in academia. I hope to continue to bridge these fields of thought so that we can answer and address some of the questions and problems that society faces. I also hope to inspire folks to get out there and be active in your communities on all levels, from local to national to international. Some of us veterans left a war hoping to come home to peace, only to find that there were fights to be fought here. We will continue to fight for what we believe is right, so that we may all live in a better society that represents us all.

In conclusion, there is a long history of veteran activism, from the Bonus Army of the First World War, to Vietnam Veterans Against the War, to the contemporary group About Face: Veterans Against War (formerly IVAW). Veteran activism continues today, and that activism is a critique of the state as well as a function of the Soldiers' Contract. The veterans I interviewed who were once geocorporeal actors in times of war continue to be so, though in different ways, as they interact and often resist the very institutions that they were part of as soldiers. They all seek to continue the long journey of fighting for what is right, both at home and abroad. Veterans should be encouraged to join these politically active communities that are not only seeking to make positive change, but also to critically engage with the state; in doing so they reclaim their geocorporeality, while also healing from the wounds of war. Secondly, we see that many of the veterans involved in social justice movements are seeking to expose the militarization of the state-finance nexus. The critique that comes about through their activism shows the clash between neoliberalism and the ideals of Western liberal democracy. The codependent relationship between capitalism and militarization has become an obstinate aspect of modernity. Be that as it may, a space of demilitarization is possible as the imbrication of the two becomes clear. This interaction between the state and the veterans' embodied experience also rearticulates leftist dissent from something that is contentious into something that is patriotic and necessary for demilitarization. Finally, the act of healing—and activism around healing—works to create communities of demilitarization, as they work on the self and issues of moral injury. The activism also works to transform the state, which has created the conditions for that moral injury. In this way, a number of issues that come about in the processes of militarization range from dealing with PTS to issues of masculinity.[9] It bears repeating that the military does a poor job dealing with these issues once a soldier comes home from combat, as there is little time to heal and no real attempt to deprogram a soldier from the training meant to dehumanize and lead them to kill the perceived enemies of the state. These communities use the very tools and tactics created to militarize the soldier in order to demilitarize the veteran (i.e., behavioral conditioning, deconstruction of identity, etc.). And again, as Enloe points out, that which is militarized can be demilitarized.[10] There is a great need for more spaces of demilitarization, where soldiers can heal and come home to a safe environment. Activist organizations often provide that space as they disrupt the processes of militarization, and all that comes with it: racism, sexism, hypermasculinity, and dehumanization. Activism not only gives veterans a sense of agency, it also creates healing communities where they can reflect on their experiences and heal from the traumas of war. This political framing makes veterans the subjects of change rather than the objects of it; thus, they are pushing back against the trauma of militarization, against the inevitability of neoliberalism, and against becoming the excess of the security dispositif. As veteran, poet, and activist Paul Abernathy puts it:

> Never again must we fall into the belief that a "band of brothers" is something only achievable while making war on others. . . . We must see a brotherhood for what it truly is, an ultimate expression of love, and we must remember it is not something we can enforce and foster with a rifle.[11]

Notes

Introduction

1. Erin P. Finley, *Fields of Combat: Understanding PTSD among Veterans of Iraq and Afghanistan*, 1st ed. (Ithaca, NY: ILR Press, 2012). I am utilizing post-traumatic stress (PTS) rather than the normative post-traumatic stress disorder (PTSD), as I am among a growing community of veterans who wish to disrupt the idea that it is or should be labeled as a "disorder."

2. See also Sarah Bulmer and David Jackson, "'You Do Not Live in My Skin': Embodiment, Voice, and the Veteran," *Critical Military Studies* 2, nos. 1–2 (2016): 25–40.

3. Dahr Jamail, *The Will to Resist: Soldiers Who Refuse to Fight in Iraq and Afghanistan* (Chicago: Haymarket Books, 2009); Lisa Leitz, *Fighting for Peace: Veterans and Military Families in the Anti–Iraq War Movement* (Minneapolis: University of Minnesota Press, 2014).

4. Victoria Basham, *War, Identity and the Liberal State: Everyday Experiences of the Geopolitical in the Armed Forces*. Interventions Series (London: Routledge, 2013).

5. Benjamin Schrader, "The Affect of Veteran Activism," *Critical Military Studies* (2017).

6. Victoria Basham, Aaron Belkin, and Jess Gifkins, "What Is Critical Military Studies," *Critical Military Studies* 1, no. 1 (2015).

7. See volume 1, issue 1 of the journal *Critical Military Studies*, specifically the editorial by Victoria Basham, Aaron Belkin, and Jess Gifkins, as well as the articles by Cynthia Enloe, Zoë Wool, Matthew Rech, Daniel Bos, K. Neil Jenkings, Alison Williams, and Rachel Woodward. See also Annick Wibben, "Why We Need to Study (US) Militarism: A Critical Feminist Lens," *Security Dialogue* 49, nos. 1–2 (2018).

8. Basham et al., "What Is Critical Military Studies."

9. Synne Dyvik, "Of Bats and Bodies: Methods for Reading and Writing Embodiment," *Critical Military Studies* 2, nos. 1–2: 56. See also Christine Sylvester, "War Experiences/War Practices/War Theory," *Millennium-Journal of International*

Studies 40, no. 3 (2012): 483–503; Christine Sylvester, *War as Experience: Contributions from International Relations and Feminist Analysis* (Abingdon, UK: Routledge, 2013); Swati Parashar, "What Wars and 'War Bodies' Know about International Relations," *Cambridge Review of International Affairs* 26, no. 4 (2013): 615–630; Linda Åhäll and Thomas Gregory, eds., *Emotions, Politics and War* (Abingdon, UK: Routledge, 2015), and Lauren Wilcox, *Bodies of Violence: Theorizing Embodied Subjects in International Relations* (Oxford: Oxford University Press, 2015).

10. Synne Dyvik, "'Valhalla Rising': Gender, Embodiment, and Experience in Military Memoirs," *Security Dialogue* 47, no. 2: 148.

11. Claire Duncanson, "What Can We Learn from Soldiers' Narratives? Methodologies and Methods," in *Forces for Good? Rethinking Peace and Conflict Studies* (London: Palgrave Macmillan), 52–71.

12. Giorgio Agamben, "What Is an Apparatus?" *And Other Essays*, trans. David Kishik and Stefan Pedatella (Stanford, CA: Stanford University Press, 2009); Michel Foucault, *Power/Knowledge: Selected Interviews and Other Writings, 1972–1977*, ed. Colin Gordon, 1st American ed., stained (New York: Vintage, 1980).

13. Michel Foucault, *Power/Knowledge: Selected Interviews and Other Writings, 1972–1977*, ed. Colin Gordon, 1st American ed., stained (New York: Vintage, 1980).

14. Anna Stavrianakis and Maria Stern, "Militarism and Security: Dialogue, Possibilities and Limits," *Security Dialogue* 49, nos. 1–2: 3.

15. Chris Cuomo, "War Is Not Just an Event: Reflections on the Significance of Everyday Violence," *Hypatia* 11, no. 4 (Autumn 1996): 30–45.

16. Laura Sjoberg and Sandra Via, *Gender, War, and Militarism: Feminist Perspectives* (Santa Barbra, CA: ABC-CLIO, 2010), 7.

17. Ibid., 41.

18. This is also illustrated by Annick Wibben in "Why we need to study (US) militarism."

19. Michael J. Shapiro, *Studies in Trans-Disciplinary Method: After the Aesthetic Turn*, 1st. ed. (New York: Routledge, 2012), 154.

20. Ibid.

21. Ibid.

22. Zoe H. Wool, *After War: The Weight of Life at Walter Reed* (Durham, NC: Duke University Press. 2015).

23. Ibid., 146.

24. Cynthia Enloe, *Maneuvers: The International Politics of Militarizing Women's Lives*, 1st ed. (Berkeley: University of California Press, 2000), 3.

25. See also Aaron Belkin, *Bring Me Men: Military Masculinity and the Benign Facade of American Empire, 1898–2001* (New York: Oxford University Press, 2012); Harold Braswell and Howard I. Kushner, "Suicide, Social Integration, and Masculinity in the U.S. Military," *Social Science & Medicine* (Part Special Issue: Men, Masculinities and Suicidal Behavior) 74, no. 4 (February 2012): 530–536; Victoria Basham, *War, Identity and the Liberal State*; Benjamin Schrader, "The Affect of Veteran Activism."

26. Joanna Tidy, "Gender, Dissenting Subjectivity and the Contemporary Military Peace Movement in Body of War," *International Feminist Journal of Politics* 17, no. 3 (2015): 454–472; Jonna Tidy, "The Gender Politics of 'Ground Truth' in the Military Dissent Movement: The Power and Limits of Authenticity Claims Regarding War," *International Political Sociology* (2016).

27. Laura Sjoberg, "Gendering the Empire's Soldiers: Gender Ideologies, the U.S. Military, and the 'War on Terror,'" in *Gender, War, and Militarism: Feminist Perspectives*, eds. Laura Sjoberg and Sandra Via; Thomas Beaumont, "A survivor's response to sacrifice," *Critical Military Studies* 3, no. 3 (2017); Mia Fischer, "Commemorating 9/11 NFL-Style: Insights into America's Culture of Militarism," *Journal of Sport and Social Issues* 38, no. 3 (2014): 199–221; Eugenie Almeida and Jessica Hafner, "Heroes versus Traitors: U.S. and Afghani Soldiers in the U.S. Press," *Global Journal of Human-Social Science* 14, no. 1 (2014).

28. Lisa Leitz, "Oppositional Identities: The Military Peace Movement's Challenge to Pro-Iraq War Frames," *Social Problems* 58, no. 2 (May 2011): 235–256.

29. Leonie Huddy and Nadia Khatib, "American Patriotism, National Identity, and Political Involvement," *American Journal of Political Science* 51, no. 1 (2007); Qiong Li and Marilynn Brewer, "What Does It Mean to Be an American? Patriotism, Nationalism, and American Identity after 9/11," *Political Psychology* 25, no. 5 (2004).

30. Lisa Leitz, "Oppositional Identities."

31. Thomas Hobbes, *Leviathan* (New York: Penguin Classics, 2003), 103.

32. Bryan Mabee, "From 'Liberal War' to 'Liberal Militarism': United States Security Policy as the Promotion of Military Modernity," *Critical Military Studies* 2, no. 3 (2016).

33. Everett Carl Dolman, "Obligation and the Citizen-Soldier: Machiavellian Virtu Versus Hobbesian Order," *Journal of Political and Military Sociology* 23 (Winter 1995): 191.

34. Ibid., 192.

35. Ibid., 196.

36. Ibid., 198.

37. Aaron Ettinger, "Ending the Draft in America: The Coevolution of Military Manpower and the Capitalist State, 1948–1973," *Critical Military Studies* 15 (August 2016). While it is considered an "all-volunteer army" many, including myself, show how there is a poverty draft in the US that forces many with no other option into joining the military.

38. Charles Mills, *The Racial Contract* (Ithaca, NY: Cornell University Press, 1997), 10.

39. Carl Bogus, "The Hidden History of the Second Amendment," *UC Davis Law Review* (1998).

40. Mills, *Racial Contract*, 12.

41. Carole Pateman and Charles Mills, *Contract and Domination* (Malden, MA: Polity, 2007), 41–44.

42. Lura Headle, "Grants of Land by the United States to Our Soldiers of Past Wars," *Advocate of Peace Through Justice* 84, no. 5 (May 1922): 176–178; Act of the 14th United States Congress, Session I, Chapter 164, April 19, 1816.

43. Bellesiles, *A Peoples History of the U.S. Military*, 110.

44. Ernest A. McKay, *The Civil War and New York City* (Syracuse, NY: Syracuse University Press, 1990).

45. David Stannard, *American Holocaust: The Conquest of the New World* (London: Oxford University Press).

46. This is not to say that the reasons for war were right and justifiable, as oftentimes the reasons were deeply racist and problematic, but to be clear that when faced with danger up close, particular sets of outcomes, rationalities, and irrationalities can be expected.

47. Smedley Butler. *War Is a Racket*, 1935, https://ratical.org/ratville/CAH/warisaracket.html.

48. Bellesiles, *A Peoples History of the U.S. Military*, 220.

49. While the fight for rights was racially desegregated, the benefits that were received were not equally distributed, as white soldiers benefited most from the GI Bill and other veterans' benefits.

50. Kimberly Phillips, *War! What Is It Good For? Black Freedom Struggles & the U.S. Military from World War II to Iraq* (Chapel Hill: University of North Carolina Press, 2012).

51. Ibid. See also Morris MacGregor, *Integration of the Armed Forces: 1940–1965* (Alexandria, VA: Library of Alexandria, 1985).

52. Phillips, *War!*

53. Laura Pulido, *Black, Brown, Yellow, and Left: Radical Activism in Los Angeles* (Berkeley: University of California Press, 2006), 34.

54. Maya Eichler, "Citizenship and the Contracting out of Military Work: From National Conscription to Globalized Recruitment," *Citizenship Studies* 18, nos. 6–7 (2014); Ettinger, "Ending the Draft in America."

55. Susan Jeffords, *Hard Bodies: Hollywood Masculinity in the Reagan Era* (New York: Rutgers University Press, 1994); Michael Shapiro, *Violent Cartographies: Mapping Cultures of War* (Minneapolis: University of Minnesota Press, 1997).

56. Schrader, "The Affect of Veteran Activism."

57. See also David Flores, "Politicization Beyond Politics: Narratives and Mechanisms of Iraq War Veterans' Activism," *Armed Forces & Society* 43, no. 1 (2017). This framework can extend beyond a US context as well. Many other countries' military formations create an interesting outlook on the relationships between the Soldiers' Contract and the Social Contract. From the ways in which rape and sexual assault have been used as weapons of war to the use of soldiers to perpetuate apartheid states, we find there are interesting and often horrifying constructions of the sexual, racial, Soldiers', and Social contracts. Furthermore, there are soldier and

veteran activists working to expose the flaws within these contracts, as the soldiers are not just an extension of the sovereign but are also comprised of the people.

58. Though if one were to broaden their idea of activism it could come to encompass veteran organizations such as the American Legion and Veterans of Foreign Wars. Also, more conservative groups such as the Tea Party and different militias can be seen as activists, but that is not the focus of this particular study, but rather an aspect that can be looked at in the future research.

59. Some veterans were participants in multiple forms of activism, thus parts of their interviews were put in different categories.

60. There were, at times, differences due to branches of the military, but there were often relatable terms. For example, the US Army has medics while the US Marines have corpsmen; both fulfill the same duties, but many of these differences are often known throughout the different branches.

61. Foucault, *Society Must Be Defended*, 8.

62. Frank Fischer, *Reframing Public Policy: Discursive Politics and Deliberative Practices* (Oxford: Oxford University Press, 2003), 38.

Chapter 1

1. Michel Foucault, *The Hermeneutics of the Subject: Lectures at the Collège de France 1981–1982*, trans. Graham Burchell, reprint (New York: Picador, 2005), 333.

2. Christian G. Appy, *Working-Class War: American Combat Soldiers and Vietnam* (Chapel Hill: University of North Carolina Press, 1993), 60.

3. Project Pat, "Chicken Head," *Mista Don't Play: Everythangs Workin*, Three 6 Mafia, 2001, CD.

4. The song was actually aimed at another rapper, likening him to a woman who gives oral sex to a man, thus making the degradation toward women obvious.

5. A battle buddy is an assigned soldier that you are supposed to do everything with. In some ways, this arrangement acts as a support system, but it also it works as an accountability system, because if one soldier messes up, then both mess up and both are punished.

6. Paul Higate, *Military Masculinities* (New York: Praeger, 2002).

7. Foucault et al., *Psychiatric Power: Lectures at the Collège de France, 1973–1974* (New York: Picador, 2008), 146–147.

8. John Protevi, *Political Affect: Connecting the Social and the Somatic* (Minneapolis: University of Minnesota Press, 2009), 156.

9. William McNeil, *Keeping Together in Time: Dance and Drill in Human History* (Cambridge, MA: Harvard University Press, 1995), 2.

10. Ibid.

11. Ibid.

12. Basham, *War, Identity and the Liberal State*, 132.

13. Since my departure from the military, they have switched to a tan suede boot that does not require shining, but the shining of boots serves as a good example of just one way in which soldiers' needs are managed.

14. Headquarters Department of the Army, *The Soldier's Blue Book: The Guide for Initial Entry Training Soldiers*, TRADOC Pamphlet 600-4 (2010). Fort Monroe, VA.

15. Foucault et al., *Psychiatric Power*, 154.

16. Michel Foucault, *Discipline and Punish: The Birth of the Prison* (New York: Vintage Books, 1995), 162.

17. Protevi, *Political Affect*, 147.

18. Michael J. Shapiro, *War Crimes, Atrocity and Justice*, 1st ed. (Oxford: Polity, 2015), 104.

19. Ibid., 151.

20. Ibid., 155.

21. For another account of military field training see James Der Derian's experience in *Virtuous War: Mapping the Military-Industrial-Media-Entertainment Network*, 2nd ed. (New York: Basic Books, 2009).

22. Ibid., 156.

23. Ibid., 155.

24. Ibid., 155–157.

25. Pink Floyd, "The Gunner's Dream," *The Final Cut*, Capitol Records, 1982, CD.

Chapter 2

1. Iraq Veterans Against the War, *Winter Soldier: Iraq and Afghanistan: Eyewitness Accounts of the Occupations*, ed. Aaron Glantz (Chicago: Haymarket Books, 2008), 57.

2. Foucault, *The Hermeneutics of the Subject*.

3. Foucault, *Society Must Be Defended*, 270.

4. For a more normative, but excellent, social movements analysis of IVAW, see Lisa Leitz, *Fighting for Peace*.

5. Much of the following information is drawn from a number of sources, including my personal experience as a member of Iraq Veterans Against the War. I was a participant in many of the activities and events discussed.

6. "Founding of IVAW," Iraq Veterans Against the War, accessed February 6, 2013, http://www.ivaw.org/about/founding-ivaw.

7. Jamail, *The Will to Resist*, 172.

8. Iraq Veterans Against the War, *Winter Soldier*, 3.

9. "Tired to the Bone," *Huffington Post*, accessed February 6, 2013, http://www.huffingtonpost.com/cindy-sheehan/tired-to-the-bone_b_6652.html.

10. "History," Iraq Veterans Against the War, accessed February 6, 2013, http://www.ivaw.org/about/history.

11. Ibid.

12. Steve Vogel and Michael Alison Chandler, "4 Years After Start of War, Anger Reigns," *Washington Post*, March 18, 2007, http://www.washingtonpost.com/wp-dyn/content/article/2007/03/17/AR2007031700539.html.

13. This was a slogan that the IVAW strategy team came up with.

14. "Operation First Casualty," *Washington Post*, March 19, 2007, http://www.washingtonpost.com/wp-dyn/content/video/2007/03/19/VI2007031901446.html. It should be noted that Operation First Casualty was a re-creation of VVAW (Vietnam Veterans Against the War) events that took place in the 1960s and 1970s.

15. For another account and theoretical framing, see Cami Rowe, *The Politics of Protest and US Foreign Policy: Performative Construction of the War on Terror (War, Politics and Experience)* (London: Routledge, 2013).

16. Protevi, *Political Affect*, 49.

17. Pasi Väliaho, "Affectivity, Biopolitics and the Virtual Reality of War," *Theory, Culture & Society* 29, no. 2 (March 1, 2012): 63–83, doi:10.1177/0263276411417461.

18. "Winter Soldier," Iraq Veterans Against the War," accessed February 6, 2013, http://www.ivaw.org/wintersoldier.

19. Iraq Veterans Against the War, *Winter Soldier*, 4.

20. "Winter Soldier," Iraq Veterans Against the War.

21. A couple of interesting facets to this: first and foremost, we did not tell the police of any of our intentions about having a march, which made many of us who were close to the situation believe that there was either an informant within the Denver group or that they were conducting surveillance on us, thus showing the threat we posed to the Denver police and the DNC. Second is the use of a "free speech zone" as a designated place to conduct protests, which is still being debated as to its unconstitutionality by many groups including the ACLU.

22. Jamail, *The Will to Resist*, 212.

23. "Resolution Against the War in Afghanistan," Iraq Veterans Against the War, accessed February 7, 2013, http://www.ivaw.org/resolution-against-war-afghanistan.

24. "History," Iraq Veterans Against the War.

25. "Service Members Have the Right to Heal," Iraq Veterans Against the War, accessed February 7, 2013, http://www.ivaw.org/blog/service-members-have-right-heal.

26. "Veterans Return Medals during NATO Protest," Iraq Veterans Against the War, accessed February 7, 2013, http://www.ivaw.org/blog/veterans-return-medals-during-nato-protest.

27. "NATO/CANG8 on Democracy Now! Carlos Montes, Aaron Hughes IVAW, Other Activists," *WAMMToday*, accessed May 22, 2013, http://wammtoday.

org/2012/05/16/natocang8-on-democracy-now-carlos-montes-aaron-hughes-ivaw-other-activists/.

28. Iraq Veterans Against the War, "Operation Recovery," *Operation Recovery*, accessed August 20, 2014, http://forthoodtestimonies.com/.

29. Iraq Veterans Against the War, *Winter Soldier*, 17–18.

30. Michel Foucault, *The Government of Self and Others: Lectures at the College de France, 1982–1983*, ed. Arnold I. I. Davidson, trans. Graham Burchell (New York: Picador, 2011), 154.

31. Ibid., 154.

32. "Democracy Now! Newscast for October 14, 2014," *Democracy Now!*, accessed November 5, 2014, http://www.democracynow.org/shows/2014/10/14.

33. Ibid.

34. Foucault, *Society Must Be Defended*, 270.

35. Iraq Veterans Against the War, *Winter Soldier*, 83.

36. Ibid., 84.

37. M. Uğur Ersen and Cinar Özen, *Use of Force in Countering Terrorism* (Amsterdam: IOS Press, 2010), 41–47.

38. Iraq Veterans Against the War, *Winter Soldier*, 50–51.

39. An exception would be Faye Donnelly's *Securitization and the Iraq War: The Rules of Engagement in World Politics* (New York: Routledge, 2013), where she utilizes Wittgenstein to show the replacement of rules of engagement, and how that became the norm in Iraq.

40. Foucault, *The Government of Self and Others*, 155.

41. Michel Foucault, *Wrong-Doing, Truth-Telling: The Function of Avowal in Justice*, ed. Fabienne Brion and Bernard E. Harcourt, trans. Stephen W. Sawyer, annotated ed. (Chicago: University of Chicago Press, 2014), 19.

42. Ibid.

43. Foucault, *The Government of Self and Others*, 25.

44. Joshua Goldstein, *War and Gender: How Gender Shaped the War System and Vice Versa* (Cambridge: Cambridge University Press, 2001).

45. Brianne Gallagher, "Burdens of Proof: Veteran Frauds, PTSD Pussies, and the Spectre of the Welfare Queen," *Critical Military Studies* 2: 139–154.

46. During the process of my writing this book, Bradley Manning chose to transition to a female identity, Chelsea Manning. While I am describing events that occurred before this transition, I will continue to refer to her as Chelsea Manning. I do this in order to honor Chelsea's decision of her identity and pronouns.

47. "Collateral Murder," WikiLeaks, accessed June 28, 2013, https://collateral murder.wikileaks.org

48. Derek Sweetman, "Bradley Manning, Collateral Murder, Truth, and Power," *Unrest Magazine*, accessed July 24, 2013, http://www.unrestmag.com/bradley-manning-collateral-murder-truth-and-power/.

49. Ibid.

50. Gene Sharp, *The Politics of Nonviolent Action* (Boston: Porter Sargent, 1973), 12.

51. Jean Baudrillard, *The Gulf War Did Not Take Place* (Bloomington: Indiana University Press, 1995), 34–36.

52. "U.S. Lifts Photo Ban on Military Coffins," *New York Times*, accessed February 17, 2013, http://www.nytimes.com/2009/02/27/world/americas/27iht-photos.1.20479953.html?_r=0.

53. Joanna Tidy, "Visual Regimes and the Politics of War Experience: Rewriting War 'from above' in WikiLeaks' 'Collateral Murder,'" *Review of International Studies* 43, part 1 (2016): 95–111.

54. Iraq Veterans Against the War, *Winter Soldier*, 212; COINTELPRO was a series of primarily illegal and brutal attacks by the FBI against different activist groups during the 1960s civil rights movement. These groups ranged from antiwar groups like IVAW to nationalistic groups like the Black Panthers.

55. Tidy, "Visual Regimes."

56. Sweetman, "Bradley Manning, Collateral Murder, Truth, and Power."

57. Iraq Veterans Against the War, *Winter Soldier*, 212.

58. Tidy, "The Gender Politics of 'Ground Truth' in the Military Dissent Movement."

59. Andreas Folkers, "Daring the Truth: Foucault, Parrhesia, and the Genealogy of Critique," *Theory, Culture & Society* 33, no. 1 (2016): 3–28.

60. Enloe, *Maneuvers*, 291.

61. Iraq Veterans Against the War, *Winter Soldier: Iraq and Afghanistan*, 482–483.

Chapter 3

1. "Oath of Enlistment," About.com US Military, accessed December 5, 2012, http://usmilitary.about.com/od/joiningthemilitary/a/oathofenlist.htm.

2. Leitz, *Fighting for Peace*, 91–92.

3. Harvey, *The Enigma of Capital*, 204.

4. Thomas Interview, 2014.

5. I would like to note that this description from Shamar Thomas is not meant to perpetuate the stereotype of the "absent" black father; rather it is an observation by Thomas of those he knew who fell into gang violence.

6. Michael Levitin, "Occupying War: A Marine Vet Finds His Mission," *The Occupied Wall Street Journal*, accessed December 5, 2012, http://occupiedmedia.us/2012/03/occupying-war-a-marine-vet-finds-his-mission/.

7. Ibid.

8. As of June 2018, https://www.youtube.com/watch?v=WmEHcOc0Sys.

9. Eugene Holland, *Nomad Citizenship: Free-Market Communism and the Slow-Motion General Strike* (Minneapolis: University of Minnesota Press, 2011), xx.

10. Johan Galtung, "Violence, Peace, and Peace Research," *Journal of Peace Research* 6, no. 3 (1969): 167–191.

11. Karl Marx and Friedrich Engels, *The Marx-Engels Reader*, ed. Robert C. Tucker, 2nd ed., revised and enlarged (New York: W. W. Norton & Company, 1978), 438.

12. Galtung, "Violence, Peace, and Peace Research," 168.

13. Levitin, "Occupying War: A Marine Vet Finds His Mission."

14. Ibid.

15. Ibid.

16. Thomas Interview, 2014.

17. Ibid.

18. Harvey, *The Enigma of Capital*, 239–241.

19. Antonio Gramsci, *Selections from the Prison Notebooks*, ed. Quintin Hoare and Geoffrey Nowell Smith (New York: International Publishers Co., 1971).

20. Levitin, "Occupying War: A Marine Vet Finds His Mission."

21. Ibid.

22. Ibid.

23. Ibid.

24. Scott Olsen, "Casualty of the Occupation," *Rollingstone.com*, accessed December 5, 2012, http://www.rollingstone.com/politics/news/scott-olsen-casualty-of-the-occupation-20120119.

25. Ibid.

26. Ibid.

27. Ibid.

28. Alain Badiou, *The Rebirth of History: Times of Riots and Uprisings*, trans. Gregory Elliott, 1st ed. (New York: Verso, 2012), 18.

29. Ibid.

30. "US Military Veterans Heed Occupy Rallying Cry," Associated Press, November 3, 2011, http://www.foxnews.com/us/2011/11/03/us-military-veterans-heed-occupy-rallying-cry/.

31. Badiou, *The Rebirth of History*, 20.

32. Olsen, "Casualty of the Occupation."

33. Jorma Jussila and Pertti Normia, "International Law and Law Enforcement Firearms," *Medicine, Conflict and Survival* 20, no. 1 (January 2004): 55–69.

34. Charles Tilly, "War Making and State Making as Organized Crime," in *Bringing the State Back In*, eds. Peter Evans, Dietrich Rueschmeyer, and Theda Skocpol (Cambridge: Cambridge University Press, 1985), 169–187.

35. Ibid., 171.

36. "Interview," RT America, October 28, 2011, https://www.youtube.com/watch?v=vhW-seBVpOs (Accessed 8/20/2017).

37. Interestingly enough, there are parallels between what the Occupy movement is fighting for and what the Tea Party was fighting for. While an in-depth analysis is not the focus of this chapter, it should be noted that the Tea Party was demonstrating against the government, whereas the Occupy movement is protesting against corporate entities. While Tea Partiers carried weapons to protests, no violence was reported because the demonstrations were most often against the state. The Occupiers, on the other hand, carried no weapons apart from a few rocks and bottles—the majority were nonviolent, unarmed protestors—yet they have been met with riot gear and violence because their protest is against capitalist entities. Interestingly, this state-finance nexus seems more concerned about protecting capitalist interests, which seem to be more vulnerable to resistance. I have often heard it said in jest that if members of the Occupy movement had come to the different actions armed with weapons, like the Tea Partiers did, they would have more than likely been shot by the police, a very sad and disturbing hypocrisy that highlights the differences between the reactions of the state in relation to protests against capitalism. I cover some of the connections and hypocrisies of the Tea Party in my master's thesis, "The Tea Party: The Discourse of Race, Class, and Gender/Sexuality," which can be found on Academia.edu.

38. "Board of Directors Statement on the Occupy Movement: We Are the 99%," Iraq Veterans Against the War, accessed December 5, 2012, http://www.ivaw.org/blog/board-directors-statement-occupy-movement-we-are-99.

39. Though I would say that it is solely made up of the 99 percent, there may be a multimillionaire hiding among the ranks of soldiers, most likely some high-ranking officer.

40. Appy, *Working-Class War*.

41. "Transcript of the Constitution of the United States," accessed December 5, 2012, http://www.archives.gov/exhibits/charters/constitution_transcript.html.

42. Aaron Glantz, *The War Comes Home: Washington's Battle against America's Veterans*, 1st ed. (Berkeley: University of California Press, 2010), 159.

43. Robert Gibbons, C. Hendricks Brown, and Kwan Hur, "Is the Rate of Suicide Among Veterans Elevated?" *American Journal of Public Health* 102, no. S1 (2012).

44. "Board of Directors Statement on the Occupy Movement: We Are the 99%," Iraq Veterans Against the War.

45. Project on Government Oversight, Bad Business: Billions of Taxpayer Dollars Wasted on Hiring Contractors, September 13, 2011, page 1, accessed November 28, 2012, http://pogoarchives.org/m/co/igf/bad-business-report-only-2011.pdf.

46. "Cost Review of Military Contractors Would Be Revealing," *Mining Journal*, accessed December 5, 2012, http://www.miningjournal.net/page/content.detail/id/579311/Cost-review-of-military-contractors-would-be-revealing.html?nav=5003.

47. "Contractor Distrust Costs DOD Billions, Study Says," *Washington Technology*, accessed December 5, 2012, http://washingtontechnology.com/Articles/2012/07/12/efficiency-dod-contractor-relationship.aspx?Page=1.

48. "Board of Directors Statement on the Occupy Movement," Iraq Veterans Against the War.

49. Ibid.

50. Tilly, "War Making and State Making," 183.

Chapter 4

1. Schrader, "The Affect of Veteran Activism."

2. Jane Lunchenco, "Entering the Century of the Environment: A New Social Contract for Science," *Science* 279, no. 5350 (1998); Karen O'Brien, Bronwyn Hayward, and Fikret Berkes, "Rethinking Social Contracts: Building Resilience in a Changing Climate," *Ecology and Society* 14, no. 2 (2009).

3. This title, "Letters from Iraq," would later become a song by the Bouncing Souls, which was primarily a poem written by Garett Reppenhagen.

4. "Nobel Peace Laureates Conference, 1998," accessed July 3, 2014, http://www.virginia.edu/nobel/laureates/bios/muller_bio.html.

5. My time as a river raft guide had already taught me of the dangers of the tamarisk, which is an invasive species that was introduced at the turn of the twentieth century to help stop erosion. That strategy, however, has backfired, as it has killed much of the biodiversity of the Colorado River because of its high release of salts into the soil and the large amounts of water it uses to sustain itself. Furthermore, the rapid rate in which it repopulates makes it very difficult to eradicate.

6. "Mission, Vision, Values," Veterans Green Jobs, accessed February 18, 2013, http://veteransgreenjobs.org/about/mission-vision-values. Sadly, VGJ is no longer an organization due to poor management by the board of directors.

7. Kristin G. Wurster, A. P. Rinaldi, T. S. Woods, and W. M. Liu, "First-Generation Student Veterans: Implications of Poverty for Psychotherapy," *Journal of Clinical Psychology* 69, no. 2 (2013): 127–137.

8. Ibid.

9. "Mission, Vision, Values," Veterans Green Jobs.

10. Michel Foucault et al., *Psychiatric Power: Lectures at the Collège de France, 1973–1974* (New York: Picador, 2008), 47.

11. Kevin McSorley, "Doing Military Fitness: Physical Culture, Civilian Leisure, and Militarism," *Critical Military Studies* (2016); Paul Higate, "'Switching It On' for Cash: The Private Militarized Security Contractor," in K. McSorley, ed., *War and the Body: Militarisation, Practice and Experience* (Abingdon, UK: Routledge), 106–127; Michael Mann, "The Roots and Contradictions of Modern Militarism," *New Left Review* 162 (March–April): 35–50.

12. McSorley, "Doing Military Fitness."

13. Wurster et al., "First-Generation Student Veterans"; Bill Briggs, "Fewer Homeless Vets This Year, but Advocacy Group Sees 'Alarming' Rise in Younger

Ex-Service Members," NBC News, accessed February 19, 2013, http://usnews.nbc news.com/_news/2012/12/10/15761391-fewer-homeless-vets-this-year-but-advocacy-group-sees-alarming-rise-in-younger-ex-service-members.

14. Higate, "'Switching It On' for Cash."

15. Michael Dillon and Luis Lobo-Guerrero, "Biopolitics of Security in the 21st Century: An Introduction," *Review of International Studies* 34, no. 02 (2008): 265–292, esp. 269.

16. Giorgio Agamben, *"What Is an Apparatus?" And Other Essays*, trans. David Kishik and Stefan Pedatella (Stanford, CA: Stanford University Press, 2009); Michel Foucault, *Power/Knowledge: Selected Interviews and Other Writings, 1972–1977*, ed. Colin Gordon, 1st American ed., stained (New York: Vintage, 1980).

17. Jon Gensler, OpFree Vet Interview, October 28, 2013.

18. Ibid.

19. "Deaths at W.Va. Coal Mine Raise Safety Issues," *New York Times*, accessed July 6, 2014, http://www.nytimes.com/2010/04/07/us/07westvirginia. html?pagewanted=all&_r=1&.

20. "Our Mission: Secure America with Clean Energy," Operation Free, accessed February 18, 2013, http://www.operationfree.net/our-mission/.

21. Michel Foucault, *"Society Must Be Defended": Lectures at the Collège de France, 1975–1976*, trans. David Macey, reprint (New York: Picador, 2003), 16.

22. Brad Evans, "Foucault's Legacy: Security, War and Violence in the 21st Century," *Security Dialogue* 41, no. 4 (August 1, 2010): 413–433.

23. Ibid.

24. Ibid., 424.

25. Ibid., 421–422.

26. Liam Downey, Eric Bonds, and Katherine Clark, "Natural Resource Extraction, Armed Violence, and Environmental Degradation," *Organization & Environment* 23, no. 4 (2010): 417–445.

27. *The Burden*, accessed July 6, 2014, http://www.theburdenfilm.com/film.

28. For more on these types of connections, see Killian McCormack, "Governing 'Ungoverned' Space: Humanitarianism, Citizenship, and the Civilian Sphere in the Territorializing Practices of the US National Security Complex," *Critical Military Studies* 4, no. 2 (2018).

29. Richard Kidd IV, "Mission Critical: Clean Energy and the U.S. Military," *Environmental Entrepreneurs*, Law Offices of Simpson Thacher & Bartlett, October 29, 2013.

30. Ibid.

31. Stacy Bare, "Veterans Expeditions to Wilderness and Regaining Health," *International Journal of Wilderness* 18, no. 1 (April 2012), http://ijw.org/april-2012/.

32. The program was called Huts for Vets, a program seeking to get veterans out in the wilderness by taking them up to the WWII 10th Mountain Division Huts, in the middle of the Rocky Mountains. It is discussed later in the chapter.

33. As well as other books such as Aaron Glantz, *The War Comes Home.*

34. Brock McIntosh, OpFree Vet Interview, October 25, 2013.

35. Peter Salmon, "Effects of Physical Exercise on Anxiety, Depression and Sensitivity to Stress—A Unifying Theory," *Clinical Psychology Review* 21, no. 1 (2001): 33–61.

36. Bum-Jin Park et al., "Physiological Effects of Shinrin-Yoku (Taking in the Atmosphere of the Forest)—Using Salivary Cortisol and Cerebral Activity as Indicators," *Journal of Physiological Anthropology* (2006): 122–128.

37. Ibid.

38. Hal Arkowitz and Scott Lilienfeld, "EMDR: Taking a Closer Look," *Scientific American*, December 6, 2007, http://www.scientificamerican.com/article/emdr-taking-a-closer-look/.

39. Ibid.

40. "What Is EMDR?," EMDR Institute, Inc., accessed July 10, 2014, http://www.emdr.com/general-information/what-is-emdr.html.

41. "Huts for Vets," accessed July 10, 2014, http://hutsforvets.org/.

42. Michel Foucault, *Technologies of the Self: A Seminar with Michel Foucault*, ed. Luther H. Martin, Huck Gutman, and Patrick H. Hutton (Amherst: University of Massachusetts Press, 1988).

43. I put the word "debate" in quotes because while it is a political debate within the United States, it is not a scientific debate.

44. Grégoire Chamayou, *A Theory of the Drone* (New York: The New Press, 2015), 181.

Chapter 5

1. To clarify the vocabulary, sexual violence is an umbrella term that covers crimes such as sexual assault, rape, sexual contact, stalking, and sexual abuse. It is a non-legal term as the legality shifts depending upon locality. For complete definitions of the terms that fall under sexual violence, according to UCMJ, see http://www.sapr.mil/public/docs/ucmj/UCMJ_Article120_Rape_Sexual_Assault.pdf.

2. See Cynthia Cockburn, *From Where We Stand: War, Women's Activism and Feminist Analysis* (London: Zed Books, 2007); Cynthia Cockburn, "The Continuum of Violence: A Gender Perspective on War and Peace," in W. Giles and J. Hyndman, eds., *Sites of Violence: Gender and Conflict* (Berkeley: University of California Press, 2004); Cynthia Enloe, *Globalisation and Militarism. Feminists Make the Link* (London: Rowman & Littlefield, 2007); Cynthia Enloe, *Maneuvers*; Cynthia Enloe, *Does Khaki Become You? The Militarization of Women's Lives* (London: Pandora, 1998); Jeff Hearn, "On Men, Women, Militarism and the Military," in P. Higate, ed., *Military Masculinities: Identity and the State* (Westport, CT: Praeger, 2003), xi–xv; Paul Higate, *Military Masculinities* (New York: Praeger, 2002); John Hockey, "No

More Heroes: Masculinity in the Infantry," in P. Higate, ed., *Military Masculinities: Identity and the State* (Westport, CT: Praeger, 2003); Annica Kronsell and Erika Svedberg, eds., *Making Gender, Making War: Violence, Military and Peacekeeping Practices* (London: Routledge Advances in Feminist Studies and Intersectionality, 2010); Christine Sylvester, ed., *Experiencing War* (London: Routledge, 2010); Ben Wadham, "Brotherhood: Homosociality, Totality, and Military Subjectivity," *Australian Feminist Studies* 28, no. 76 (2013).

3. Steve Pond, "Military Rape Documentary 'Invisible War' Leads to Policy Changes Before Its Opening," *TheWrap*, accessed September 18, 2014, http://www.thewrap.com/movies/column-post/military-rape-documentary-invisible-war-leads-policy-changes-its-opening-44671/.

4. "About," *Not Invisible*, accessed September 18, 2014, http://www.notinvisible.org/the_movie.

5. Jessica Kenyon, MST.org Interview, November 25, 2013.

6. "Fact Sheet," Service Women's Action Network, Rape, Sexual Assault and Sexual Harassment in the Military, July 2012, http://servicewomen.org/media/publications/#factSheet.

7. Kenyon Interview.

8. Extra duty in the military is an additional two to six hours of work a day. Lower-ranking enlisted soldiers will usually have to do manual labor, from yard work to cleaning common areas. Upper enlisted soldiers and officers who receive extra duty usually only have to supervise the lower enlisted soldiers conducting extra duty, or spend time doing office work. So really it is just a slap on the wrist.

9. Kenyon Interview.

10. Madeline Morris, "By Force of Arms: Rape, War, and Military Culture," *Duke Law Journal* 45, no. 4 (February 1996); Aaron Belkin, *Bring Me Men*.

11. Paul Kirby, "How Is Rape a Weapon of War? Feminist International Relations, Modes of Critical Explanation and the Study of Wartime Sexual Violence," *European Journal of International Relations*, 2012.

12. Ruth Seifert, "The Second Front: The Logic of Sexual Violence in Wars," in Manfred B. Steger and Nancy S. Lind, eds., *Violence and Its Alternatives: An Interdisciplinary Reader* (New York: Palgrave Macmillan, 1999), 146.

13. Cynthia Cockburn, "Gender Relations as Causal in Militarization and War: A Feminist Stand Point," in *Making Gender, Making War Violence, Military and Peacekeeping Practices*, 41–42.

14. Sjoberg and Via, *Gender, War, and Militarism*.

15. Ibid., 20–24.

16. Ibid., 23.

17. Ramon Hinohosa, "Doing Hegemony: Military, Men, and Constructing Hegemonic Masculinity," *Journal of Men's Studies*, March 2010; Aaron Belkin, *Bring Me Men*, 29–30.

18. Iraq Veterans Against the War, *Winter Soldier*, 264.

19. Chris Cuomo, "War Is Not Just an Event: Reflections on the Significance of Everyday Violence," *Hypatia* 11, no. 4 (Autumn 1996): 32.

20. Military sexual trauma is a designation of post-traumatic stress that specifically occurred in the military. For a legal definition according to the VA, see https://www.ptsd.va.gov/public/types/violence/military-sexual-trauma-general.asp.

21. "Trial of Fort Hood NCO Accused of Setting Up Prostitution Ring Starts Wednesday," *Stars and Stripes*, March 9, 2015, https://www.stripes.com/news/trial-of-fort-hood-nco-accused-of-setting-up-prostitution-ring-starts-wednesday-1.333414.

22. "SFC Sentenced for Organizing Fort Hood Prostitution Ring," Associated Press, *Army Times*, March 11, 2015.

23. Rachel Weiner and Matt Zapotosky, "Air Force Colonel Acquitted in Assault Trial," *Washington Post*, November 12, 2013.

24. See Anthony King, "The Female Combat Soldier," *European Journal of International Relations* 22, no. 1 (2015); Helen Thorpe, *Soldier Girls* (New York: Scribner, 2015); Helen Benedict, *The Lonely Soldier: The Private War of Women Serving in Iraq* (New York: Beacon Press, 2010).

25. Brian Lewis Interview, 2017.

26. Ibid.

27. Ibid.

28. Ibid.

29. "Section 8" is a historical expression in the military meaning mentally unfit for duty; this designation is no longer used.

30. See Aaron Belkin's *Bring Me Men*.

31. Nathaniel Penn, "'Son, Men Don't Get Raped,'" *GQ*, accessed November 15, 2014, http://www.gq.com/long-form/male-military-rape.

32. Ibid.

33. "Annual Report on Sexual Assault in the Military: Fiscal Year 2015," US Department of Defense, 2015.

34. Belkin, *Bring Me Men*, 98; Penn, *GQ*.

35. Belkin, *Bring Me Men*, 40–41; Penn, *GQ*.

36. Belkin, *Bring Me Men*, 86.

37. Ibid., 92.

38. Rachel Kimerling, Kerry Makin-Byrd, Samantha Louzon, Rosalinda Ignacio, and John McCarthy, "Military Sexual Trauma and Suicide Mortality," *American Journal of Preventive Medicine* 50, no. 6 (June 2016): 684–691.

39. Harold Braswell and Howard I. Kushner, "Suicide, Social Integration, and Masculinity in the U.S. Military," *Social Science & Medicine*, Part Special Issue: Men, Masculinities and Suicidal Behaviour 74, no. 4 (February 2012): 530–536, doi:10.1016/j.socscimed.2010.07.031.

40. Ibid.

41. Herman, *Trauma and Recovery*, 101.

42. Ibid.

43. Kenyon, MST.org Interview.

44. Penn, "'Son, Men Don't Get Raped.'"

45. Ibid.

46. Herman, *Trauma and Recovery*, 215.

47. Ibid., 215–216.

48. Basham, *War, Identity and the Liberal State*, 13.

49. *Heath's Story of Surviving Military Sexual Assault*, 2012, https://www.youtube.com/watch?v=_4J8Z09zHXA&feature=youtube_gdata_player.

50. Belkin, *Bring Me Men*, 86.

51. Enloe, *Maneuvers*, 285.

Chapter 6

1. Craig R. Shagin, "Deporting Private Ryan: The Less than Honorable Condition of the Noncitizen in the United States Armed Forces," *Widener Law Journal* 17 (2007): 245.

2. "Immigrants in the US Armed Forces," *The Migration Information Source*, accessed January 24, 2013, http://www.migrationinformation.org/feature/display.cfm?ID=683.

3. The term "war imaginary" is broad, as it has primarily been connected to connotations of the Cold War, i.e., Cold War imaginary. It has been used in other places similar to how I describe it above, but with no real specific definition as I outline here; with the exception of Lilie Chouliaraki (see Lilie Chouliaraki, "Liberal Ethics and the Spectacle of War," in *Ethics of Media*, edited by N. Couldry, M. Madianou, and A. Pinchevski [London: Palgrave Macmillan, 2013]), who describes it more as a spectacle. However, my definition goes beyond that and is affectual within the personal understandings and experiences of war. Another close usage of the term is Sean Lawson's terminology of "military imaginaries," in his article "Articulation, antagonism, and intercalation in Western military imaginaries," *Security Dialogue* 42, no. 1 (2011). While our construction of the term is similar, I feel that "war imaginary" is a term that is a bit broader than "military imaginary," one that military imaginary would fall under. I think that a broader conception of the term is necessary because as militarism has become embedded within our everyday thought and actions, war is also as prevalent, and while militaries primary focus is war, war often extends beyond militaries.

4. Manfred Steger, *The Rise of the Global Imaginary: Political Ideologies from the French Revolution to the Global War on Terror* (New York: Oxford University Press, 2009), 6.

5. Charles Taylor, *Modern Social Imaginaries* (Durham, NC: Duke University Press, 2003), 25.

6. Cynthia Weber, *Imagining America at War: Morality, Politics, and Film* (New York: Taylor & Francis, 2006), 2.

7. Ibid., 5.

8. Luis Alberto Urrea and Erin Siegal McIntyre, "Mexican Soldiers Fight for US Army but Still Deported," *Playboy*, accessed November 8, 2013, http://www.playboy.com/playground/view/deported-warriors-us-soldiers.

9. Hector Beragas, Banished Veterans Interview, September 30, 2013.

10. Lisa Daniel, "Defense.gov News Article: Recruiters Recall Patriotism of Post-9/11 America," accessed January 27, 2013, http://www.defense.gov/News/News Article.aspx?ID=65272.

11. Carlos Valdez, "Defense.gov News Article: Face of Defense: Soldiers Keep Up Family Tradition," accessed January 27, 2013, http://www.defense.gov/News/NewsArticle.aspx?ID=54384.

12. Daniel, "Defense.gov News Article: Recruiters Recall Patriotism of Post-9/11 America."

13. The training is often substandard, often leaving the soldier unprepared for civilian life and in need of retraining once they exit the military.

14. "Military Benefits," *Today's Military*, accessed January 27, 2013, http://www.todaysmilitary.com/main/military-benefits.

15. Lizette Alvarez, "More Americans Joining Military as Jobs Dwindle," *New York Times*, January 18, 2009, http://www.nytimes.com/2009/01/19/us/19recruits.html.

16. James Tracy, *The Military Draft Handbook: A Brief History and Practical Advice for the Curious and Concerned* (San Francisco: Manic D Press, 2005), 50–53. The only academic that I know of who addresses this is Teresia Teaiwa, who is addressing it in the context of it being a way out for many Pacific Islanders. It was also a prominent part of the documentary *When I Came Home*, the story of a young black man from the Bronx who joined to escape poverty and came home from war, only to become homeless again.

17. Cordula Meyer, "Fighting for a New Homeland: US Army Lures Foreigners with Promise of Citizenship," *Spiegel Online*, accessed January 27, 2013, http://www.spiegel.de/international/world/fighting-for-a-new-homeland-us-army-lures-foreigners-with-promise-of-citizenship-a-512384.html.

18. "Media Archives," *Banished Veterans*, accessed January 27, 2013, http://www.banishedveterans.info/MEDIA-ARCHIVES.html.

19. Melissa Cook, "Banished for Minor Crimes: The Aggravated Felony Provision of the Immigration and Nationality Act as Human Rights Violation," *Boston College Third World Law Journal* 23 (2003): 293.

20. "World Gazetteer: America—Largest Cities (per Geographical Entity)," September 30, 2007.

21. "BTS: Border Crossing/Entry Data: Query Detailed Statistics," accessed November 16, 2013, http://transborder.bts.gov/programs/international/transborder/TBDR_BC/TBDR_BCQ.html.

22. Theo Gonzalves, "'We Hold a Neatly Folded Hope': Filipino Veterans of World War II on Citizenship and Political Obligation," *Amerasia Journal* 21, no. 3 (Winter 1995–96): 155–174.

23. Priscilla Juan-Sneden, "We Fight over There, so We Don't Have to Fight Here," *MarinesBlog: The Official Blog of the United States Marine Corps*, accessed January 27, 2013, http://marines.dodlive.mil/2011/05/02/osamabinladendead/.

24. Steger, *The Rise of the Global Imaginary*, 218–220.

25. Shapiro, *Violent Cartographies*, 21–22.

26. Jules Tindugan, War Resisters Interview, November 20, 2013.

27. Ibid.

28. Tindugan, War Resisters Interview.

29. "Courage to Resist—Kimberly Rivera," accessed May 10, 2014, http://couragetoresist.org/kimberly-rivera.html.

30. Bob Meola and Michael McKee, "Courage to Resist: Giving Birth behind Bars," accessed May 10, 2014, http://couragetoresist.org/kimberly-rivera/1017-birth-behind-bars.html.

31. Ibid.

32. Ibid.

33. Matt Zeller, No One Left Behind Interview, October 24, 2013.

34. "No One Left Behind," *No One Left Behind*, accessed August 25, 2014, http://www.nooneleft.org/.

35. The Truman Foundation is the same umbrella group that runs Operation FREE, discussed in the environmental activism chapter.

Chapter 7

1. Protevi, *Political Affect*, 155.

2. This work was not originally started by Warrior Writers and Lovella, but rather has been happening for a long time. One of the first to deeply engage in this work is Maxine Hong Kingston, who began by working with Vietnam veterans in the early 1990s, trying to turn their traumas into poetry.

3. Drew Cameron, Combat Paper Interview, October 5, 2013.

4. Ibid.

5. Justine Browning, "Turning the Page, U.S. Soldiers Home from War Rebound through Writing," *Occupy.com*, March 7, 2014, http://www.occupy.com/article/turning-page-us-soldiers-home-war-rebound-through-writing.

6. Kathy E. Ferguson, "Shocking Us to Thought: Anarchist Art and Poetry Concerning Political Prisoners," Western Political Science Association, 2014.

7. Protevi, *Political Affect*, 187.

8. Ibid., 90.

9. Enloe, *Maneuvers*, 291.

10. "Veterans Book Project," accessed April 26, 2014, http://www.veteransbookproject.com/.

11. Cameron, Combat Paper Interview.

12. Paula Howie, *Art Therapy with Military Populations: History, Innovation, and Applications* (New York: Routledge, 2017), 2.

13. Ibid.

14. "Why Soldiers Miss War," *FUNKER530*, accessed January 22, 2015, http://www.funker530.com/why-soldiers-miss-war/.

15. Cameron, Combat Paper Interview.

16. Ibid.

17. Because I knew Eli fairly well, I chose not to interview him for my project, as I had decided to not interview anyone that I had a close friendship with—though subsequently I have made many close friends with many of the participants.

18. For another view of this event, as well as a great analysis of Warrior Writers, see Brianne Gallagher, "Aesthetic Interventions: The Biopolitics of the U.S. Soldier's Wounded Body and Horror of Nothing to See" (PhD diss., University of Hawaii, 2014).

19. Andrew Hunt, *The Turning: A History of Vietnam Veterans against the War* (New York: New York University Press, 2001).

20. "Combat Paper Project," accessed December 9, 2013, http://www.combat paper.org/about.html.

21. Roland Barthes, "An Introduction to the Structural Analysis of Narrative," *New Literary History* 6, no. 2 (Winter 1975): 261.

22. Christine Sylvester, "The Art of War/The War Question in (Feminist) IR," *Millennium: Journal of International Studies* 33, no. 3 (2005): 875–876.

23. Michael Daly Hawkins, "Coming Home: Accommodating the Special Needs of Military Veterans to the Criminal Justice System," *Ohio State Journal of Criminal Law* 7 (2010 2009): 563; Moni Basu, "Why Suicide Rate among Veterans May Be More than 22 a Day," *CNN*, accessed April 19, 2014, http://www.cnn.com/2013/09/21/us/22-veteran-suicides-a-day/index.html.

24. Ibid.

25. Sarah Bulmer and Maya Eichler, "Unmaking Militarized Masculinity: Veterans and the Project of Military-to-Civilian Transition," *Critical Military Studies* 3, no. 2 (2017).

Conclusion

1. For a full account of how we met, see Benjamin Schrader, "My Best/Craziest/Funniest Story . . . Ever!!" *Ben-Schrader*, October 5, 2017, http://www.ben-schrader.com/the-past/2017/10/5/my-bestcraziestfunniest-story-ever.

2. "The KKK and American Veterans—Part 1, United States," *VICE*, accessed January 23, 2015, http://www.vice.com/video/the-kkk-and-american-veterans-part-1-666.

3. "Soldier's Heart: Remembering Jacob George, Afghan War Vet Turned Peace Activist Who Took Own Life," *Democracy Now!*, accessed January 23, 2015, http://www.democracynow.org/2014/9/29/soldiers_heart_remembering_jacob_george_afghan.

4. Basu, "Why Suicide Rate among Veterans May Be More than 22 a Day."

5. Tiqqun, *This Is Not a Program*, trans. Joshua David Jordan (Cambridge, MA: Semiotext, 2011).

6. Foucault, *The Politics of Truth*, 143.

7. Molly Osberg, "The Military Has a Serious White Nationalist Problem," *Splinter News*, October 25, 2017, accessed October 25, 2017, http://readersupportednews. org/opinion2/277-75/46488-the-military-has-a-serious-white-nationalist-problem.

8. For a closer examination, see my blog post about it, online at http://www. ben-schrader.com/blog-1/myweekatstandingrock.

9. Gallagher, "Burdens of Proof."

10. Enloe, *Maneuvers*.

11. Iraq Veterans Against the War, *Warrior Writers: Re-making Sense: A Collection of Artwork*, 1st ed. (Philadelphia: Iraq Veterans Against the War, 2008).

Bibliography

"About." *Not Invisible*. Accessed September 18, 2014. http://www.notinvisible.org/the_movie.

"About That 99 Percent . . ." *New York Times* Economix Blog. Accessed December 5, 2012. http://economix.blogs.nytimes.com/2011/10/10/about-that-99-percent/.

Agamben, Giorgio. *"What Is an Apparatus?" and Other Essays*. Translated by David Kishik and Stefan Pedatella. Stanford, CA: Stanford University Press, 2009.

Åhäll, Linda, and Thomas Gregory, eds. *Emotions, Politics and War*. Abingdon, UK: Routledge, 2015.

Almeida, Eugenie, and Jessica Hafner. "Heroes versus Traitors: U.S. and Afghani Soldiers in the U.S. Press." *Global Journal of Human-Social Science* 14, no. 1 (2014).

Alvarez, Lizette. "More Americans Joining Military as Jobs Dwindle." *New York Times*, January 18, 2009. http://www.nytimes.com/2009/01/19/us/19recruits.html.

Appy, Christian G. *Working-Class War: American Combat Soldiers and Vietnam*. Chapel Hill: University of North Carolina Press, 1993.

Arnold, Roger. "Occupy Wall Street and the 1-9-90 Rule—The Street." Accessed December 5, 2012. http://www.thestreet.com/story/11280871/1/occupy-wall-street-and-the-1-9-90 rule.html.

Associated Press. "SFC Sentenced for Organizing Fort Hood Prostitution Ring." *Army Times*, March 11, 2015.

Badiou, Alain. *The Rebirth of History: Times of Riots and Uprisings*, 1st ed. Translated by Gregory Elliott. London: Verso, 2012.

Barthes, Roland. "An Introduction to the Structural Analysis of Narrative." *New Literary History* 6, no. 2 (Winter 1975).

Basham, Victoria. *War, Identity and the Liberal State: Everyday Experiences of the Geopolitical in the Armed Forces*. Interventions series. London: Routledge, 2013.

Basham, Victoria, Aaron Belkin, and Jess Gifkins. "What Is Critical Military Studies." *Critical Military Studies* 1, no. 1 (2015).

Basu, Moni. "Why Suicide Rate among Veterans May Be More than 22 a Day." *CNN*. Accessed April 19, 2014. http://www.cnn.com/2013/09/21/us/22-veteran-suicides-a-day/index.html.

Baudrillard, Jean. *The Gulf War Did Not Take Place*. Bloomington: Indiana University Press, 1995.

Baumgold, Deborah. "Subjects and Soldiers: Hobbes on Military Service." *History of Political Thought* 4, no. 1 (1983): 43–64.

Beaumont, Thomas. "A Survivor's Response to Sacrifice." *Critical Military Studies* 3, no. 3 (2017).

Belkin, Aaron. *Bring Me Men: Military Masculinity and the Benign Facade of American Empire, 1898–2001*. New York: Oxford University Press, 2012.

Benedict, Helen. *The Lonely Soldier: The Private War of Women Serving in Iraq*. New York: Beacon Press, 2010.

Benjamin, Walter. *Illuminations: Essays and Reflections*. New York: Random House Digital, Inc., 1969.

Beragas, Hector. Banished Veterans Interview, September 30, 2013.

Bellesiles, Michael. *A Peoples History of the U.S. Military*. New York: The New Press, 2013.

Blecher, Ivy Kenneth. "Three Centuries of American War." Accessed July 30, 2017. http://www.history-of-american-wars.com/revolutionary-war-soldiers.html.

Bogus, Carl. "The Hidden History of the Second Amendment." *UC Davis Law Review*. 1998.

Braswell, Harold, and Howard I. Kushner. "Suicide, Social Integration, and Masculinity in the U.S. Military." *Social Science & Medicine, Part Special Issue: Men, Masculinities and Suicidal Behaviour* 74, no. 4 (February 2012): 530–536. doi:10.1016/j.socscimed.2010.07.031.

Browning, Justine. "Turning the Page, U.S. Soldiers Home from War Rebound through Writing." *Occupy.com*, March 7, 2014. http://www.occupy.com/article/turning-page-us-soldiers-home-war-rebound-through-writing.

"BTS: Border Crossing/Entry Data: Query Detailed Statistics." Accessed November 16, 2013. http://transborder.bts.gov/programs/international/transborder/TBDR_BC/TBDR_BCQ.html.

Bulmer, Sarah, and David Jackson. "'You Do Not Live in My Skin': Embodiment, Voice, and the Veteran." *Critical Military Studies* 2, no. 1–2 (2016).

Bulmer, Sarah, and Maya Eichler. "Unmaking Militarized Masculinity: Veterans and the Project of Military-to-Civilian Transition." *Critical Military Studies* 3, no. 2 (2017).

Butler, Smedley. *War Is a Racket: The Antiwar Classic by America's Most Decorated Soldier*. Port Townsend, WA: Feral House, 2003.

Cameron, Drew. Combat Paper Interview, October 5, 2013.

Chamayou, Grégoire. *A Theory of the Drone*. New York: The New Press, 2015.

Chouliaraki, Lilie. "Liberal Ethics and the Spectacle of War." In *Ethics of Media*, edited by N. Couldry, M. Madianou, and A. Pinchevski. London: Palgrave Macmillan, 2013.

Cockburn, Cynthia. *From Where We Stand: War, Women's Activism and Feminist Analysis*. London: Zed Books, 2007.

———. "The Continuum of Violence: A Gender Perspective on War and Peace." In *Sites of Violence: Gender and Conflict*, edited by W. Giles and J. Hyndman. Berkeley: University of California Press, 2004.

———. "Gender Relations as Causal in Militarization and War: A Feminist Stand Point." In *Making Gender, Making War: Violence, Military and Peacekeeping Practices*, edited by A. Kronsell and E. Svedberg. London: Routledge, 2011.

"Combat Paper Project." Accessed December 9, 2013. http://www.combatpaper.org/about.html.

"Contractor Distrust Costs DOD Billions, Study Says—Washington Technology." Accessed December 5, 2012. http://washingtontechnology.com/Articles/2012/07/12/efficiency-dod-contractor-relationship.aspx?Page=1.

Cook, Melissa. "Banished for Minor Crimes: The Aggravated Felony Provision of the Immigration and Nationality Act as Human Rights Violation." *Boston College Third World Law Journal* 23 (2003): 293.

Cooper, Helene. "Pentagon Study Finds 50% Increase in Reports of Military Sexual Assaults." *New York Times*, May 1, 2014. http://www.nytimes.com/2014/05/02/us/military-sex-assault-report.html.

"Cost Review of Military Contractors Would Be Revealing." *Mining Journal*. Accessed December 5, 2012. http://www.miningjournal.net/page/content.detail/id/579311/Cost-review-of-military-contractors-would-be-revealing.html?nav=5003.

"Courage to Resist: Kimberly Rivera." Accessed May 10, 2014. http://couragetoresist.org/kimberly-rivera.html.

Cuomo, Chris. "War Is Not Just an Event: Reflections on the Significance of Everyday Violence." *Hypatia* 11, no. 4 (Autumn 1996): 30–45.

Daniel, Lisa. "Defense.gov News Article: Recruiters Recall Patriotism of Post-9/11 America." Accessed January 27, 2013. http://www.defense.gov/News/NewsArticle.aspx?ID=65272.

"Democracy Now! Newscast for October 14, 2014." Democracy Now! Accessed November 5, 2014. http://www.democracynow.org/shows/2014/10/14.

Department of Defense. "Annual Report on Sexual Assault in the Military: Fiscal Year 2015." 2015.

Der Derian, James. *Virtuous War: Mapping the Military-Industrial-Media-Entertainment Network*. 2nd ed. New York: Routledge, 2009.

Dillon, Michael, and Luis Lobo-Guerrero. "Biopolitics of Security in the 21st Century: An Introduction." *Review of International Studies* 34, no. 02 (2008): 265–292. doi:10.1017/S0260210508008024.

Dolman, Everett Carl. "Obligation and the Citizen-Soldier: Machiavellian Virtu Versus Hobbesian Order." *Journal of Political and Military Sociology* 23 (Winter 1995).

Donnelly, Faye. *Securitization and the Iraq War: The Rules of Engagement in World Politics*. New York: Routledge, 2013.

Downey, Liam, Eric Bonds, and Katherine Clark. "Natural Resource Extraction, Armed Violence, and Environmental Degradation." *Organization & Environment* 23, no. 4 (December 2010): 417–445.

Duggan, Lisa. *The Twilight of Equality? Neoliberalism, Cultural Politics, and the Attack on Democracy*. Boston: Beacon Press, 2004.

Duncanson, Claire. "What Can we Learn from Soldiers' Narratives? Methodologies and Methods." In *Forces for Good? Rethinking Peace and Conflict Studies*, 52–71. London: Palgrave Macmillan.

Dyvik, Synne. "Of Bats and Bodies: Methods for Reading and Writing Embodiment." *Critical Military Studies* 2, nos. 1–2.

———. "'Valhalla Rising': Gender, Embodiment, and Experience in Military Memoirs." *Security Dialogue* 47, no. 2 (2016): 133–150.

Eichler, Maya. "Citizenship and the Contracting out of Military Work: From National Conscription to Globalized Recruitment." *Citizenship Studies* 18, no. 6–7 (2014).

Enloe, Cynthia. *Does Khaki Become You? The Militarization of Women's Lives*. London: Pandora, 1998.

———. *Maneuvers: The International Politics of Militarizing Women's Lives*. 1st ed. Berkeley: University of California Press, 2000.

———. *Globalisation and Militarism. Feminists Make the Link*. London: Rowman & Littlefield, 2007.

"Environmental Costs: Costs of War," August 3, 2012. http://costsofwar.org/article/environmental-costs.

Ersen, M. Uğur, and Cinar Özen. *Use of Force in Countering Terrorism*. New York: IOS Press, 2010.

Ettinger, Aaron. "Ending the Draft in America: The Coevolution of Military Manpower and the Capitalist State, 1948–1973." *Critical Military Studies* 4, no. 1: 1–16. doi: 10.1080/23337486.2016.1215075.

Fathi, Riyad Abdullah, Lilyan Yaqup Matti, Hana Said Al-Salih, and Douglas Godbold. "Environmental Pollution by Depleted Uranium in Iraq with Special Reference to Mosul and Possible Effects on Cancer and Birth Defect Rates." *Medicine, Conflict and Survival* 29, no. 1 (March 1, 2013): 7–25. doi:10.1080/13623699.2013.765173.

Ferguson, Kathy E. *Oh, Say, Can You See: The Semiotics of the Military in Hawai'i*. 1st ed. Minneapolis: University of Minnesota Press, 1998.

———. "Shocking Us to Thought: Anarchist Art and Poetry Concerning Political Prisoners." Western Political Science Association, Annual Meeting 2014.

Finley, Erin P. *Fields of Combat: Understanding PTSD among Veterans of Iraq and Afghanistan*. 1st ed. Ithaca, NY: ILR Press, 2012.

Fischer, Frank. *Reframing Public Policy: Discursive Politics and Deliberative Practices*. Oxford and New York: Oxford University Press, 2003.

Fischer, Mia. "Commemorating 9/11 NFL-Style: Insights into America's Culture of Militarism." *Journal of Sport and Social Issues* 38, no. 3 (2014): 199–221.

Flores, David. "Politicization Beyond Politics: Narratives and Mechanisms of Iraq War Veterans' Activism." *Armed Forces & Society* 43, no. 1 (2017).

Folkers, Andreas. "Daring the Truth: Foucault, Parrhesia, and the Genealogy of Critique." *Theory, Culture & Society* 33, no. 1 (2016): 3–28.

"Food Deserts: Food Empowerment Project." Accessed May 20, 2013. http://www.foodispower.org/food-deserts/.

Foucault, Michel. *Discipline and Punish: The Birth of the Prison*. New York: Vintage Books, 1995.

———. *Power/Knowledge: Selected Interviews and Other Writings, 1972–1977*. Edited by Colin Gordon. 1st American ed., New York: Vintage, 1980.

———. *"Society Must Be Defended": Lectures at the Collège de France, 1975–1976*. Translated by David Macey. Reprint. New York: Picador, 2003.

———. *Technologies of the Self: A Seminar with Michel Foucault*. Edited by Luther H. Martin, Huck Gutman, and Patrick H. Hutton. Amherst: University of Massachusetts Press, 1988.

———. *The Birth of Biopolitics: Lectures at the Collège de France, 1978–1979*. Reprint ed. New York: Picador, 2010.

———. *The Government of Self and Others: Lectures at the College de France, 1982–1983*. Edited by Arnold I. I. Davidson. Translated by Graham Burchell. New York: Picador, 2011.

———. *The Hermeneutics of the Subject: Lectures at the Collège de France 1981–1982*. Translated by Graham Burchell. Reprint. New York: Picador, 2005.

———. *The History of Sexuality, Vol. 1: An Introduction*. Translated by Robert Hurley. 5th ed. New York: Vintage, 1990.

———. *The Politics of Truth*. Edited by Sylvère Lotringer. 2nd ed. Cambridge, MA: MIT Press, 2007.

———. *Wrong-Doing, Truth-Telling: The Function of Avowal in Justice*. Edited by Fabienne Brion and Bernard E. Harcourt. Translated by Stephen W. Sawyer. Annotated ed. Chicago, London, and Louvain-la-Neuve: University of Chicago Press, 2014.

———. *Psychiatric Power: Lectures at the Collège de France, 1973–1974*. Edited by Jacques Lagrange, Graham Burchell, and Arnold I Davidson. New York: Picador, 2008.

Gallagher, Brianne. "Burdens of Proof: Veteran Frauds, PTSD Pussies, and the Spectre of the Welfare Queen." *Critical Military Studies* 2 (2016): 139–54. doi:10.1080/23337486.2016.1155861.

———. "Aesthetic Interventions: The Biopolitics of the U.S. Soldier's Wounded Body and Horror of Nothing to See." PhD diss., University of Hawaii, 2014.

Gensler, Jon. OpFree Vet Interview, October 28, 2013.

Gibbons, Robert, C. Hendricks Brown, and Kwan Hur. "Is the Rate of Suicide Among Veterans Elevated?" *American Journal of Public Health* 102, no. S1 (2012): S17–S19. doi:10.2105/AJPH.2011.300491.

Glantz, Aaron. *The War Comes Home: Washington's Battle against America's Veterans.* 1st ed. Berkeley: University of California Press, 2010.

Goldstein, J. *War and Gender: How Gender Shaped the War System and Vice Versa.* Cambridge: Cambridge University Press, 2001.

Gonzalves, Theo. "'We Hold a Neatly Folded Hope': Filipino Veterans of World War II on Citizenship and Political Obligation." *Amerasia Journal* 21, no. 3 (Winter 1995–96): 155–174.

Gramsci, Antonio. *Selections from the Prison Notebooks.* Edited by Quintin Hoare and Geoffrey Nowell Smith. New York: International Publishers Co, 1971.

———. *Selections from the Prison Notebooks of Antonio Gramsci.* ElecBook, 2001.

———. *The Antonio Gramsci Reader: Selected Writings 1916–1935.* Edited by David Forgacs. New York: NYU Press, 2000.

"Guatemalan War Rape Victims Break Silence in Genocide Trial." Accessed May 23, 2013. http://www.trust.org/item/20130510144558-362tb.

Hanssen, Beatrice. *Critique of Violence: Between Poststructuralism and Critical Theory.* New York: Routledge, 2000.

Harvey, David. *The Enigma of Capital: And the Crises of Capitalism.* 2nd ed. Oxford: Oxford University Press, 2011.

Hawkins, Michael Daly. "Coming Home: Accommodating the Special Needs of Military Veterans to the Criminal Justice System." *Ohio State Journal of Criminal Law* 7 (2010): 563.

Heath's Story of Surviving Military Sexual Assault, 2012. https://www.youtube.com/watch?v=_4J8Z09zHXA&feature=youtube_gdata_player.

Hearn, Jeff. "On Men, Women, Militarism and the Military." In *Military Masculinities: Identity and the State,* edited by P. Higate. Westport, CT: Praeger, 2002.

Headle, Lura. "Grants of Land by the United States to Our Soldiers of Past Wars." *Advocate of Peace through Justice* 84, no. 5 (May 1922): 176–178.

Herman, Judith. *Trauma and Recovery: The Aftermath of Violence—from Domestic Abuse to Political Terror.* New York: Basic Books, 1997.

Higate, Paul. *Military Masculinities.* New York: Praeger 2002.

———. "'Switching it on' for Cash: The Private Militarized Security Contractor." In *War and the Body: Militarisation, Practice and Experience,* edited by K. McSorley, 106–127. Abingdon, UK: Routledge.

Hinohosa, Ramon. "Doing Hegemony: Military, Men, and Constructing Hegemonic Masculinity." *Journal of Men's Studies* (March 2010).

Hlad, Jennifer. "Military Grapples with Stigma of Men Reporting Sexual Assault— News Stripes." Accessed December 11, 2014. http://www.stripes.com/news/military-grapples-with-stigma-of-men-reporting-sexual-assault-1.318203.

Hobbes, Thomas. *Leviathan.* New York: Penguin Classics, 2003.

Hockey, John. "No More Heroes: Masculinity in the Infantry." *Military Masculinities: Identity and the State*, edited by P. Higate. Westport, CT: Praeger, 2002.

Holland, Eugene W. *Nomad Citizenship: Free-Market Communism and the Slow-Motion General Strike*. Minneapolis: University of Minnesota Press, 2011.

Howie, Paula. *Art Therapy with Military Populations: History, Innovation, and Applications*. New York: Routledge, 2017.

Huddy, Leonie, and Nadia Khatib. "American Patriotism, National Identity, and Political Involvement." *American Journal of Political Science* 51, no. 1 (2007): 63–77.

Hunt, Andrew. *The Turning: A History of Vietnam Veterans against the War*. New York: NYU Press. 2001.

Hunter, Dard. *Papermaking: The History and Technique of an Ancient Craft*. Mineola, NY: Dover Publications, 1978.

"Immigrants in the US Armed Forces." The Migration Information Source. Accessed January 24, 2013. http://www.migrationinformation.org/feature/display.cfm?ID=683.

"Iraq Sanctions Kill Children, U.N. Reports." *New York Times*. Accessed May 20, 2013. http://www.nytimes.com/1995/12/01/world/iraq-sanctions-kill-children-un-reports.html.

Iraq Veterans Against the War. *Winter Soldier: Iraq and Afghanistan: Eyewitness Accounts of the Occupations*. Edited by Aaron Glantz. Chicago: Haymarket Books, 2008.

———. "Board of Directors Statement on the Occupy Movement: We Are the 99%." Accessed December 5, 2012. http://www.ivaw.org/blog/board-directors-statement-occupy-movement-we-are-99.

———. "Founding of IVAW." Accessed February 6, 2013. http://www.ivaw.org/about/founding-ivaw.

———. "History." Accessed February 6, 2013. http://www.ivaw.org/about/history.

———. "Operation Recovery." Accessed August 20, 2014. http://forthoodtestimonies.com/.

———. "Resolution against the War in Afghanistan." Accessed February 7, 2013. http://www.ivaw.org/resolution-against-war-afghanistan.

———. "Service Members Have the Right to Heal." Accessed February 7, 2013. http://www.ivaw.org/blog/service-members-have-right-heal.

———. "Veterans Return Medals during NATO Protest." Accessed February 7, 2013. http://www.ivaw.org/blog/veterans-return-medals-during-nato-protest.

———. *Warrior Writers: Re-making Sense: A Collection of Artwork*. 1st ed. Philadelphia: Iraq Veterans Against the War, 2008.

———. "Winter Soldier." Accessed February 6, 2013. http://www.ivaw.org/winter soldier.

Jamail, Dahr. *The Will to Resist: Soldiers Who Refuse to Fight in Iraq and Afghanistan*. Chicago: Haymarket Books, 2009.

Jeffords, Susan. *Hard Bodies: Hollywood Masculinity in the Reagan Era*. New York: Rutgers University Press, 1994.

Jonas, Lara. "Mad Lonely World." Accessed February 7, 2014. http://www.warrior writers.org/Artists/jonasCW.html.

Juan-Sneden, Priscilla. "We Fight over There, so We Don't Have to Fight Here." *MarinesBlog: The Official Blog of the United States Marine Corps*. Accessed January 27, 2013. http://marines.dodlive.mil/2011/05/02/osamabinladendead/.

Junger, Sebastian. "Why Soldiers Miss War." FUNKER530. Accessed January 22, 2015. http://www.funker530.com/why-soldiers-miss-war/.

Jussila, Jorma, and Pertti Normia. "International Law and Law Enforcement Firearms." *Medicine, Conflict and Survival* 20, no. 1 (January 2004): 55–69.

Kenyon, Jessica. MST.org Interview, November 25, 2013.

Kidd IV, Richard, Russell LaChance, Kitt Kennedy, and Scott Sklar. "Mission Critical: Clean Energy and the U.S. Military." Presented at the Environmental Entrepreneurs, Law Offices of Simpson Thacher & Bartlett, October 29, 2013.

Kimerling, Rachel, Kerry Makin-Byrd, Samantha Louzon, Rosalinda Ignacio, and John McCarthy. "Military Sexual Trauma and Suicide Mortality." *American Journal of Preventive Medicine* 50, no. 6 (June 2016): 684–691.

King, Anthony. "The Female Combat Soldier." *European Journal of International Relations* 22, no. 1 (2015).

Kirby, Alex. "Climate Change? Makes Violence Likelier?" Climate News Network. Accessed November 14, 2014. http://www.climatenewsnetwork.net/climate-change-makes-violence-likelier/.

Kirby, Paul. "How Is Rape a Weapon of War? Feminist International Relations, Modes of Critical Explanation and the Study of Wartime Sexual Violence." *European Journal of International Relations* 19, no. 4 (2013).

Kronsell, Annica, and Erika Svedberg, eds. *Making Gender, Making War: Violence, Military and Peacekeeping Practices: Routledge Advances in Feminist Studies and Intersectionality*. London: Routledge, 2011.

Lawson, Sean. "Articulation, Antagonism, and Intercalation in Western Military Imaginaries." *Security Dialogue* 42, no. 1 (2011).

Leitz, Lisa. *Fighting for Peace: Veterans and Military Families in the Anti–Iraq War Movement*. Minneapolis: University of Minnesota Press, 2014.

———. "Oppositional Identities: The Military Peace Movement's Challenge to Pro-Iraq War Frames." *Social Problems* 58, no. 2 (May 2011): 235–256.

Lewis, Brian. Mr. MST. Interview, October 28, 2017.

Lenin, V. I. *What Is to Be Done?* Edited by S. V. Utechin. Peking: Foreign Languages Press, 1975.

Levitin, Michael. "Occupying War: A Marine Vet Finds His Mission." *Occupied Wall Street Journal*. Accessed December 5, 2012. http://occupiedmedia.us/2012/03/occupying-war-a-marine-vet-finds-his-mission/.

Li, Qiong, and Marilynn Brewer. "What Does It Mean to Be an American? Patriotism, Nationalism, and American Identity after 9/11." *Political Psychology* 25, no. 5 (2004).

Lunchenco, Jane. "Entering the Century of the Environment: A New Social Contract for Science." *Science* 279, no. 5350 (1998).

Mabee, Bryan. "From 'Liberal War' to 'Liberal Militarism': United States Security Policy as the Promotion of Military Modernity." *Critical Military Studies* 2, no. 3 (2016).

Mac Bica, Camillo. "Should Veterans Become Activists?" *Truthout*, July 4, 2013. http://www.truth-out.org/opinion/item/17356-should-veterans-become-activists.

———. "The Invisible Wounds of War." *Truthout*, October 24, 2011. http://www.truth-out.org/opinion/item/3770:the-invisible-wounds-of-war.

MacGregor, Morris. *Integration of the Armed Forces: 1940–1965*. Alexandria: Library of Alexandria, 1985.

Mann, Michael. "The Roots and Contradictions of Modern Militarism." *New Left Review* 162 (March–April): 35–50.

Marx, Karl, and Friedrich Engels. *The Marx-Engels Reader*. Edited by Robert C. Tucker. 2nd ed., revised and enlarged. W. W. Norton & Company, 1978.

McCormack, Killian. "Governing 'Ungoverned' Space: Humanitarianism, Citizenship, and the Civilian Sphere in the Territorializing Practices of the US National Security Complex." *Critical Military Studies* 4, no. 2 (2018).

McIntosh, Brock. OpFree Vet Interview, October 25, 2013.

McKay, Ernest A. *The Civil War and New York City*. Syracuse, NY: Syracuse University Press, 1990.

McNeil, William. *Keeping Together in Time: Dance and Drill in Human History*. Cambridge, MA: Harvard University Press, 1995.

McSorley, Kevin. "Doing Military Fitness: Physical Culture, Civilian Leisure, and Militarism." *Critical Military Studies* 2, nos. 1–2 (2016).

———. *War and the Body: Militarisation, Practice and Experience*. London: Routledge, 2013.

———. "Towards an Embodied Sociology of War." *Sociological Review* 62, no. 2 (2014): 107–128. doi:10.1111/1467-954X.12194.

"MEDIA ARCHIVES." *Banished Veterans*. Accessed January 27, 2013. http://www.banishedveterans.info/MEDIA-ARCHIVES.html.

Meola, Bob, and Michael McKee. "Courage to Resist: Giving Birth behind Bars." Accessed May 10, 2014. http://couragetoresist.org/kimberly-rivera/1017-birth-behind-bars.html.

Meyer, Cordula. "Fighting for a New Homeland: US Army Lures Foreigners with Promise of Citizenship." *Spiegel Online*. Accessed January 27, 2013. http://www.spiegel.de/international/world/fighting-for-a-new-homeland-us-army-lures-foreigners-with-promise-of-citizenship-a-512384.html.

"Military Benefits." Today's Military. Accessed January 27, 2013. http://www.todays military.com/main/military-benefits.

Mills, Charles. *The Racial Contract*. Ithaca, NY: Cornell University Press, 1997.

Morris, Madeline. "By Force of Arms: Rape, War, and Military Culture." *Duke Law Journal* 45, no 4 (February 1996).

"NATO/CANG8 on Democracy Now! Carlos Montes, Aaron Hughes IVAW, Other Activists." WAMMToday. Accessed May 22, 2013. http://wammtoday. org/2012/05/16/natocang8-on-democracy-now-carlos-montes-aaron-hughes-ivaw-other-activists/.

"No One Left Behind." *No One Left Behind*. Accessed August 25, 2014. http://www.nooneleft.org/.

"Oath of Enlistment." About.com, US Military. Accessed December 5, 2012. http://usmilitary.about.com/od/joiningthemilitary/a/oathofenlist.htm.

O'Brien, Karen, Bronwyn Hayward, and Fikret Berkes. "Rethinking Social Contracts: Building Resilience in a Changing Climate." *Ecology and Society* 14, no. 2 (2009).

"Operation First Casualty." *Washington Post*, March 19, 2007. http://www.washington post.com/wpdyn/content/video/2007/03/19/ VI2007031901446.html.

Parashar, Swati. "What Wars and 'War Bodies' Know about International Relations." *Cambridge Review of International Affairs* 26, no. 4 (2013): 615–630. doi:1 0.1080/09557571.2013.837429.

Penn, Nathaniel. "'Son, Men Don't Get Raped.'" *GQ*. Accessed November 15, 2014. http://www.gq.com/long-form/male-military-rape.

Phillips, Kimberly. *War! What Is It Good For? Black Freedom Struggles & the U.S. Military from World War II to Iraq*. Chapel Hill: University of North Carolina Press, 2012.

Pond, Steve. "Military Rape Documentary 'Invisible War' Leads to Policy Changes Before Its Opening." *TheWrap*. Accessed September 18, 2014. http://www.thewrap.com/movies/column-post/military-rape-documentary-invisible-war-leads-policy-changes-its-opening-44671/.

Protevi, John. *Political Affect: Connecting the Social and the Somatic*. Minneapolis: University of Minnesota Press, 2009.

Pulido, Laura. *Black, Brown, Yellow, and Left: Radical Activism in Los Angeles*. Berkeley: University of California Press, 2006.

Rowe, Cami. *The Politics of Protest and US Foreign Policy: Performative Construction of the War on Terror (War, Politics and Experience)*. London: Routledge, 2013.

Schrader, Benjamin. "The Affect of Veteran Activism." *Critical Military Studies*. 2017.

———. "My Best/Craziest/Funniest Story . . . Ever!!" *Ben-Schrader*. October 5, 2017. http://www.ben-schrader.com/the-past/2017/10/5/my-bestcraziest funniest-story-ever.

———. "My Week at Standing Rock." *Ben-Schrader*. December 3, 2016. http://www.ben-schrader.com/blog-1/myweekatstandingrock.

"Scott Olsen: Casualty of the Occupation." Rollingstone.com. Accessed December 5, 2012. http://www.rollingstone.com/politics/news/scott-olsen-casualty-of-the-occupation-20120119.

Service Women's Action Network. "Rape, Sexual Assault and Sexual Harassment in the Military," July 2012. http://servicewomen.org/media/publications/#factSheet.

Sharp, Gene. *The Politics of Nonviolent Action*. Boston: Porter Sargent, 1973.

Shagin, Craig R. "Deporting Private Ryan: The Less than Honorable Condition of the Noncitizen in the United States Armed Forces." *Widener Law Journal* 17 (2007): 245.

Shapiro, Michael J. *Studies in Trans-Disciplinary Method: After the Aesthetic Turn*. 1st ed. London and New York: Routledge, 2012.

———. *Violent Cartographies: Mapping Cultures of War*. Minneapolis: University of Minnesota Press, 1997.

———. *War Crimes, Atrocity and Justice*. 1st ed. Oxford: Polity, 2015.

Sjoberg, Laura, and Sandra Via. *Gender, War, and Militarism: Feminist Perspectives*. Santa Barbara, CA: ABC-CLIO, 2010.

Sjoberg, Laura. "Gendering the Empire's Soldiers: Gender Ideologies, the U.S. Military, and the 'War on Terror.'" In *Gender, War, and Militarism: Feminist Perspectives*, edited by Laura Sjoberg and Sandra Via. Santa Barbara, CA: ABC-CLIO, 2010.

"Soldier's Heart: Remembering Jacob George, Afghan War Vet Turned Peace Activist Who Took Own Life." *Democracy Now!* Accessed January 23, 2015. http://www.democracynow.org/2014/9/29/soldiers_heart_remembering_jacob_george_afghan.

Springer, Simon. "Neoliberalism as Discourse: Between Foucauldian Political Economy and Marxian Poststructuralism." *Critical Discourse Studies* 9, no. 2 (May 1, 2012): 133–147. doi:10.1080/17405904.2012.656375.

Stars and Stripes. "Trial of Fort Hood NCO Accused of Setting Up Prostitution Ring Starts Wednesday." March 9, 2015. https://www.stripes.com/news/trial-of-fort-hood-nco-accused-of-setting-up-prostitution-ring-starts-wednesday-1.333414.

Stannard, David. *American Holocaust: The Conquest of the New World*. Oxford: Oxford University Press, 1992.

Stavrianakis, Anna, and Maria Stern. "Militarism and Security: Dialogue, Possibilities and Limits." *Security Dialogue* 49, no. 1–2: 3–8.

Steger, Manfred B. *The Rise of the Global Imaginary: Political Ideologies from the French Revolution to the Global War on Terror*. Oxford: Oxford University Press, 2009.

Steger, Manfred B., and Nancy S. Lind, eds. *Violence and Its Alternatives: An Interdisciplinary Reader*. London: Palgrave Macmillan, 1999.

Sweetman, Derek. "Bradley Manning, Collateral Murder, Truth, and Power." *Unrest Magazine*. Accessed July 24, 2013. http://www.unrestmag.com/bradley-manning-collateral-murder-truth-and-power/.

Sylvester, Christine, ed. *Experiencing War*. London: Routledge, 2010.

———. "The Art of War/The War Question in (Feminist) IR." *Millennium: Journal of International Studies* 33, no. 3 (2005): 855–878.

———. "War Experiences/War Practices/War Theory." *Millennium-Journal of International Studies* 40, no. 3 (2012): 483–503. doi:10.1177/0305829812442211.

———. *War as Experience: Contributions from International Relations and Feminist Analysis.* Abington, UK: Routledge, 2013.

Tarrow, Sydney. *The New Transnational Activism.* Cambridge: Cambridge University Press. 2005.

Taylor, Charles. *Modern Social Imaginaries.* Durham, NC: Duke University Press, 2003.

"The KKK and American Veterans—Part 1." VICE. Accessed January 23, 2015. http://www.vice.com/video/the-kkk-and-american-veterans-part-1-666.

Thomas, Shamar. Occupy Vets Interview, October 27, 2013.

Thorpe, Helen. *Soldier Girls: The Battles of Three Women at Home and at War.* New York: Scribner, 2015.

Tidy, Joanna. "Gender, Dissenting Subjectivity and the Contemporary Military Peace Movement in Body of War." *International Feminist Journal of Politics* 17, no. 3 (2015): 454–472.

———. "The Gender Politics of 'Ground Truth' in the Military Dissent Movement: The Power and Limits of Authenticity Claims Regarding War." *International Political Sociology* 10, no. 2 (2016): 99–114.

———. "Visual Regimes and the Politics of War Experience: Rewriting War 'from above' in WikiLeaks' 'Collateral Murder.'" *Review of International Studies* 43, part 1 (2016): 95–111.

Tilly, Charles. "War Making and State Making as Organized Crime." In *Bringing the State Back In*, edited by Peter Evans, Dietrich Rueschmeyer, and Theda Skocpol. Cambridge: Cambridge University Press, 1985.

Tindugan, Jules. War Resistors Interview, November 20, 2013.

Tiqqun. *This Is Not a Program.* Translated by Joshua David Jordan. Los Angeles and Cambridge, MA: Semiotext, 2011.

"Tired to the Bone." *Huffington Post.* Accessed February 6, 2013. http://www.huffingtonpost.com/cindy-sheehan/tired-to-the-bone_b_6652.html.

Tracy, James. *The Military Draft Handbook: A Brief History and Practical Advice for the Curious and Concerned.* New York: Manic D Press, 2005.

"Transcript of the Constitution of the United States—Official Text." Accessed December 5, 2012. http://www.archives.gov/exhibits/charters/constitution_transcript.html.

"United States Guilty of Genocide in Guatemala Should Be Real Headline." IPS. Accessed May 23, 2013. http://www.ips-dc.org/articles/united_states_genocide_guatemala.

Urrea, Luis Alberto, and Erin Siegal McIntyre. "Mexican Soldiers Fight for US Army but Still Deported." *Playboy.* Accessed November 8, 2013. http://www.playboy.com/playground/view/deported-warriors-us-soldiers.

"U.S. Lifts Photo Ban on Military Coffins." *New York Times*. Accessed February 17, 2013. http://www.nytimes.com/2009/02/27/world/americas/27iht-photos.1.20479953.html?_r=0.

"US Military Veterans Heed Occupy Rallying Cry." Text. Article. Associated Press, November 3, 2011. http://www.foxnews.com/us/2011/11/03/us-military-veterans-heed-occupy-rallying-cry/.

Valdez, Carlos. "Defense.gov News Article: Face of Defense: Soldiers Keep Up Family Tradition." Accessed January 27, 2013. http://www.defense.gov/News/NewsArticle.aspx?ID=54384.

Väliaho, Pasi. "Affectivity, Biopolitics and the Virtual Reality of War." *Theory, Culture & Society* 29, no. 2 (March 1, 2012): 63–83. doi:10.1177/0263276411417461.

Veterans Administration. "Military Sexual Trauma." Accessed June 19, 2018. https://www.ptsd.va.gov/public/types/violence/military-sexual-trauma-general.asp.

"Veterans Book Project." Accessed April 26, 2014. http://www.veteransbookproject.com/.

Vogel, Steve, and Michael Alison Chandler. "4 Years After Start of War, Anger Reigns." *Washington Post*, March 18, 2007, sec. Nation. http://www.washingtonpost.com/wp-dyn/content/article/2007/03/17/AR2007031700539.html.

Wadham, Ben. "Brotherhood: Homosociality, Totality, and Military Subjectivity." *Australian Feminist Studies* 28, no. 76 (2013).

Waltzer, Michael. *Obligations: Essays on Disobedience, War, and Citizenship*. Cambridge, MA: Harvard University Press. 1970.

Weber, Cynthia. *Imagining America at War: Morality, Politics, and Film*. New York: Taylor & Francis US, 2006.

Weiner, Rachel, and Matt Zapotosky. "Air Force Colonel Acquitted in Assault Trial." *Washington Post*, November 12, 2013.

Wibben, Annick. "Why We Need to Study (US) Militarism: A Critical Feminist Lens." *Security Dialogue* 49, nos. 1–2 (2018): 136–148.

Wikileaks. "Collateral Murder." Accessed June 28, 2013. https://collateralmurder.wikileaks.org.

Wilcox, Lauren. *Bodies of Violence: Theorizing Embodied Subjects in International Relations*. Oxford: Oxford University Press, 2015.

Wool, Zoe. *After War: The Weight of Life at Walter Reed*. Durham, NC: Duke University Press, 2015.

"World Gazetteer: America—Largest Cities (per Geographical Entity)," September 30, 2007.

Zeller, Matt. No One Left Behind Interview, October 24, 2013.

Index